Fusion

MELIAM TRAVEL & TAX SERVICE

The Monacelli Press

Fusion
The Performance of Architecture

Payette

Foreword by Z Smith
Introduction by Kevin B. Sullivan

Contents

Foreword

Z Smith

Payette is an architectural practice that is both unique and exemplary. They concentrate their efforts on just a few building types—science laboratories and healthcare facilities—yet the excellence of their design work has been widely recognized as relevant to all. They are leaders in the application of building science to science and healthcare buildings, but their fusion of design with performance has meaning for us all.

These buildings driven by science are in fact delightfully humane places for people, bringing together old and new, social and solitary, light and shadow, science and art.

Many of us are drawn to architecture by its power to make a difference in the lives of people, to shape beautiful and nurturing places from mere stone and wood and glass and steel. The fact that buildings endure for decades or even centuries offers the possibility that our efforts can have lasting impact.

This lasting impact of architecture can be positive, negative, or both at the same time. The structures we design can shelter and delight, and can support the uniquely human pursuits of learning and healing. At the same time, the construction and operation of buildings today is the single largest contributor to climate change of any human activity.

The work of Payette is the story of a group of people working to bring these seemingly opposite kinds of effects into positive alignment. They specialize in high-impact buildings, buildings that host research that can change the lives of millions or that foster the recovery to health of thousands. These same building types—research labs and healthcare facilities—have also typically been demanding in terms of their use of materials and energy. The work of Payette has shown that it's possible to produce these intensive buildings with a radically lower environmental footprint. They inverted the negative of "environmental impact" into the positive of "performance."

Payette has also had another kind of impact on the design profession. It's common to assume that some building types afford the most opportunity for great design—say, art museums or signature towers or high-end homes. Payette shows through its work that building types that many firms might treat as formulaic or overly constrained by programmatic requirements can offer just as much opportunity for beauty, inspiration, and delight.

Over the past few decades, there has been a split within our profession as to whether we should honor beautiful design or buildings that are environmentally responsible. Some firms show one project when they want to talk about design, and another when asked about performance. Payette takes a different approach. For them, every project is a "design project." Every project is a "performance project."

Payette shows every firm that it's possible to make beautiful buildings that perform beautifully. They demonstrate that historic preservation, sustainability, and design excellence are not in conflict—they can work together. Their projects exemplify how forgotten, unloved spaces can be transformed into people's favorite places to be. They aren't afraid of the bold gesture, providing a strangely welcome otherworldly presence at the end of a typical Boston street. Yet these exciting forms don't come at the expense of performance—in fact, the forms are essential to the performance.

These projects work at the scale of the city, literally bridging the tracks linking an old campus to a new front door, providing a new center for student life while inviting the city in. Instead of making big buildings, Payette makes small cities. They shape an academic common as a street, where classes from calculus to film studies may go on side by side, with research on display as students head to class.

Payette's projects work at all scales—from the doorknob to the city. For Payette, the edge of a building is a place you design to be occupied by people. Their practice breaks down the barriers between building and landscape, landscape and city.

Their buildings engage individuals at the most intense moments of their lives—birth, death, healing, discovery. Payette's work shows that even in program types with strict functional constraints there is the opportunity to make spaces that are humane for occupants, inspiring for visitors, and a positive contribution to the urban fabric.

Payette's work in healthcare demonstrates that good design can produce spaces that promote healing—not just a place for doctors and equipment, but places for families and friends that rebuild our connection to the outside world—and that a fragrant garden can help those on their path to recovery as much as a state-of-the-art piece of analytical equipment. We need both.

Their work shows that even in projects of colossal scale, it is possible to envision, simulate, and prototype a design element that is at once a solar shading strategy and a place for families to gather in each patient room. Instances such as these are a nice illustration of how good design works at every scale, and that for all the skill needed to deftly shape steel and glass and concrete, the greatest challenge is to shape the spaces that can foster a healing conversation, the touch of a hand over a cup of tea.

The culture, the firm

While the buildings Payette has designed offer much to learn from, the firm itself has become a model as well. In 2019, the American Institute of Architects bestowed upon Payette the highest honor that can be conferred upon a practice: the Architecture Firm Award. Payette's projects have won plenty of design awards, and individual staff members have been recognized for their singular contributions to the profession. Yet the Firm Award is different. It is the AIA signaling to its membership: "Here is a firm you could learn from, with lessons you could apply to your own practice."

This recognition is a story of transformation—the story of a quiet, decades-old, mid-sized firm that became a leader in design, performance, and firm culture, and that shows a way forward for the institute and the profession.

Our profession faces two great challenges: to attract, cultivate, and advance a pool of talent as diverse as our nation, and to transform design such that buildings, instead of being the single largest contributors to climate change, become part of the solution. Payette is at the forefront of both challenges. They lead through a combination of research and commitment.

It is perhaps not surprising that a firm that designs places for research would become a leader in research themselves. Payette developed an easy-to-use tool that helps designers around the world develop building enclosures that don't just save energy—they provide a comfortable environment in which occupants can be more productive. This expertise has allowed them to develop expressive high-performance building envelopes that simultaneously reveal and protect those at work behind it.

Their research goes beyond the gears of physics into the realm of human behavior. Every architect says they design spaces to promote collaboration. Payette studies—and freely discloses—when their intuitions were right, and when they weren't.

They understand that open-source research is a "gift society"—where you gain esteem not by hoarding knowledge, but by giving it away. Staff at all levels of their firm present and teach. Their model of design/observe/share is one that more and more firms, large and small, are now adopting.

This excellence in design at all scales has garnered increased recognition. Over the last few decades in their home region of New England—a region of extraordinary design talent—they have won more awards for design than any other firm. Each successive year, as the number of design awards has piled up, the energy use of their buildings has been reduced. While they work with building types that are typically the most intense users of energy, Payette, as a long-term participant in the AIA 2030 Commitment, has shown portfolio performance far better than the average of all reporting firms. Payette was the first practice to be nominated for the Firm Award by both the AIA

Committee on Design and the AIA Committee on the Environment. That sent an incredible message.

How do they do this? As you wander through their offices, you can't help but notice, tacked at the corner of each project alcove, the energy and daylighting performance metrics complementing the evocative sketch and the quick study model. Payette has established itself as a leader among firms who do not design "by the numbers"—but with the numbers. They bring an astonishing level of rigor to the mysterious process of design.

The architectural press loves personalities—the more dynamic, the more charismatic, the more elegant, the better. Where some firms may be energized by a cult of personality, Payette has created a personality of culture, a spirit of collective authorship.

We know our profession faces a huge challenge in the mismatch between the demographics of those leading our firms, of those entering our profession, and of the country as a whole. Payette models for all AIA members how firms can, through conscious action, bring about the transition to the profession we want to become.

Their firm culture provides support toward licensure that has been recognized twice with national awards. And although the office can have the buzz of a university design studio, Payette has cultivated a culture of work/life balance that is a model for the profession, where a young father can leave early to pick up the kids without having his commitment to the work questioned.

They show you can have a culture of design excellence without a culture of continual all-nighters. You can change the world and still have time for your family and community. They have established a firm culture dedicated to the joy of making, and of making a difference.

Their firm is structured around continuous engagement where all voices can participate and be heard. Every firm can look to Payette as an example of how existing firms can transform themselves.

This human-centered, all-voices design culture manifests itself in the firm's engagement in the design community of their home city of Boston, their work nationally promoting diversity and equity in the profession, and in their pro bono projects locally to internationally, from their work with local high school students, to working with a community to reenergize forgotten downtown spaces into inviting gathering places, to engaging with a nonprofit to envision, design, and raise funds for a project promoting local food security and nutrition, to the design and construction of a maternity ward in Haiti. Their practice is emblematic of efforts around the world to harness the power of design to improve communities.

When we're at our best, good architecture seems like magic—taking a mundane assignment and making a place that lifts the spirit while meeting program and being frugal with resources.

Payette shows that through the fusion of design and performance—grounded in research, energized by equity and inclusion—we can transform architectural practice, and transform the world.

The Fusion of Design and Performance

Kevin B. Sullivan

We are a collective of designers driven to create boldly original buildings for science and health-care that are as profoundly humane in their accommodation of needs as they are pioneering in their pursuit of environmental performance.

These building types have a lot in common. They're complex, loaded with constraints. In them, people do the same, precise things over and over—a scientist titrates a solution, a nurse adjusts an IV drip. It's a challenge to make them places that enliven human experience. That challenge drives us.

Individually, we're drawn to designing hospitals, laboratories, and research centers for many reasons: some of us are gearheads at heart, driven to understand the inner workings of complex organisms; others have found ourselves in a hospital at a life-changing moment. Together, we cherish the close relationships we build with clients and collaborators—who include eight Nobel Prize–winning scientists—on the journey from design to reality. Perhaps our passion stems from the quiet awareness that many of these buildings are typically destined to become unassuming settings for some of life's most momentous

The solar veil at Northeastern University

events: scientific discovery, illness and recovery, birth and death. We aim to elevate these spaces.

The architecture that responds to these needs is, above all, people-centric. The impressions it leaves are of abundant daylight and fresh air, embedded nature, nuanced social geometry, and carefully considered craft that delights both the eye and the hand. Payette buildings do not share a common style or "look" yet they are linked in spirit by how they "feel" and reflect the culture of place. At the same time, they must fulfill intricate programs, integrate complex technologies, and wrestle with intense energy use. It demands a holistic interaction of design and performance. This fusion is what we seek.

The roots of these values took hold in 1932, when Fred Markus and Paul Nocka founded the firm now known as Payette. Trained as industrial engineers when "scientific management" was the dominant manufacturing and production theory, Markus and Nocka began their practice with a singular purpose: to apply these techniques to the improvement of healthcare facilities. Among the fruits of their research was the Parallel Services Plan (1942), a radical and widely influential rethinking of the hospital layout.

Shadow study documenting patterns of researchers conducting stem cell research

In the late 2000s, we found ourselves engaged in a similar study of academic science labs, observing interactions of professors and students while researching ways to tame this building type's colossal energy use. From our study emerged a new planning model that layers the social space of the lab and the zoning of conditioned air, encouraging productive interactions while conserving critical resources.

Though separated by decades, the similarities between these two paradigm-shifting moments are not accidental. Together they demonstrate a remarkable continuity of design philosophy and leading-edge expertise, a continuity made possible by an enduring practice ethos.

This ethos can be traced to the moment in 1965 when thirty-three-year-old Tom Payette became president of the firm, well before the founders retired. This early advancement gave Tom decades to explore new possibilities, not just maintain a legacy. He embraced this precedent, taking on younger partners to expand the practice from its then dozen employees to the 175 we number today. The pattern of multigenerational leadership he set in motion has shaped our collaborative, entrepreneurial culture, and it underlies the dynamic between expertise and innovation that has led to the rapid advancement of the practice over the last two decades.

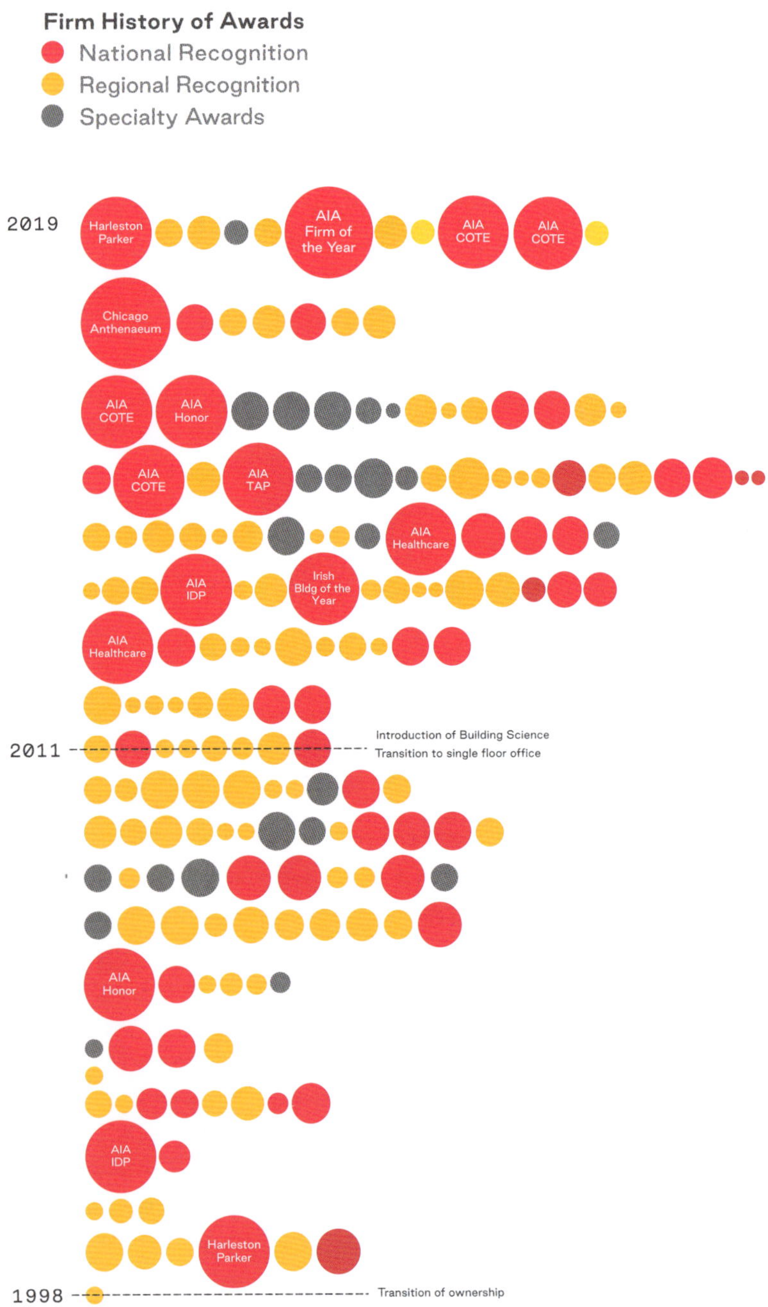

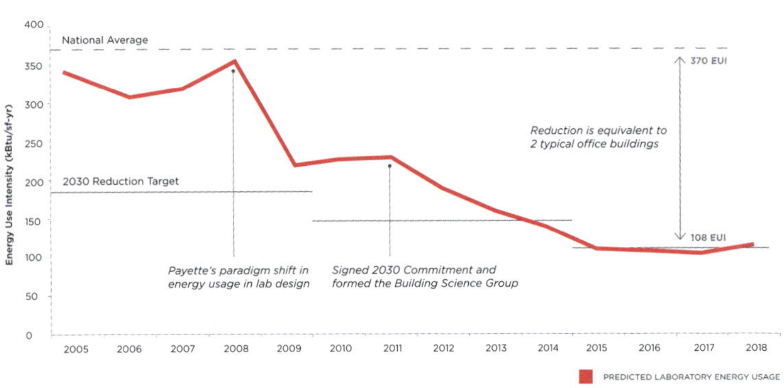

Reduction in Payette Labs Energy Use Intensity

Performalism: A New Definition of Beauty

The foundation for the fusion of design and performance started to become a more visible part of our process with the formation of our Building Science Group in 2011. This focused effort helped us clarify the framework for our internal dialogue, including the vocabulary, metrics, and goals we use to discuss our work with each other. The idea of high-performance architecture has always been important to us, particularly given our typological focus, but it was more a value we held—a latent part of our culture—than a practice of tracking measurable building performance. The Aga Khan University Medical Center in Pakistan from the 1970s, in which we employed a natural ventilation and evaporative cooling strategy for the entirety of the campus, is a particularly good example of this type of thinking. We hadn't articulated a philosophy; we just felt that it was simply the right thing to do for that client in that climate in that culture. While *performance* had not been fundamentally a part of our everyday dialogue, informing every design decision, the curiosity was always there.

With the emergence of our Building Science Group as an integral part of our design process, the lexicon of our performance-based design discussions began to evolve, becoming more nuanced and particular, addressing compositional and performance issues in tandem as part of a singular organic whole. We also realized that we were embedded in a rather significant and exciting moment in architectural discourse, in which the definition of beauty was being redefined. Our eyes and our brains were becoming conditioned to see things differently and standards would come to bear on aesthetics; for example, it was becoming unacceptable to have an all-glass facade facing south or west without an integrated strategy to deal with the exposure, nor was it acceptable to have a building with more than 40 percent glazing without a larger sustainable strategy or an idea about the systemic logic of the composition. Was formalism a thing of the past, and might *performalism* provide a more meaningful and dynamic theoretical framework for our work going forward? We began to use this term to describe our approach and how we define the meaning of beauty. As Z Smith has often said, "If it is not beautiful, it is not performing and if it is not performing, it is not beautiful."

Many of us were educated in a formalist tradition in which buildings were explored as objects that reveal the ethic of their making and compositional terms form the basis for discourse. Formalism has been a theoretical underpinning for architecture for a thousand years. It is based on the deep logic of geometry and proportion and the belief that everything necessary to determine a building's form can be derived from the work itself. Architects delight in the rigor associated with formalism, in how it makes logic visible, and in the deep roots it taps in its enlistment and transformation of precedent.

Missing from this approach, however, is the concept of performance, how a building responds to stimuli. We are fascinated by how a building functions for its intended use, in terms of both its social geometry and its environmental impact, and we love to measure and study these things to inform our work. Their importance is heightened in our chosen typologies, programmatically intense buildings for healthcare and science, in which human interaction is often procedurally constrained, and in which a single building may use more energy than a small city. For these reasons we believe that performance cannot be separated from beauty. Performance brings greater meaning to architecture when it becomes integral with composition, hence *performalism*.

Our definition of *Performalism* expands beyond the realm of digital architecture previously defined by Yasha J. Grobman and Eran Neuman.[1] *Performalism* asserts the inseparability of design and performance in our practice. It acknowledges the context of the project and explores how the building responds to stimuli. It considers the role of the environment, social geometry, and functionality in forming an organic unity, conceived and made evident in the integration of materiality and composition.

In Boston each year, a single building receives the Harleston Parker Medal, recognizing the most beautiful building in Boston built in the past ten years. In 2019, the Interdisciplinary Science and Engineering Complex at Northeastern University received this award. Recently, Paul Pettigrew, a Massachusetts Institute of Technology faculty member who chaired the jury, described how the jury typically defines for itself the meaning of beauty before beginning deliberations, and he revealed some interesting things about how the idea of performance came into those deliberations. Because of all the integrated performance measures, such as the solar veil, that were essential to both the visual language of the ISEC and its extreme energy efficiency, the jury was forced to rethink the definition of beauty they had only recently agreed upon. It was a delight to hear of this debate and the important role performance played in the selection of the ISEC for the Harleston Parker Medal, and to help redefine the jury's understanding of beauty in the process.

Payette has been fortunate to have been recognized with a significant number of design awards over the past fifteen years, but even more impressive has been the reduction of energy use in our buildings for science and healthcare over this same period. As one curve goes up, the other goes down, each entwined with the other, the fusion of design and performance.

1 In the first chapter of their book, Grobman and Neuman state, "Performalism proposes that computer-based architecture transforms notions in the architectural discourse from function to performance."

Performalism: Form and Performance in Digital Architecture, (Routledge, 2012), 5

Analytical Tools

We have come to see that the tools and techniques we use to integrate performance into our design process have become an essential part of our studio culture. For different questions, we employ different tools, and if the tools don't yet exist, we invent them. Our office is filled with architects and designers, but we also employ data scientists, building scientists, coders/programmers, and fabrication specialists to help us develop the tools, apps, and techniques essential for each project. Among our inventions are our SkinDesigner plug-in for Grasshopper, Winter Comfort Tool, Summer Comfort Tool, and Pulse, a campus planning app to measure how students and faculty move through buildings and across campus. We believe in and support the open-source community, so we make the digital analysis and design tools that we develop freely available to fellow architects.

In many of our projects, there are moments in the design process that vividly illustrate the fusion of design and performance, such as the solar veil at Northeastern University and the Family Nest at the Fifth Xiangya Hospital in Changsha, China. The Family Nest is a vessel that contains the typical patient room window and a niche in which several family members can sit. It is a room within a room, a building within a building, and it is precisely tuned to optimize environmental performance and the patient experience. The Fifth Xiangya Hospital is a massive, 5,600,000 square-foot facility with a seemingly infinite expanse of patient rooms, so the patient room windows are a highly repetitive design element with an enormous impact.

Results of Payette's internal data analysis initiatives for the patient rooms at the Fifth Xiangya Hospital

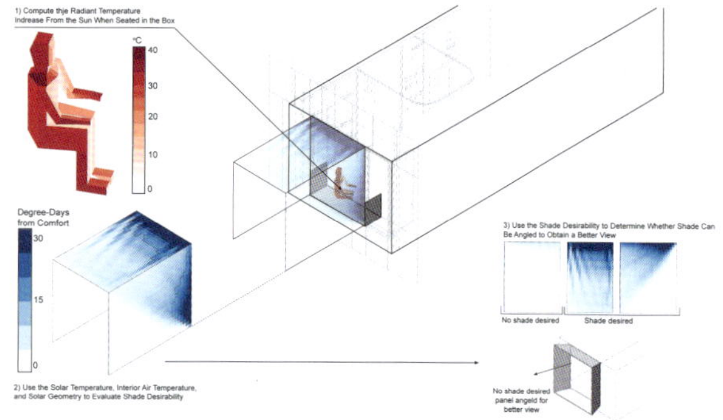

Analysis showing where the most comfort and energy benefit is coming from on the shading

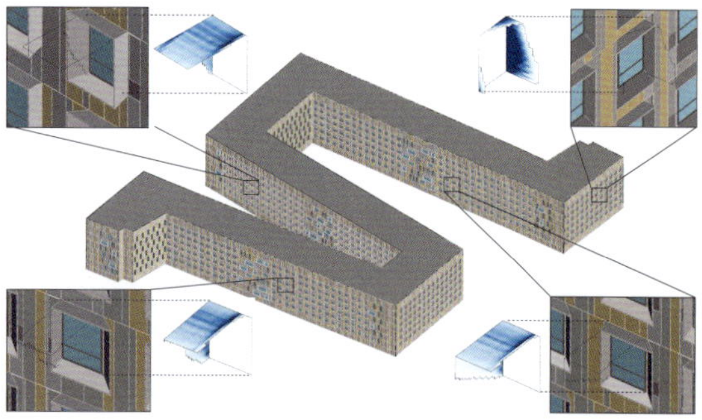

The shading benefit by orientation and facade

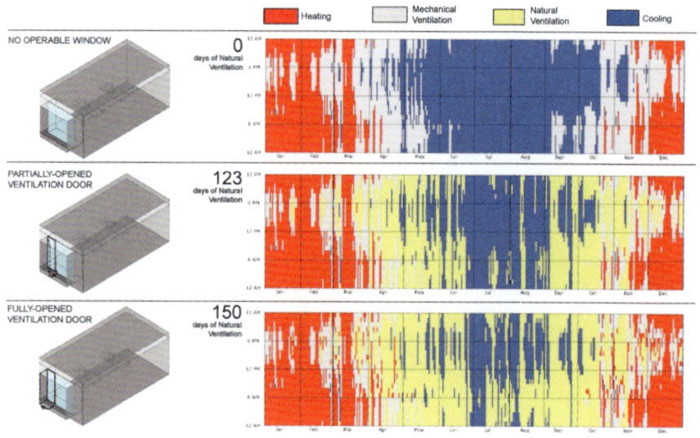

Analysis of strategies to increase natural ventilation in patient room

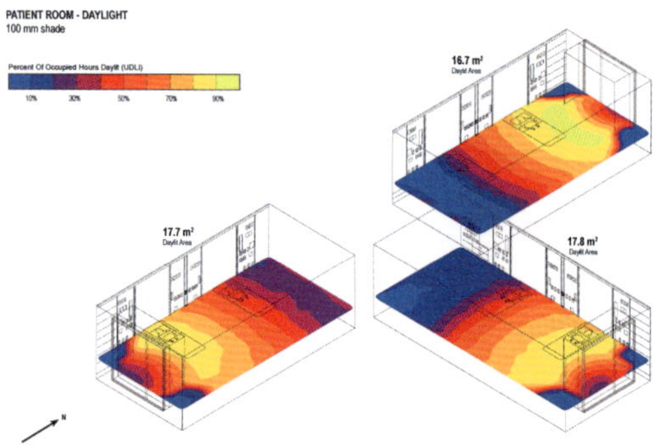

Useful daylight

We studied the Family Nest in several ways, first through shoebox-model building simulation studies, to test the effectiveness of different daylighting and natural ventilation strategies, and then through full-size physical mock-ups, which we built in our fabrication lab to test the physical attributes of the room and the architectural details of the Family Nest. When we began our performance analysis, we had several basic questions:

Should the shape of the window change based on the varied exposures? Can we create a comfortable experience in the Family Nest? Can we protect performance and design in value engineering? Can we naturally ventilate the hospital patient rooms for ten months of the year?

The answer to all of these questions was "yes." The simulations and the mock-up were invaluable in demonstrating the effectiveness of the Family Nest and its importance in the overall design—so important was it, in fact, that the contractor from China visited our office at the request of the owner to ensure that the design intent and performance goals for the Family Nest could be realized when it was built.

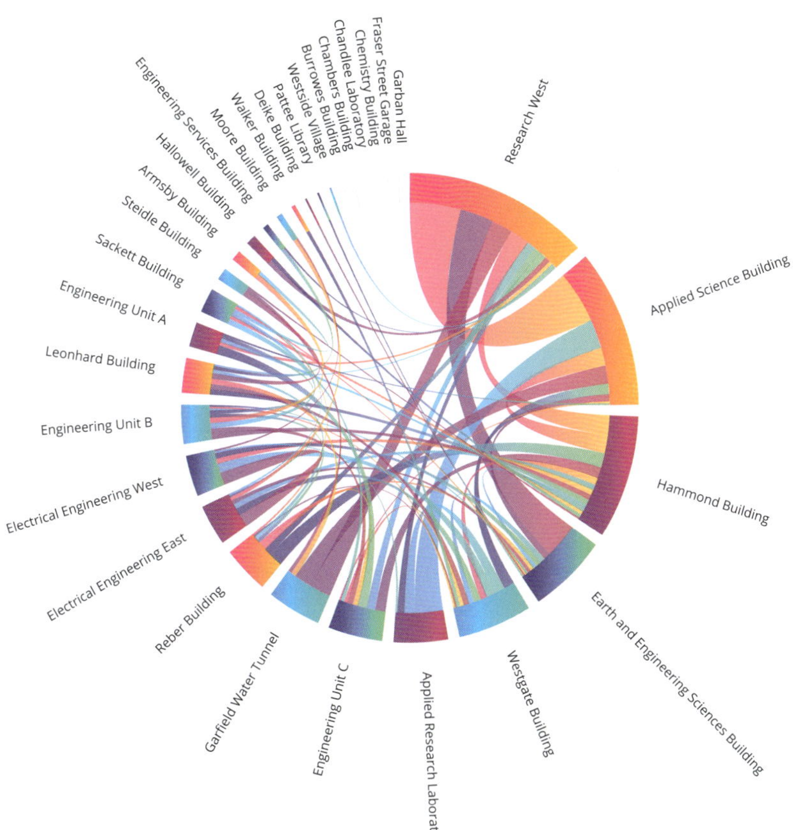

Example insight from Pulse, a Payette-built spatial surveying app. We gave the survey to the Penn State College of Engineering in 2019 to help inform the design of new buildings on the School's West Campus

Prototyping, Models, and Mock-Ups

The ability to fabricate prototypical elements like the Family Nest has become an essential part of our design process. The components we study range from entire patient rooms to fenestration details, to furnishings and fixtures. We believe in the importance of having architectural artifacts all around the office to fuel our curiosity, inspire us to refine our craft, and provide a healthy level of competitiveness. We also fabricate just because we can, to have fun, and because we love to build and make well-crafted things.

For a part of our office we call the Lido Deck, because it has a great view of Boston Harbor, we needed to address the duality of its use. It was a useful meeting area during most of the week, and it was also a location for informal group gatherings such as happy hour on Friday afternoons. But the furniture we had at the time wasn't optimal for any of these uses, so we decided to start over. We couldn't pass up the opportunity to invent something, so we designed and fabricated a conference table that can transform into a mobile bar to free up space on Fridays. The kinetic table is beautiful and clever; it provides inspiration for similar moments and opportunities in the other buildings we design. Furniture and product design have been part of our practice since the beginning. Founding principals Markus and Nocka's Bowditch desk is part of MoMA's permanent collection. This transforming table is the latest embodiment of this approach.

We developed many full-scale prototypes of the solar veil to test the form and feel of what was to become a critical component in the formal language of the ISEC project.

This conceptual model for the Northeastern design competition was used to define the formal aspirations and potential for the project. As we continued to develop the project, we were always measuring our progress against this initial vision in which the original ideas of flow, movement, and the distinct attitude about a layered facade are clearly articulated.

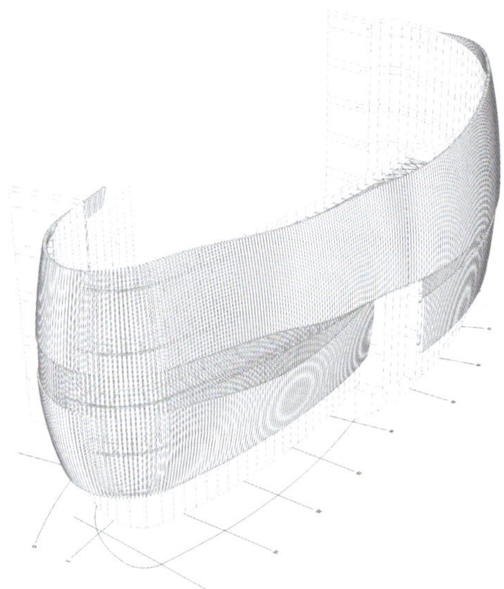

To optimize profile, form, assembly and performance, our designers developed a parametric model alongside custom compositing software to perform iterative simulations of performance and assembly techniques.

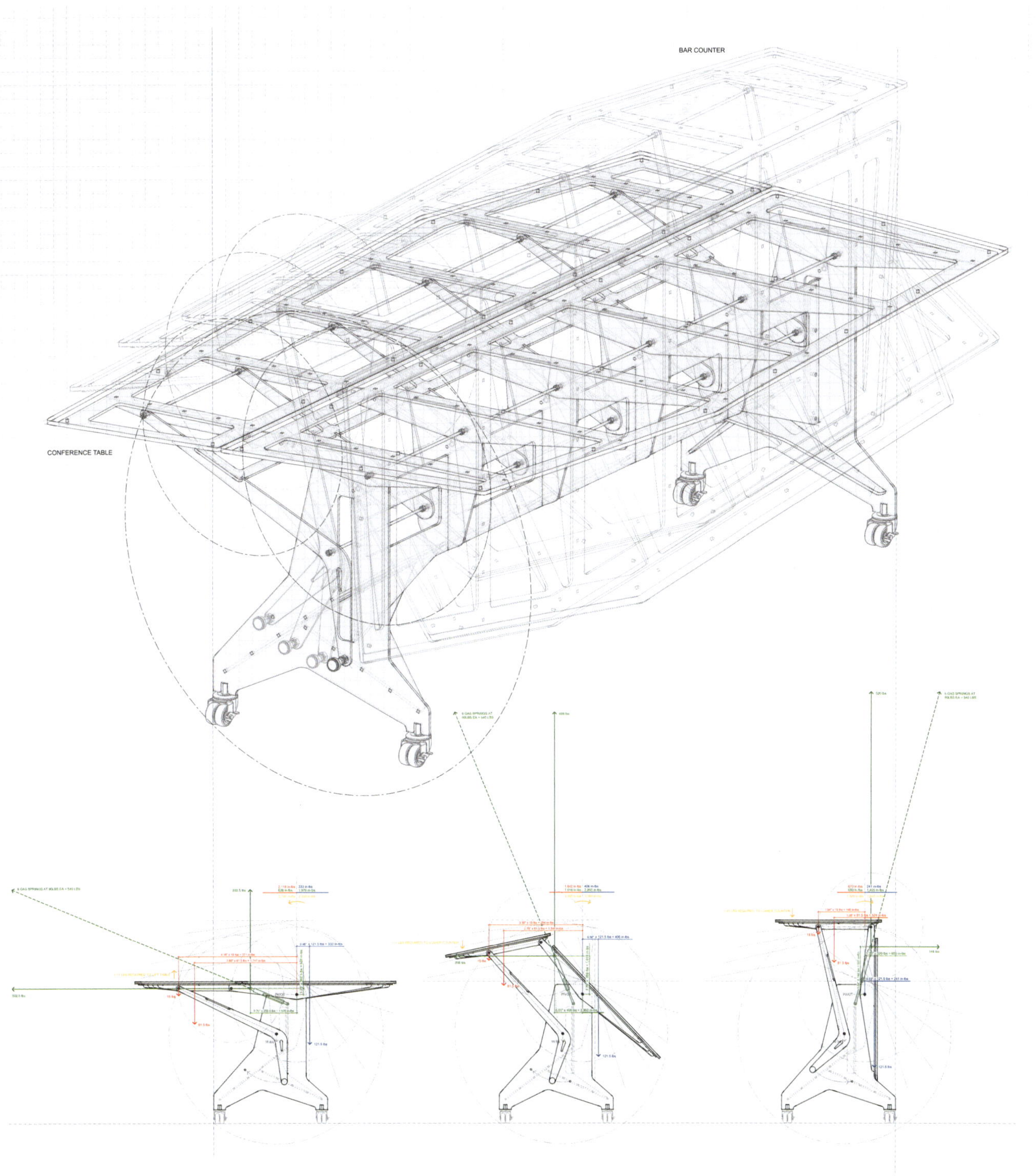
BAR COUNTER
CONFERENCE TABLE

The Art of Science

James H. Collins, Jr.

Payette sees the laboratory as a cultural institution as much as a scientific one. It is a place of imagination, not merely of procedure. Accordingly, its architecture must support the imagination, and our practice is dedicated to that end.

Despite society's fascination with the lone genius, science in the modern era (like architecture) is a collective endeavor. In 1885, author Sarah Knowles Bolton wrote of Thomas Edison,

> When one of his inventions failed—a printing machine—he took five men into the loft of his factory, declaring he would never come down till it worked satisfactorily. For two days, and nights and twelve hours—sixty hours in all—he worked continuously without sleep, until he had conquered the difficulty.

We can't help but wonder how much the other five men slept. For the architect, the more salient question is: What was the quality of their experience during those long hours? As it happens, we have some idea.

Thomas Edison Research Laboratory, 1876

When Edison's research laboratory opened in Menlo Park, New Jersey, in 1876, it was a simple, rectangular loft, with large windows for natural light—it predated, after all, the electric light bulb, which was perfected there. The windows opened for ventilation. Apparatuses weren't tethered to elaborate mechanical systems, but placed wherever was most convenient for the researchers. It was a workshop, not so different from the labs you see in paintings from the sixteenth century. Its roots were in the person and the science, with almost no engineering of the environment. It was a humane space. The same was true of turn-of-the-last-century academic teaching spaces for science: they were first of all well-proportioned, daylit rooms; technology barely shaped their design or expression.

Following World War II, things changed. The war had been won on the back of the atom bomb, developed in top secret laboratories, windowless to keep out prying eyes, compartmentalized so that only a very few knew the whole of what was going on. With the outbreak of the Cold War and the ensuing space race, technology became a driving force. Air conditioning arrived around the same time, and thinking about buildings of all sorts fundamentally changed. The laboratory changed dramatically. It came to be designed not by the researcher or the architect, but by the mechanical engineer, for the efficiency of the technical systems. Optimized around machinery, it was more like a factory, with a bulky mechanical core and ranks of fume hoods crowding out the windows. These Sputnik-era labs were closed and cramped, opaque and not at all conducive to collaboration.

Restoring the Academic Loft

This model predominated throughout the 1950s and, '60s and into the 1970s. Tom Payette first challenged it in the design of the Sherman Fairchild Biochemistry Laboratory at Harvard in 1981, reintroducing natural light and views, both to the outdoors and within the lab itself, so that the researchers could see one another at work. His goal was to make a place that would lift, rather than dampen, the human spirit—a place where scientists would enjoy working. This remains the underlying goal of all of Payette's work.

To accomplish that goal, Tom reimagined the relationship between lab spaces and the mechanical systems

Harvard University, Sherman Fairchild Biochemistry Laboratory, 1981

serving them. He moved the fume hoods to the interior and replaced the continuous, central mechanical shaft with a series of smaller shafts, between which the interior lab walls were glazed, floor to ceiling. The labs were fully transparent to the corridor, so that the connection to the outside carried all the way through the building.

Transparent to light and views, Sherman Fairchild also revealed its mechanical systems; there were no hung ceilings, no furred-out surfaces. Its concrete structure was left exposed, complemented by warm, wooden casework, rather than gray metal. It was the first lab to express its elements honestly and the first to dispel the chill, Cold War mentality.

Payette's next advance was to combine the uncomfortably small lab spaces, which were the postwar norm, into continuous, open labs, shared by several principal investigators. It took more

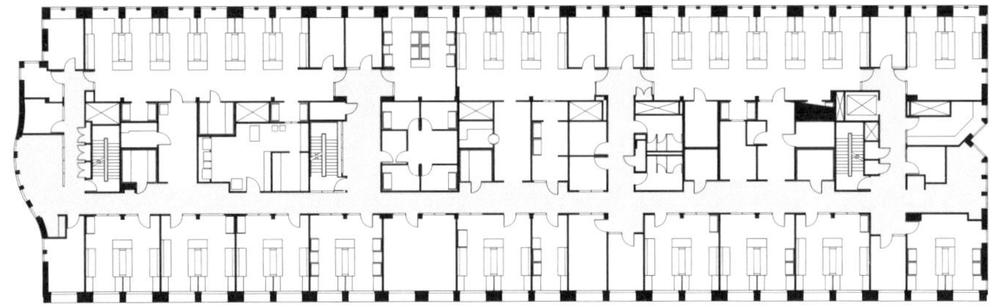

Princeton University, Lewis Thomas Laboratory, 1986

Middlebury College, McCardell Bicentennial Hall, 1999

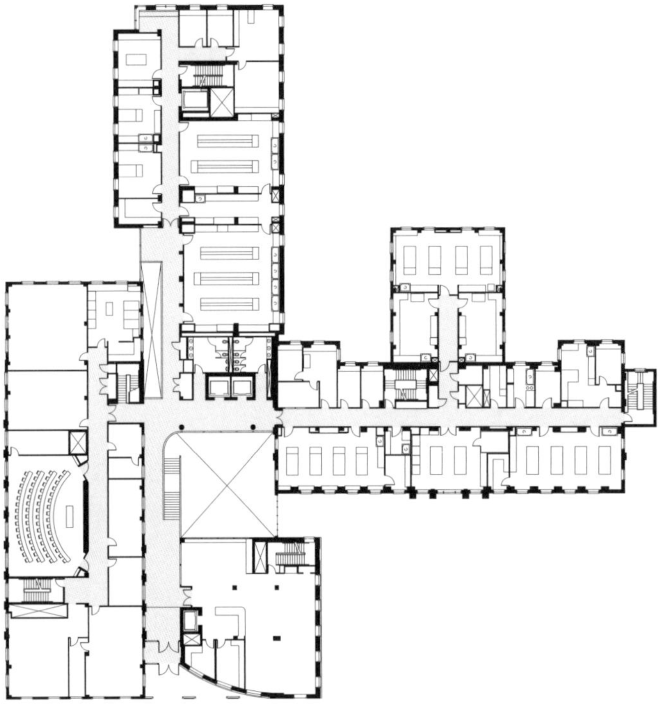

Washington and Lee University, Science Center, 1997

than simply removing walls. Architecture always requires an understanding of the relationships between natural phenomena, people, and the building itself. Technically complex buildings like labs are particularly demanding. In them, the control of air movement is critical, both for the safety of researchers and to avoid cross-contamination of experiments. To effectively control air movement in the open lab required invention: the development of precisely configured and strategically placed fume hood alcoves. The means may have been prosaic, but the result was inspiring: a bright, open, collaborative space, shaped not for the equipment but for the people.

We first realized the open lab in the Wellman Research Building at Massachusetts General Hospital in 1985. The following year, in Princeton University's Lewis Thomas Laboratory, we combined the open plan of Wellman with the transparency, expression of systems, and warmth of materials of Sherman Fairchild. To the long-diminished laboratory typology, Lewis Thomas reintroduced the energy and generosity of the academic loft.

Interaction and Discovery

In an open lab, less space is needed for corridors. At Lewis Thomas, we put some of that saved space to a novel use: we extended the ends of the remaining corridors into cozy lounges, comfortably furnished and lined with blackboards. It is now common practice for lab buildings to incorporate informal spaces for casual interaction among scientists; Lewis Thomas was the first institutionalized instance of it.

We have similarly reworked undergraduate teaching spaces to enhance interaction between faculty and students. Up until the mid-'90s, undergraduate science buildings were typically organized with large teaching labs on the entry floor and faculty offices on upper floors. Faculty research labs were rare, especially in small liberal arts colleges.

In the 1990s, many of these smaller colleges began to introduce research projects for seniors, to give them a taste of graduate school and to strengthen their admissions prospects. In two projects in the late '90s, one for Washington & Lee University (1997) and one for Middlebury College (1999), we dramatically reorganized the undergraduate science building to support this change in curriculum. At Washington & Lee, we clustered teaching labs, research labs, and faculty offices by discipline, which facilitated not only formal instruction but also informal learning. In particular, lower division students were exposed to the work of the seniors, from whom they could learn a great deal.

We took this idea further in McCardell Bicentennial Hall at Middlebury, where four arms radiate out from a central great hall. The relationship of the arms to the center is something like that of the arms of a starfish: there's an ambiguity about where the body stops and the arms begin. In McCardell Bicentennial Hall, each arm has a distinct program—wet labs in one, dry in another, with, again, the collocation of teaching labs, faculty labs, and offices—but they become less specific as they near the center, encouraging interaction between disciplines. The scheme mirrors the undergraduate experience of gradually focusing in on a specific area of study.

Efficiency and Social Geometry

McCardell Bicentennial Hall is also highly sustainable, not only in operation but also in construction. It was such a large building for the state of Vermont that it became the catalyst for the certified lumber industry in the state. As the first undergraduate science building to earn *R&D* magazine's Lab of the Year Award, which typically goes to major corporate research labs, it has become a much-emulated model.

Laboratories are expensive buildings, so we continually seek efficiencies of space, structure, materials, and systems. These efficiencies conserve resources and lower costs, but their ultimate goal is to make the building more limber, to permit richer, more productive social geometries. Such geometries—the ways that people see and meet one another, both in the midst of their work and in more casual encounters—affect, sometimes profoundly, the progress of their investigations.

Social geometry is three-dimensional. In Mass General's Wellman Research Building, for example, a structural system of less than normal depth enabled us to align the floors with the existing, adjacent Edwards Building, so that the labs in the two could operate as larger realms of collaboration. A similar strategy allowed us to carve out space for social interaction in George Washington University's Milken Institute School of Public Health in 2014.

Questioning Long-Held Assumptions

The greatest opportunity for resource conservation in labs is energy use. Laboratories, along with hospitals, are among the most energy consuming of all building types. Making a sustainable laboratory is one of today's critical challenges, one we are working hard to meet. In 2011, we established our Building Science Group to enable us to do it better, by integrating research and design. We conduct intensive investigations, shadowing researchers and metering actual energy use. We've discovered that many of the energy design loads (heating, cooling, electric) used in the industry are too high; they push you into less-sustainable systems. That's the first way to reduce energy use: get the loads right.

The optimization of HVAC systems is not merely a matter of energy savings, but also of human comfort, and

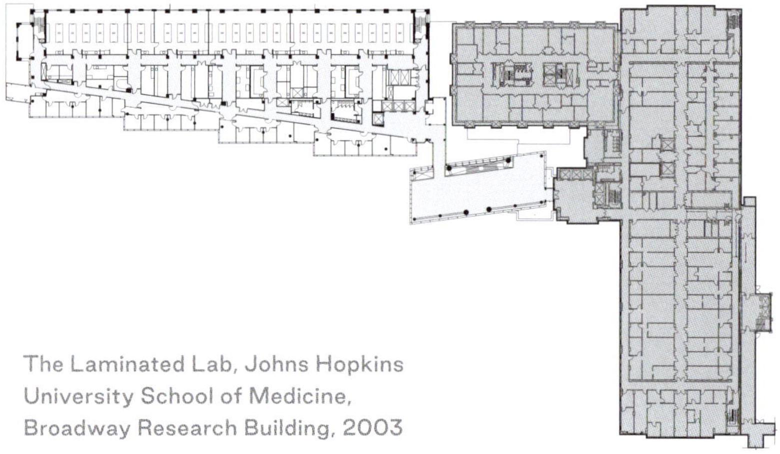

The Laminated Lab, Johns Hopkins University School of Medicine, Broadway Research Building, 2003

The Layered Laboratory Concept, National University of Ireland Galway, Biosciences Research Building, 2013

in fact the two are intimately entwined. Much of what building HVAC systems purport to do is to create a controlled environment for human comfort, yet the standard of comfort is defined in a psychrometric chart that was determined in the late 1950s, tuned to men in suits, rather than to our present population, more diverse in gender and dress. It is not surprising that most women feel that typical academic buildings are overcooled. Their voice did not contribute to that chart. We now have the ability to develop more detailed models of human comfort that track clothing worn, air temperature and movement, and radiant surface temperature differentials, and we can design systems that respond to this information. Just as the metering of actual power usage for equipment has enabled us to reduce building energy loads, so does the accurate assessment of comfort needs; together, the two reduce not only energy use but also the capital cost of construction.

Systems Differentiation and the Laminated Lab

Thinking of energy consumption as a function of human experience has allowed us to make paradigm-changing advances in laboratory architecture. Wellman's structural innovations were accompanied by an innovation in HVAC systems—separating laboratory heating, served by fan coils, from ventilation. Doing so made both more efficient. More significantly, the concept of separating the two enabled a revolutionary planning strategy, one that has further enhanced the human experience, in what have ultimately become some of the world's most energy-efficient labs.

In 1995, we introduced the "laminated lab," in which the researchers' offices, which had typically been interspersed between lab spaces, are organized as a band on one side of the building. On the other side is a band of labs, with a band of support spaces in between. This arrangement was more cost-effective, because it consolidated the expensive, high-technology spaces on one side and the less expensive office space on the other. At the same time, it gave both office and lab space direct views to the out-of-doors. Other examples of the laminated lab from this period are the Chemistry Research and Life Sciences Buildings at Penn State (2004) and the Life Sciences Building at West Virginia University (2002).

Shadow Studies and the Layered Lab

At the outset of our practice, founding partners Fred Markus and Paul Nocka used time-motion studies and extensive, firsthand observations to develop a detailed understanding of how hospitals worked and how they could be made to work better. We employ similar techniques for laboratories, shadowing researchers engaged in a wide range of activities, spending a day doing what they do, so that we understand it intimately. In recent years, we have observed a gradual change in research practice, driven by increasing reliance on specialized equipment. Whereas researchers had typically spent more time at the lab bench than in support spaces, today they spend more time in the support spaces, where this equipment is housed. When these spaces were used rarely, it was acceptable for them to be in the center of the building, without views. That is no longer the case, so we have introduced another paradigmatic change in layout. In the "layered lab," prototyped in an unbuilt project for Harvard's Allston Campus and first realized in our Biosciences Research Building at the National University of Ireland Galway (2013), the support spaces form an outside band, with the band of open laboratory spaces in the middle, looking through floor-to-ceiling glass to the non-technical workspace and the outside world beyond. Now everyone enjoys daylight and views.

At the same time, the layered lab dramatically changes the energy profile of the building. All of the spaces that don't use chemicals—the workspace layer—can have a separate, less robust mechanical system. The cost of these systems is reduced, and there's a big jump in energy efficiency. At 143 kBtu/sq.ft., the project at NUIG uses 72 percent less energy than the current baseline set for the 2030 Challenge, and was awarded a national AIA COTE Top Ten Award.

Sense Experience

As we have transformed the planning of laboratories, we have also rethought the details that intimately affect the individual researcher. For the Biomedical Sciences Tower III at the University of Pittsburgh School of Medicine (2005), we developed a modular, adaptable casework system, which allows for ease of reconfiguration. The lab's facilities department can raise and lower the benches and relocate them for better, more cost-effective arrangements, without calling in a contractor.

In our 2011 renovation of Harvard's Sherman Fairchild Biochemistry Building (for which we had designed the first wooden casework thirty years previously), we introduced a task ambient lighting strategy, using very thin strip LEDs as task lights under the shelf of the lab bench, which puts light where the researchers actually need it and reduces the power density in the lab by half. Working with a lighting manufacturer, we designed the fixture, versions of which are now produced by several manufacturers and are being used widely in the industry. The color of the benches themselves is calibrated to reduce eye strain. We treat the interiors of the labs with as much care as the lobby and office spaces, using wood and other materials that aren't only durable but also pleasant. At the Schepens Eye Research Institute for Harvard School of Medicine (2004), we use color in the laboratories to explore the depth of the visual field for scientists investigating the same concept in their research.

The Lab, the Campus, and the Wider World

The material of a bench-top is architecture at its most intimate. At its most expansive is a building's relationship to its near and distant contexts. Today, with society's renewed focus on STEM fields, colleges and universities are investing heavily in academic laboratories, which often play defining roles on the campus. They shape the experience not only of faculty and students in the sciences, but of the entire campus community and, in some cases, the city of which it is a part. This larger context is both natural and cultural, and for us the building is an opportunity to weave connections between the two.

Our recently completed New Science Center for Amherst College (2018), set against the Pelham Hills, anchors the eastern edge of the campus in the landscape. Its transparent commons, a focal point of the new campus greenway, makes its activities visible, inviting interest in the sciences. At Northeastern University, the Interdisciplinary Science and Engineering Complex (2016) is a gateway to the university's new academic precinct, connecting the Fenway and Roxbury neighborhoods of Boston. Its fluid form, sculpted to guide passage between the precincts, is rigorously tuned to dramatically reduce heating and cooling loads—a vivid demonstration of the fusion of design and performance. Its publicly accessible six-story atrium is scaled to serve as the hub of the new precinct.

Knowledge and Freedom

The true measure of a building's success is its ability to support the technical, physical, and behavioral needs of those who use it. From the sensual qualities of a surface to the social geometry of an entire research complex and the campus of which it is a part, human experience drives the disruptive actions of our practice. Introducing transparency, revealing systems, cracking open compartments, proposing new patterns of interaction, we have opened up the laboratory typology as no one had done before.

The art of design for science is knowing the science well enough to identify when such changes can occur, and knowing what the changes mean for the culture of science. The freedom to enact these changes is hard-won, a product of our deep knowledge of the type and our research into building performance and human behavior. Over the past four decades, Payette has freed the laboratory from its postwar claustrophobia, making it once again a place of imagination.

EXIT

The Hospital as a Small City

George E. Marsh, Jr.

We are privileged to live and work in Boston, where nature is embedded seamlessly throughout the city, in the famed Emerald Necklace, the series of parks, greenways, and waterways laid out by Frederick Law Olmsted between 1878 and 1895. These green spaces bring delight to the city and are crucial for its health, providing a respite from the hustle-bustle and reconnecting us to the natural world. Interwoven with the pattern of streets and squares, they also help to organize the city, to make it comprehensible.

We think of the hospital in a similar way, as a small city. The analogy is a powerful one, a continual reminder that it is first of all a place of human relationships. We conceive of it as a community of neighborhoods, formed around gardens and plazas—moments of embedded nature—connected by streets and boulevards. The clarity of these patterns is a comfort in a place of high emotion. Patient and visitor alike know where they are, where they are going, and how they will return. Throughout the journey and in the clinical spaces themselves, they experience the healing power of sunlight and foliage; they can step out for a breath of fresh air.

Hospital as a linked set of pavilions—Peter Bent Brigham Hospital, Boston, 1913

Roots in the American Tradition

This transparency to the natural world is paramount within our design process, yet it also revisits ideas that were essential to healthcare architecture over one hundred years ago. The evolution of American hospital architecture is rooted in the 1880s, when the most advanced models of the times were shaped by principles prescribed in Florence Nightingale's seminal book, *Notes on Hospitals*, of 1857. Hospitals of the late nineteenth century were organized around pavilion wards, based on Nightingale's prescription for health: sun, air, water, and evasion of infection. Nature was invited in for the health of the patient. Sunlight and ventilation studies of carefully placed beds within precisely dimensioned wards, conducted by Nightingale and, later, in 1905, by William Atkinson, were the precursors of today's performance models.

Hospitals of this generation were cadences of linked pavilions, on hills, in open fields, or by a river, and landscape architects significantly influenced their design. Olmsted had worked with H.H. Richardson on the Buffalo State Hospital of 1880, which followed the Kirkbride Plan asylum model. Based on theories of mental healthcare advanced by Philadelphia psychiatrist Dr. Thomas Story Kirkbride, this model sought healing through exposure to natural light and air, but it did so in a single, imposing building with long, narrow wings. Similar healthcare goals shaped McLean Hospital of 1895, but its form was much different. Olmsted and the civil engineer Joseph Curtis selected its site amidst the rolling hills and trees of Belmont, Massachusetts. Its patient cottages, surrounding a central administration building, were placed in concert with the land, not imposed on it. Between 1895 and 1912, Olmsted's sons, John Charles and Frederick, Jr., composed the same wonderful choreography of land and hospital at Butler Hospital in Providence, Rhode Island, to achieve a healing environment of nature, light, and air for the institution's psychiatric patient.

Typical mid-century hospital

Retreat from Nature

The next half-century saw an evolution away from hospital design that opened outward to nature, toward hermetic, inward-looking configurations. Very few hospitals were designed by exemplary architects. Far too many were designed by doctors-as-designers—like Dr. S. S. Goldwater, who consulted on administration and construction for such hospitals as the Welfare Hospital for Chronic Diseases on New York City's Roosevelt Island—or by multiple generations of hospital architects with a solely technical focus.

Technological progress contributed to the turn away from nature. The invention of the elevator, while of enormous benefit, fragmented the experience of passage and helped turn the

Leonard Morse Hospital, Patient Unit, 1971

hospital into a disorienting, three-dimensional labyrinth. The advent of air-conditioning allowed hospitals to become increasingly internalized. No longer did they have to breathe. The midcentury French term *le plateau technique* summed up the situation: the hospital had become a platform of technology, packed with program, from diagnostic radiology to surgical suites, organized around its mechanical systems. Careless, ad hoc additions exacerbated the confusion, as hospitals expanded, filling city blocks and consuming what little outdoor space remained.

Genesis of the Courtyard Hospital

In 1969, Tom Payette began to reverse this trend with groundbreaking work at Leonard Morse Hospital in Natick, Massachusetts. In the fifty years preceding this project, the partnership of landscape design and building design had, with very few exceptions, been on sabbatical. Working with landscape architect Carol R. Johnson, Tom restored this relationship, and an idea about the landscape permeated Leonard Morse's planning. Its sloped site allowed for stepped courtyards at entry areas, merging inside and outside. The hospital's sawtoothed plan, with openings carved into it for small courtyards, reintroduced light and air. Corridors ran adjacent to these courtyards, so patients always knew where they were.

A detail of the patient rooms at Leonard Morse is representative of the firm's approach to design. The challenge—a perennial one—was to bring fresh air directly into the room without compromising the view with insect screening. The solution was to separate the two functions, providing large, fixed-glass panels for light and view, with opaque operable panels below, for natural ventilation. The opaque panels conceal the screening; the view is undisturbed. A simple but unexpected idea emerged from a process of questioning long-standing assumptions.

Introducing the Cluster

Similar questioning led to a paradigm shift in the organization of patient floors, one that Tom Payette had been developing in a number of smaller projects and brought to fruition at Leonard Morse. At the time, most hospitals were organized in long bars with double-loaded corridors, with patient rooms and support spaces strung out along them. Travel times for nurses were inordinately long. Tom reconfigured these floors as aggregated clusters of rooms, spokes around a hub that contained both the nurses' station and medical support spaces. Gaps between clusters brought light into the hub, so that the new configuration changed not only how nurses worked, but also the ambience of the place. The complex geometries of the clusters engendered new possibilities of texture and detail, bringing a sense of human scale that had been lacking in the healthcare architecture of the 1960s.

Aga Khan University and Hospital, Plan for a New Campus

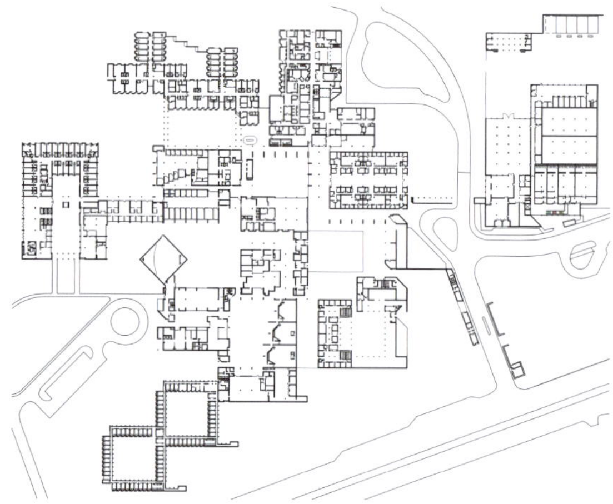

Similar thinking led to a new model for ICUs at Emerson Hospital several years later: a dual-corridor layout, with an internal corridor for the medical staff and a perimeter corridor with light and views, where visitors can relax, separate from the hubbub of staff activities.

The Courtyard Hospital Comes of Age

The successful innovations at Leonard Morse soon led to an even more radical rethinking of the hospital. In 1970 or '71, a selection committee from the Aga Khan University Hospital traveled through Europe and the United States, seeking an architect for a new hospital in Central Asia. Morgan Wheelock, landscape architect from Sasaki, Dawson & DeMay was on the committee; he had helped design Costa Smeralda in Sardinia, a resort for the Aga Khan, in which the landscape design was as important as the architecture. Wheelock recommended that the Aga Khan meet Tom Payette and visit Leonard Morse Hospital after his meeting with The

Joslin Diabetes Foundation, 1976

Architects Collaborative in Cambridge. Tom toured the hospital with the Aga Khan, who said, "Mr. Payette, this is a terrific hospital, but it is not anything that I want." Nevertheless, two days later, Tom received a letter inviting him to design the new Aga Khan University Hospital in Karachi, Pakistan. As he recounts, the Aga Khan "felt that I would listen, and that I would look, and that I would undertake to try to find a direction that would relate in a modern way to Islam."

In the Aga Khan University Hospital, the historic rules of Islamic architecture, incorporating cooling breezes and the interplay of shade and sunlight, led to an unprecedented union of building and landscape. The hospital became a choreography of landscape places, designed in collaboration with Sasaki. Courtyards are the focus, with buildings as their edges—the inverse of the platform hospital with courtyards carved into it. An oasis in the midst of one of the most chaotic cities in the world, its courtyards are its waiting rooms, with dappled shade, trees filled with birds, with cool air and cool stone benches. They provide clear entries to the clinics; orientation is easy. The idea of embedded nature had opened up the internalized hospital into a city of piazzas for health, and the idea of the courtyard hospital became an essential component of our practice.

Many commissions followed, challenging the monolithic hospital block. Most notable was the mid-1970s work at Joslin Diabetes Foundation in Boston, where a central courtyard, framed by the new building and two existing Joslin buildings, is a jewel in the city block. Also designed with Sasaki, this landscaped outdoor space allows natural light to suffuse all the buildings. It is a point of orientation for patients and a place of healing, sheltered from the urban surroundings.

Johns Hopkins Hospital with view to dome, 1996

Penn State Health Hershey Medical Center, 2009

Restorative Urbanism

The idea of the hospital as a small city is particularly clear in Payette's work at Johns Hopkins Hospital. The original campus layout, envisioned by John Billings in the 1880s, with landscape design by E. W. Bowditch, featured a central green quadrangle on axis with the institution's iconic Dome. The edges of the quadrangle were defined by a series of sunny, airy pavilions by architects Cabot and Chandler.

In the 1970s, the quad had been largely filled in to form a continuous building, violating this wonderful campus parti and severing the view along the axis to the historic Dome. A clumsy, air-conditioned mass, the hospital had forgotten its roots as a healing environment in the landscape.

In the late 1980s, healthcare strategies were changing. Overnight hospital stays were being reduced, while more care was being provided on an outpatient, or ambulatory, basis. Payette was selected to design an outpatient center and parking structure across Broadway from the Dome. The new center—the first freestanding ambulatory care facility in the country—would house a number of outpatient programs, extracting lines of services from neurology to pathology to orthopedics from the density of the complex old campus.

The Payette scheme revived ideas of placemaking that had shaped the original campus. By closing a city street, we created a new, landscaped campus mall, on axis with and once again celebrating the Dome. This was the first of perhaps eight projects in which we replaced roads with pedestrian green space, to restore the idea of campus. The edge of the mall is defined by the Outpatient Center, which opened in 1996. Internally, a central spine, flanked by small courtyards, provides a clear, simple circulation path for patient and visitor. Extending under Broadway, this spine intersects a skylit subway station before continuing on to unite the new building with the original campus.

Prefiguring the Healing Garden

In the early 2000s, the practice of healthcare architecture went through what was touted as a "revolution," with the emergence of therapeutic, or healing, gardens. Suddenly and with great publicity, the profession "discovered" this idea, through "evidence-based design." Our practice did not change its direction; embedded nature was implicit in all we designed, as was the formative use of evidence. The ideals of performance—air, sun, thermal comfort—that were now highlighted and studied in depth had been fundamental to our work since the 1960s.

We continued integrating architecture and landscape in large healthcare projects. Penn State Health's Milton S. Hershey Medical Center Master Plan (2005), Cancer Institute (2009), and Children's Hospital (2012), are united by an arc marrying land and building, together forming a garden hospital. In the continuous passage of the arc, patients and visitors understand where they are and where they are going. Woven between the building blocks that extend from the arc are six gardens, for six different patient audiences. The spirit of the early Payette courtyards is alive in these gardens, which connect inside to outside to form distinct places of healing—a garden for children, for chemotherapy infusion, for the hospital itself—piazzas in a small city.

The idea of special places nestled within the city is a theme of the Beth Israel Deaconess Medical Center New Inpatient Building, which is scheduled for completion in 2022. Adding to the 1980s Rosenberg Building, it completes a 300-by-400-foot block in the center of the Longwood Medical Area in Boston. The first five floors build the technical platform of surgeries, diagnostic imaging, and emergency services linking both buildings. The special place is the patient garden sheltered between the old and new patient wings, lofted above the city.

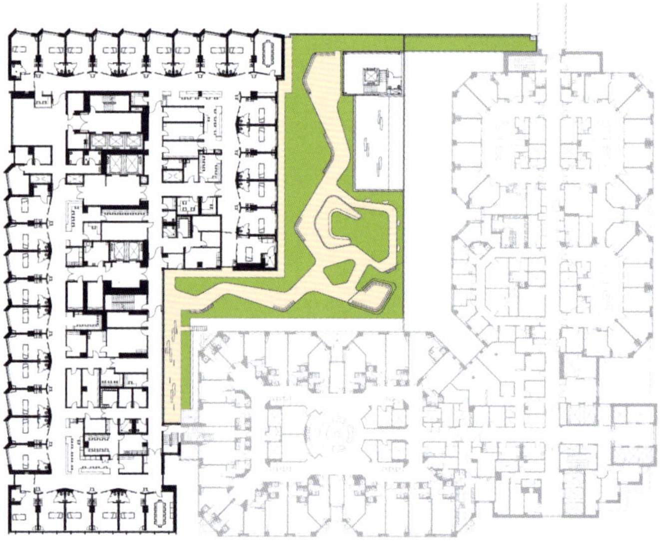

Beth Israel Deaconess Medical Center

Fifth Xiangya Hospital, Landscape Plan

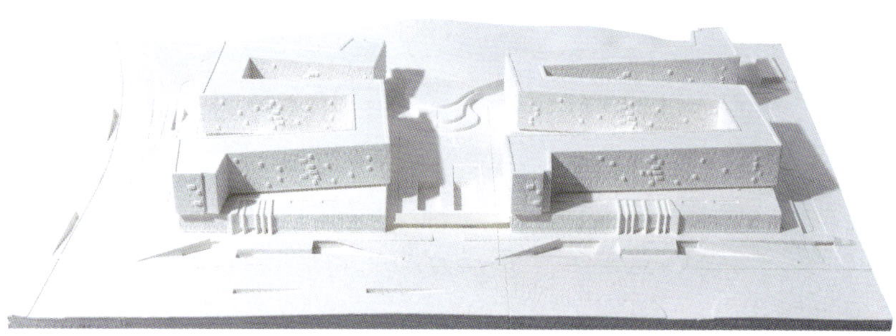

Fifth Xiangya Hospital, Design Competition Model

The patient lobbies are all glazed—sky lobbies, streetscape upper connector, and main lobby—mirroring the famed Riverway landscape that bounds the hospital campus, part of Olmsted's Emerald Necklace. The patient garden, the Francis Street gateway from the Riverway, and the landscape designed holistically for the city block are 2020 siblings of Olmsted's Riverway ideals.

The Sustainable Hospital

The largest hospital we have designed as a small city is the Fifth Xiangya Hospital in Changsha, China, which will open in 2020 as an eco-hospital in a garden. The complex is situated at the base of Xianguling Park. The landscape defines the architecture, the hillside park cascading onto the platform, a series of openings in the patient wings bringing light, air, and clarity of orientation to the lowest levels. They are a twenty-first-century reminder of the courtyards of Leonard Morse Hospital in the 1960s and Aga Khan University Hospital in the 1970s.

On the patient floors, dragon-like in plan, patient rooms face south and east. Their windows are sculpted into family niches that, expressed on the exterior, bring the huge complex—the size of Boston Common—into human scale. For Xiangya, as for Beth Israel Deaconess Medical Center and another current project, the Chelsea Soldiers' Home, we mocked up the window element at full size, through many iterations, both to fine tune how it welcomes the visiting family and to optimize solar performance. At Xiangya, the windows provide natural ventilation—something that would be good to reintroduce into the American hospital.

Sunlight and air are key factors in human experience; they are key, as well, to designing sustainable buildings. Hospitals, along with laboratories—the other focus of Payette's work—use far more energy than any other common building type. They share extraordinary technical constraints, such as contamination control, and extraordinary demands, such as the energy loads of sophisticated equipment. To design a sustainable hospital is one of the great architectural challenges of our day.

Payette is meeting this challenge with the simultaneous creation of humane places and high-performing buildings. The two are equally dependent on the building's relationship to the natural environment. We believe each advances further when they are considered together. Doing so calls for both cultivated intuition and rigorous calculation, the fusion of design and performance. This fusion can be seen in the family niches of Xiangya, where solar performance meets human comfort and interaction. They create a personal space for many different uses including a place of meditation, an area for a parent and child to be together, a space for relaxation, or just a framed view to the garden.

Why Hospitals?

Since its earliest days, our firm has measured the things that can be measured, both to optimize those things and to better shape the important things that can't, perhaps, be measured at all. When at their best, architects are both scientists and humanists; that, at least, is how we see it. The hospital offers a stern test of our capacity to be so. It is a test we welcome. We enjoy the technical and formal complexity, and we value the opportunity to shape buildings in which people encounter some of life's most difficult challenges and most remarkable discoveries, some of its greatest joys and deepest sorrows. It is a privilege to bring the gifts of architecture to the moments when we are most vulnerable. The impact of design on these life thresholds is immediate and profound. No other building type can demonstrate, so consistently and so meaningfully, the effects of good design.

One measure of a society's values is the buildings it celebrates. Historically, hospitals were among our most celebrated institutions. Iconic in form, they were sited prominently not only to welcome in natural light and air, but also as places of civic pride. Today, cities look instead to museums as signs of stature. Hospitals, more often than not, are formless aggregations, disconnected from the city, sterile mechanisms of little symbolic value. The contrast is unsettling, and our priorities are unsettled, both as a society and as architects.

The museum's value is real and significant, but we visit it by choice, and many people don't visit it at all. By contrast, we go to the hospital because we have to, and sooner or later we all have to. More people experience hospitals, more regularly, than experience museums—or courthouses or city halls or DMVs or indeed any other civic building. There is no better or more important place to demonstrate the impact of good architecture.

We take pride in designing hospitals that are humane and sustainable and that, once again, represent core values of our society: service, compassion, healing, and a common spirit and vision. We find these values most fully realized in a place that embraces the natural world within the world we have made, the hospital as a small city.

Stunned by the devastation wrought by Haiti's 2010 earthquake, our healthcare group was determined to apply our expertise to help rebuild the country. This pro bono project, a new maternity hospital for a grossly underserved community, emerged from a multiyear, pro bono design-build relief effort initiated by the firm. Located in mountainous terrain three hours west of Port-au-Prince, the St. Boniface Hospital is the only hospital in the southern peninsula, and serves a population of almost twelve thousand inhabitants.

The Aga Khan University and Hospital complex is one of the largest philanthropic projects of its kind ever initiated in a developing country. It serves as the primary institutional focus for the healthcare efforts of the Ismaili Community, operating over one hundred primary medical and health units in rural Pakistan. Payette designed the original hospital and has continued to further AKU's vision through subsequent new buildings over the past forty years, setting a new paradigm for the network of primary and secondary healthcare facilities throughout the country.

Project Stories

Flow

Northeastern University

Interdisciplinary Science and Engineering Complex

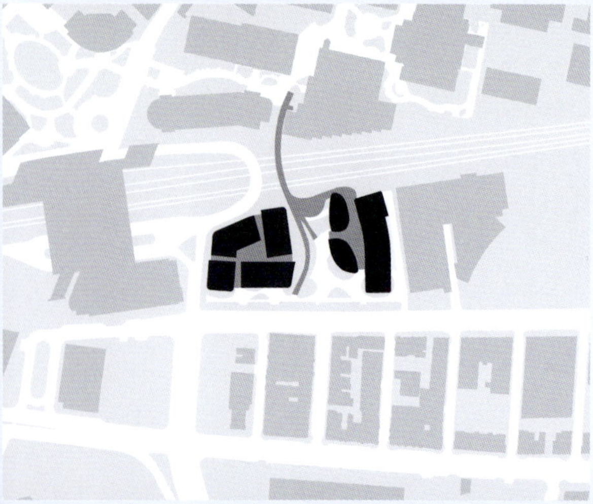

Northeastern University
Interdisciplinary Science and Engineering Complex

Historically, Northeastern University has been constrained by a sunken rail corridor along its southeast edge, separating its Huntington Avenue Campus in the Fenway from neighboring Roxbury. The university's long-anticipated expansion across this divide could have amounted to little more than a workaday footbridge leading to run-of-the-mill classroom buildings. The university president and the expansion of the research mission demanded something more powerful: an iconic gateway that would encourage movement between the two campus precincts and the two neighborhoods. The occasion for this gateway would be a new science center, intended to advance the university's cutting-edge, interdisciplinary approach to global challenges in the areas of sustainability, security, and health.

The issue from a pedestrian point of view, as we saw it, was one of flow: how to draw people to and across the landscape. This idea of flow guided our design of the Interdisciplinary Science and Engineering Complex. It suggested that the pedestrian path might depart from the rigid lines of the railway and streets, that the form of the building might yield to that path, and that the building might actually become, in a sense, a part of the path.

Northeastern University

Thus began the development of a building form that curves away from Columbus Avenue to lead you over the tracks. How many things might such a form do, and how tightly might they be synthesized, one with another? First and perhaps most obviously, the unexpected shape stands out as an icon, drawing attention both to the passage between campuses and to the role of the sciences in the university. Convex on the outside, it is an embracing void within, a soaring atrium that becomes not only a common space for the sciences but also a living room for the new campus. Like an eddy in a stream, it is as much an extension of the path as a building alongside it.

Early sketch of the design concept illustrating the idea of flow and movement through the site, creating a new urban path

The building's shape is not mere whimsy, but rather a precisely calibrated response to the course of the sun, balancing the entry of daylight with the reduction of solar heat gain. Iterative simulations, employing parametric modeling and custom compositing software developed by our Building Sciences Group, shaped the exterior shading system as an integral part of the building's form: a striking example of the fusion of design and performance.

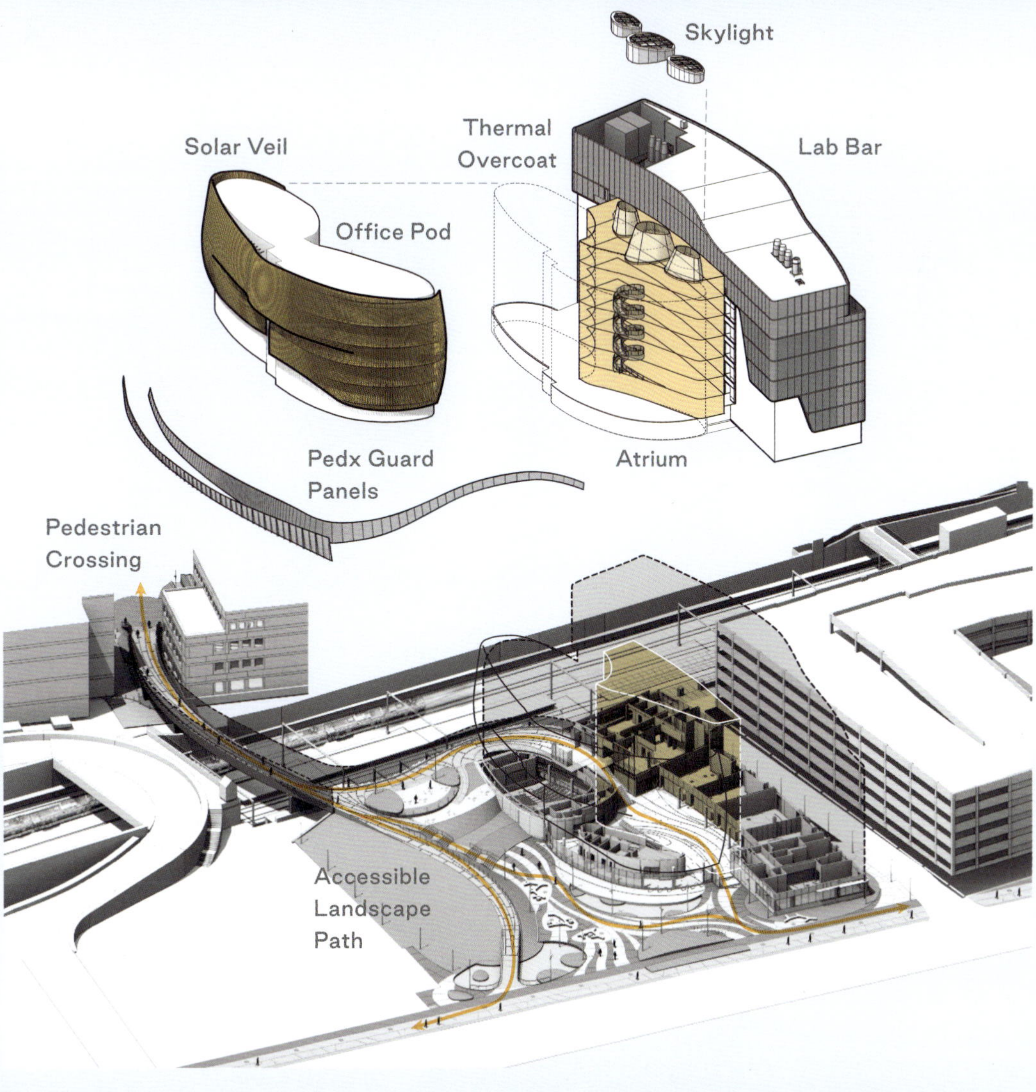
Skylight
Thermal
Overcoat
Lab Bar
Solar Veil
Office Pod
Atrium
Pedx Guard
Panels
Pedestrian
Crossing
Accessible
Landscape
Path

805

The atrium acts as a mixing chamber for a cascade ventilation system that conditions and recycles air throughout the building. It is a social mixing chamber, as well. Surrounding it are research neighborhoods of labs and intimate collaboration spaces, which encourage the fortuitous collisions and conversations that break down disciplinary divides. The labs follow the layered paradigm we first introduced in the Biosciences Research Building at the National University of Ireland in Galway, with the write-up spaces separated by glass walls from the more energy-intensive bench spaces, dramatically reducing overall energy use. In a radical departure from the typical lab, the write-up spaces face inward to the daylit atrium, so that visitors and fellow research students and faculty can see what's going on. Science is on display.

Back outside, the public pathway curves past the building, ascending the slope to a new pedestrian bridge that is anything but workaday. Its slanted, weathered steel panels, developed through full-scale mock-ups in our FabLab, lend rhythm to the passage. Spaced progressively apart, they appear solid on first approach before opening to a view of the Boston skyline. The bridge is both a dramatic embodiment of the idea of flow and an engineering and logistical feat. Its larger span—132 feet long, weighing sixteen tons—was lifted into place in the dead of night by the largest crane in New England.

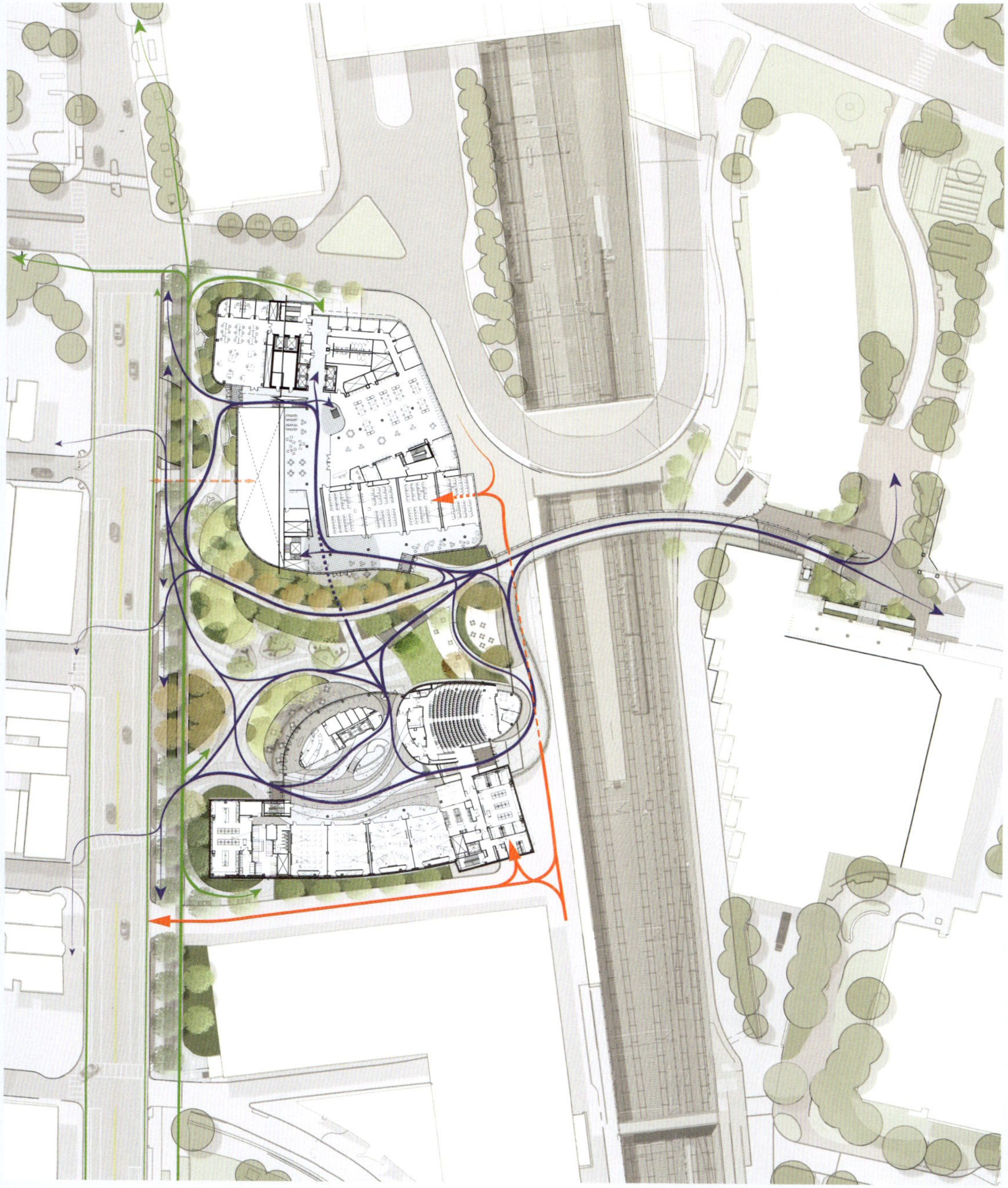

Performance Strategy

To optimize the profile, volumetric form, and performance of the sunshade system, our designers developed a parametric model, rendered with custom compositing software, that allowed us to perform iterative simulations to predict the screen's solar performance.

The laboratories are divided into high- and low-energy zones. A cascade ventilation system leverages this zoning to reduce the outside air needed for the research spaces. Outside air is supplied to perimeter offices and passively drawn into the atrium, which acts as a mixing chamber before the air flows through the write-up spaces to the research spaces. A solar wall along the southern side of the penthouse preheats the air in the winter; a high-efficiency heat recovery system captures heat exhausted from the research spaces.

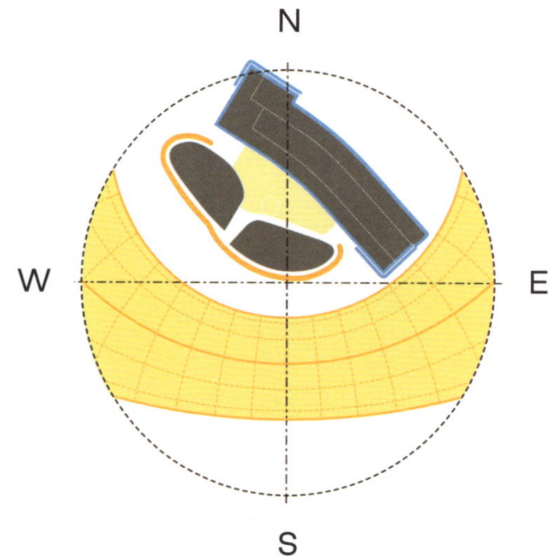

Sun Path Diagram

78% Average energy savings over typical lab/2030 baseline

91 kBtu/sq. ft.

57% Reduction in potable water use for flush and flow fixtures

1,316 Houses

Energy Reduction Equivalency to annual energy usage

LEED Gold Certified

AIA COTE Top Ten Award

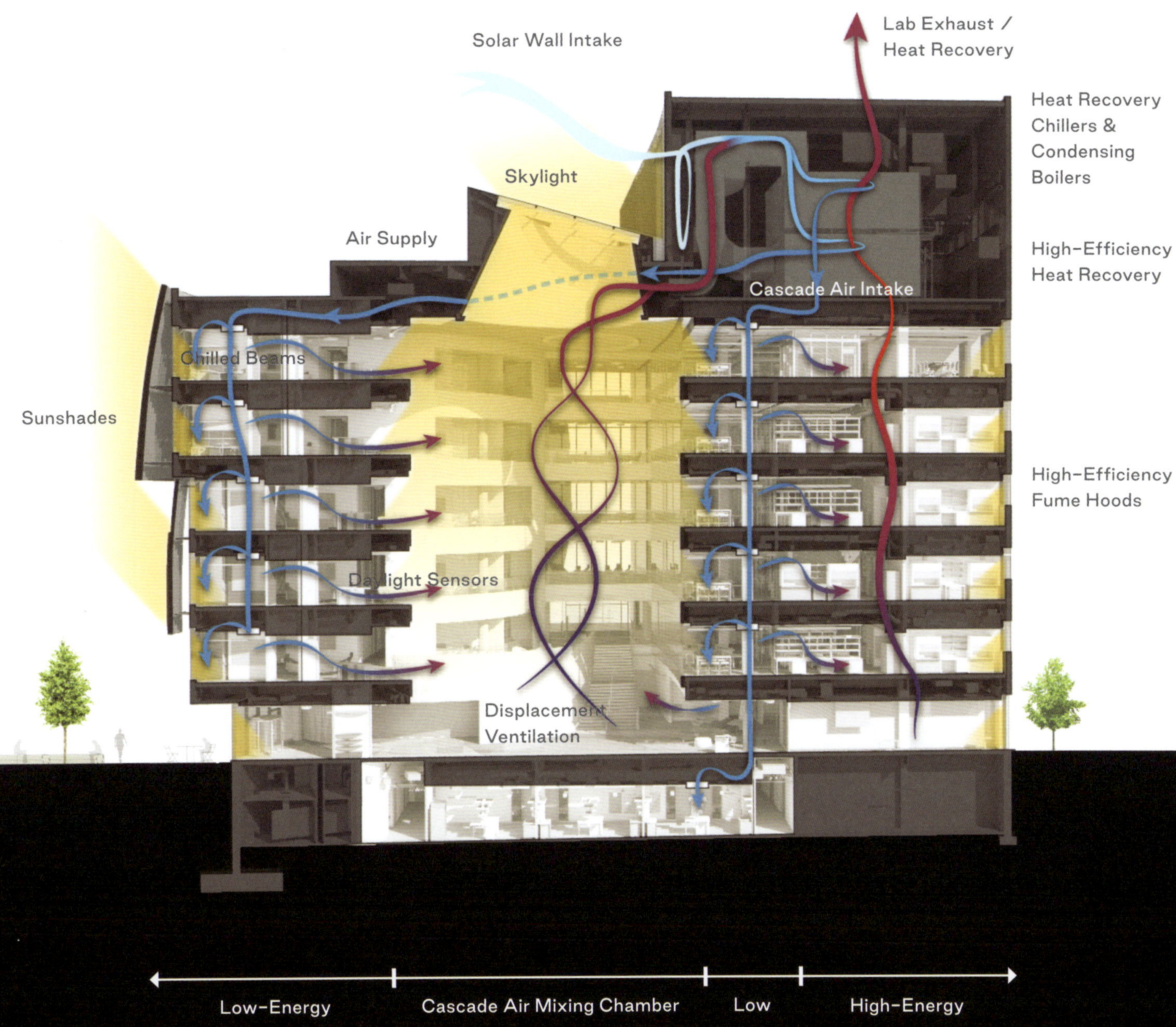

Solar Wall Intake
Lab Exhaust / Heat Recovery
Heat Recovery Chillers & Condensing Boilers
Skylight
Air Supply
High-Efficiency Heat Recovery
Cascade Air Intake
Chilled Beams
Sunshades
High-Efficiency Fume Hoods
Daylight Sensors
Displacement Ventilation
Low-Energy
Cascade Air Mixing Chamber
Low
High-Energy

Jewel Box

Tufts University

Science and Engineering Complex

Tufts University
Science and Engineering Complex

A delicate glass box floats effortlessly between two historic, redbrick bookends. Its taut skin celebrates and reflects its surroundings, complements the brick, and lends quiet dignity to the older buildings. Its contingent form shapes a nested series of interior and exterior spaces that heighten awareness of the juxtaposition of old with new.

Located three miles north of Boston, in the Mystic River Watershed, the new Science and Engineering Complex at Tufts University is an unexpected and innovative response to site and context. At its core, it is about doing more with less. Rather than relocate or demolish one of the significant historic buildings on the site, as the university's initial project description suggested, we proposed a smaller but more ambitious addition that revitalizes the existing buildings and creates an integrated complex. From the outset of the project, our team set ambitious targets for building performance. The project's sustainable solutions are integral to its architectural solution, mirroring the interdependence between sustainability and scientific research.

The Science and Engineering Complex is a dynamic, community-focused, high-tech hub for interdisciplinary research in biology, environmental science, and neuroscience. The academic precinct it has created satisfies the university's desire for a critical mass of research and teaching space to support cross-departmental collaborations in an environmentally responsible manner.

Instead of housing individual departments, the SEC allows students and faculty from different disciplines to collaborate on research themes in lab space designed to accommodate new themes as they arise. An exciting innovation for Tufts, it is the first instance here of the joint use of labs—a concept increasingly adopted by peer institutions across the country.

The building comprises two lab wings with flexible suites on each floor housing a wide array of scientific research. Inflected by the historic buildings, the wings pinwheel around an L-shaped atrium that provides a campus living room and informal communal spaces unlike any that previously existed.

HENRICKS ART WALL

The site's sloping topography allows for entrances on three levels, making the building welcoming and open to its setting. The spaces between it and the earlier buildings are now as significant as those buildings' prominent public faces, animating movement through the campus. The redevelopment of the landscape has transformed an underutilized space into a model of sustainability, planted with a variety of low-maintenance, native species to increase biodiversity, encourage habitat creation, and reduce heat island effect.

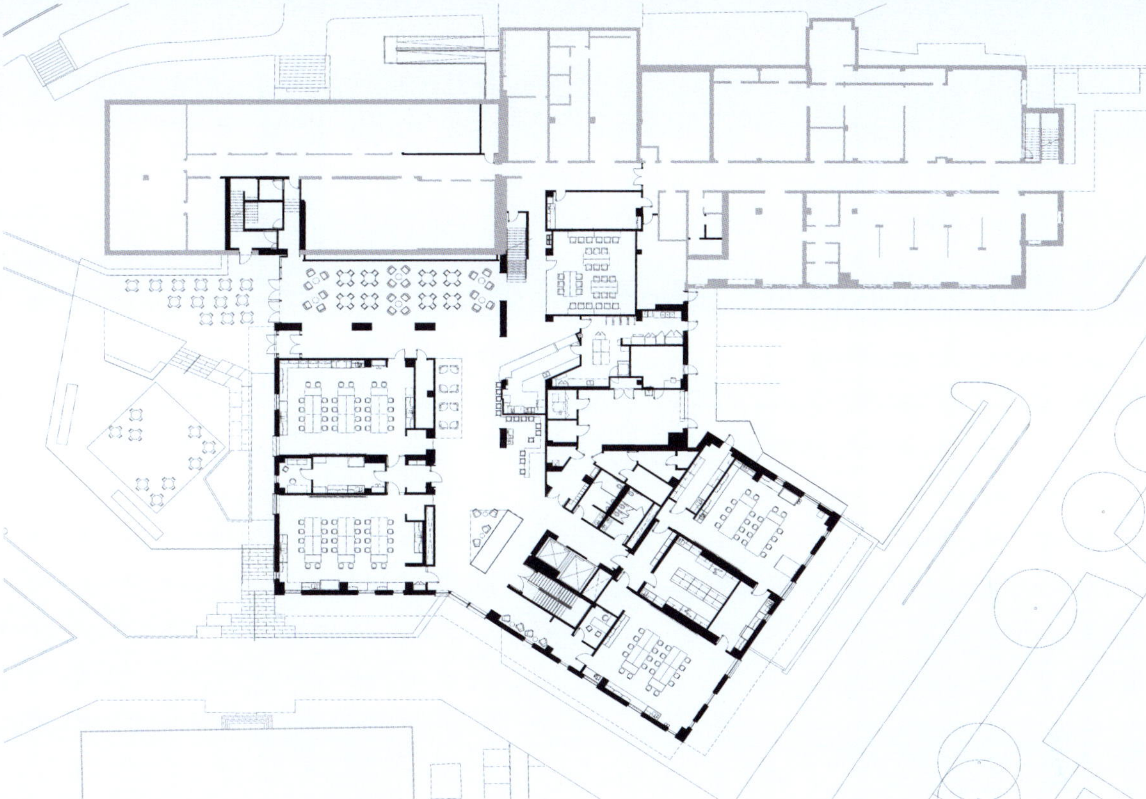

First Floor Plan

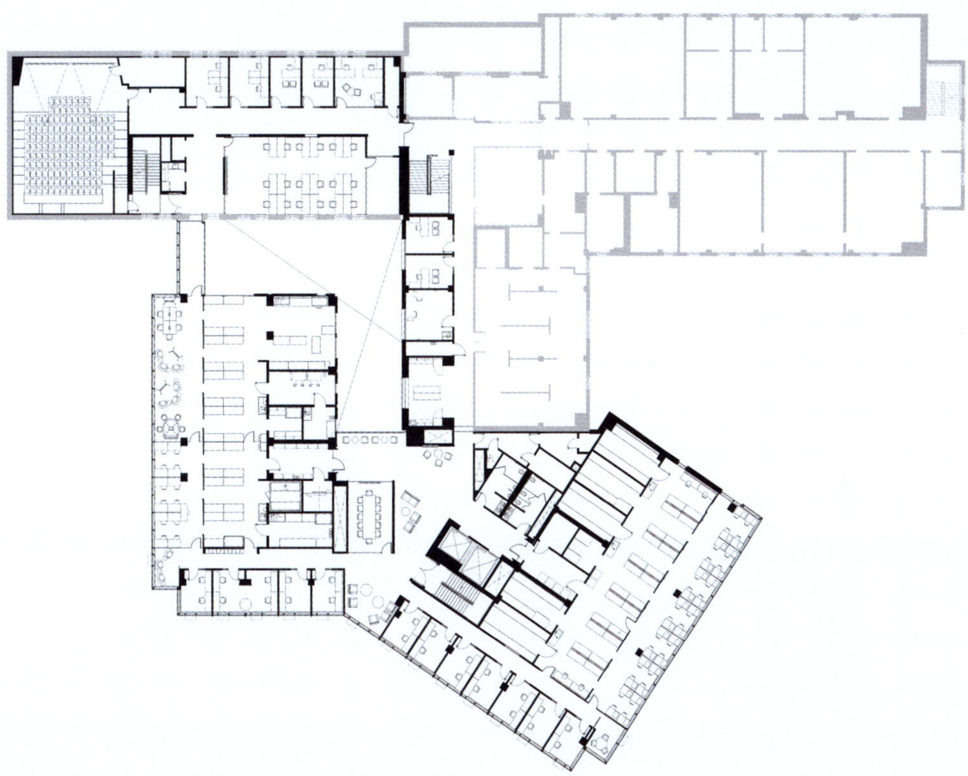

Upper Floor Plan

3W

The impact of the SEC is much greater than its size and deference to its neighbors might first suggest. Highlighting the sciences, it serves as the academic and social heart of a precinct much larger than itself, offering a renewed sense of connection to place, simply and elegantly.

Performance Strategy

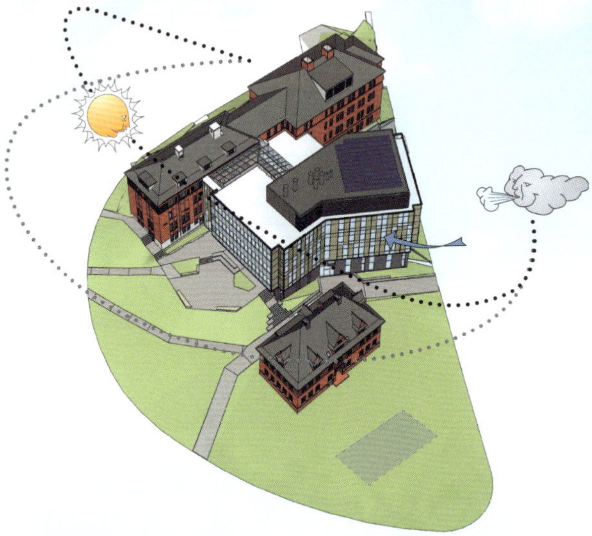

The Science and Engineering Complex provides state-of-the-art infrastructure to a three-building complex, utilizing the new atrium between the buildings as the lungs for a cascade air system. Offices can be naturally ventilated when outdoor conditions permit, assisted by otherwise dormant atrium smoke evacuation fans. This approach has mechanical systems performing double-duty, thereby reducing redundancy. Return air from offices and non-lab spaces is passively warmed as it cascades through the atrium on its way to the penthouse, where it requires only minimal preheating to supply the labs, rather than the extensive preheating that would be required for direct outside air.

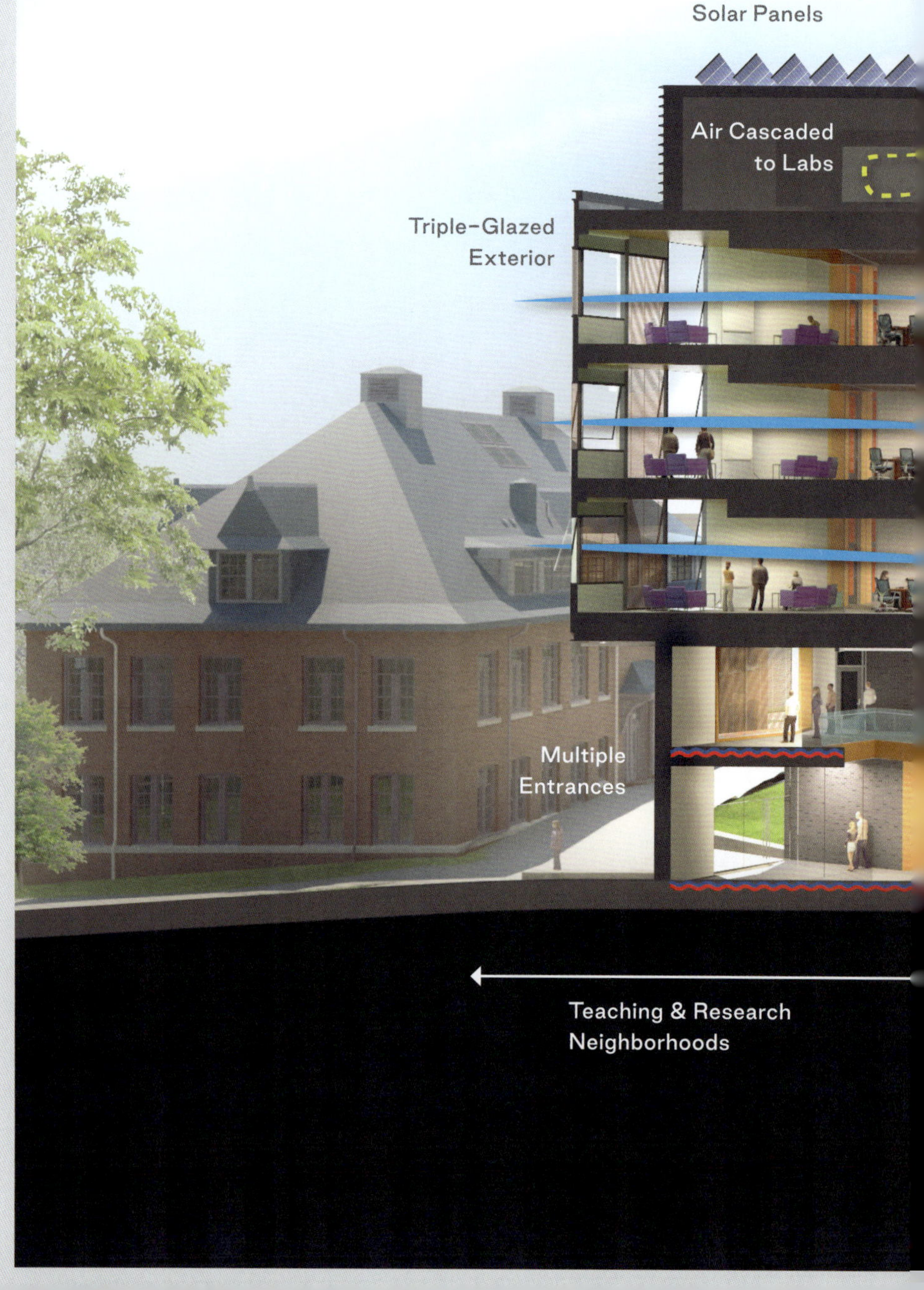

77% Average energy savings over typical lab/2030 baseline

112 kBtu/sq. ft.

87% Daylight autonomous in the atrium space

703 Houses

Energy Reduction Equivalency to annual energy usage

LEED Gold Certified

I²SL International Institute for Sustainable Laboratories® Go Beyond Award

Natural Ventilation
Progressively Opaque Roof Glazing
Thermally Improved Existing Building
Multiple Entrances
Radiant Heating and Cooling Floors
New Addition
Atrium/Cafe/Commons

Embedd Nature

Hengqin Island

Hengqin Hospital & Medical Campus

ed

门诊 out patient

Hengqin Island

Hengqin Hospital & Medical Campus

The plan of the Hengqin Hospital draws a group of large buildings into an organic unity with land and water. The flowing, intermingled forms of the buildings and landscape break down the vast facility into human-scaled spaces, as they create a cohesive campus committed to healing, embedded with nature.

The five hundred-bed hospital, located on a rapidly developing island adjacent to Zhuhai, China, is the signature component of a two-block medical campus, serving a population of over sixty million. It establishes the landscape strategy for the campus, which will also include five independently designed specialty hospitals and a residential precinct.

Our team resisted the natural inclination to distribute the large program into an aggregation of discrete components around a central garden, oriented to the south. Instead, we organized the hospital as a single, contiguous facility. Its density and integration help to accomplish two critical goals.

First, the hospital's programs are interconnected, both horizontally and vertically, with maximum

广州医科大学附属第一医院

Layers are tightly stacked to make up a well-integrated assembly of buildings and spaces.

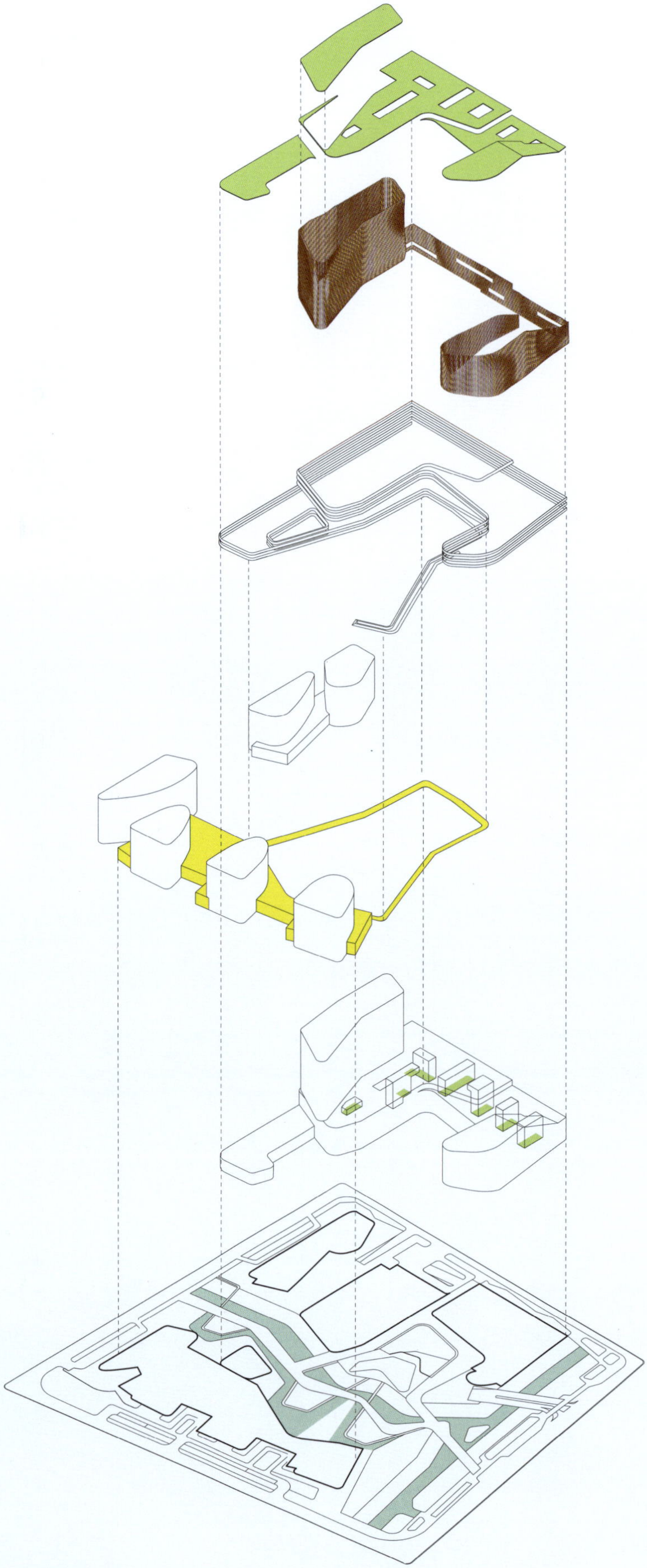

Green roofs over podium and towers

Shell enclosure faces the street and wraps the towers

Ribbons run along the heart of the site

Elevated circulation connects the General Hospital with the Specialty Hospitals' podium

Courtyards bring light and air deep into the lower levels of the podium of the General Hospital

Site: Ground plane showing building footprints and waterway

efficiency, ensuring a more rational and intuitive circulation, shorter travel distances and direct adjacency of related, critical functions.

Second, a densely designed hospital makes the best use of the land, reserving as much outdoor space as possible, so that nature can be seamlessly integrated into the life of the hospital, nurturing the well-being of patients, family, visitors, and staff.

The crescent-shaped building hugs the city street to the east and opens toward the heart of the block to the west. As it breaks down in scale toward the center of the site, the crescent embraces the outdoors, creating a grand common garden in the center of the campus. This "Green Heart" is a natural oasis, shared with the five interdependent Specialty Hospitals. A multilevel reflecting pool anchors a network of parks, promenades, and gardens along a waterway that stitches together all of the components of the campus. The wa-

Model showing the General Hospital tower to the right and four of the five Specialty Hospitals to the left

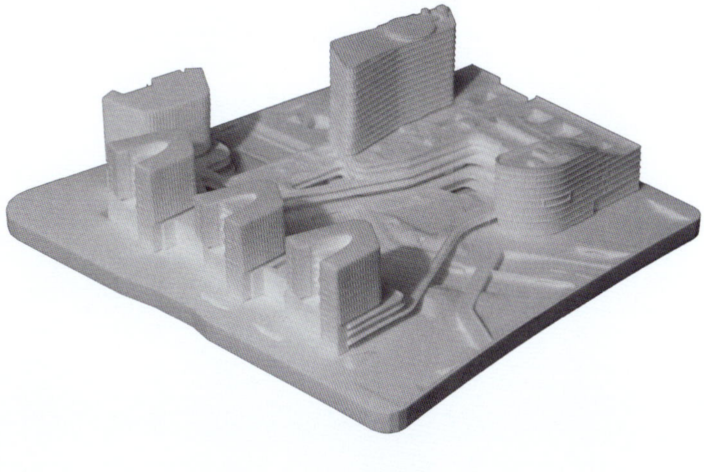

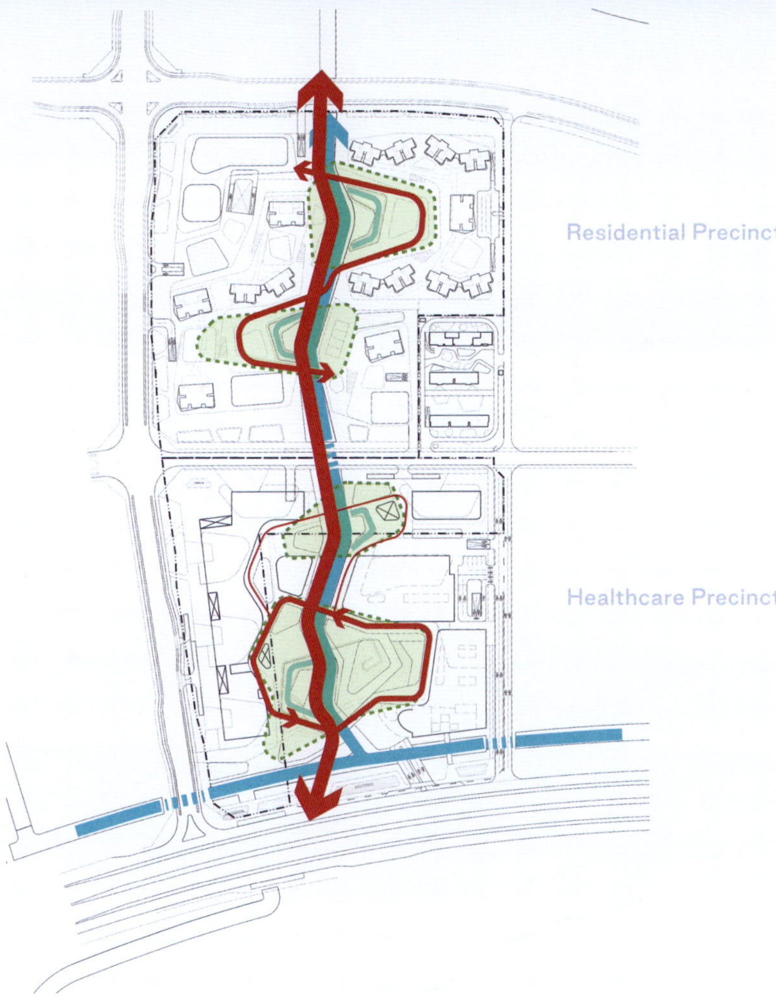
Residential Precinct
Healthcare Precinct

1 Pedestrian Entrance
2 Main Outpatient Drop-Off
3 Therapy Garden in the Green Heart
4 Patient Roof Garden

1

2

3

4

Site plan showing different landscape zones that make up the Green Heart: circulation, riverfront promenade, recreation, and Therapy Gardens

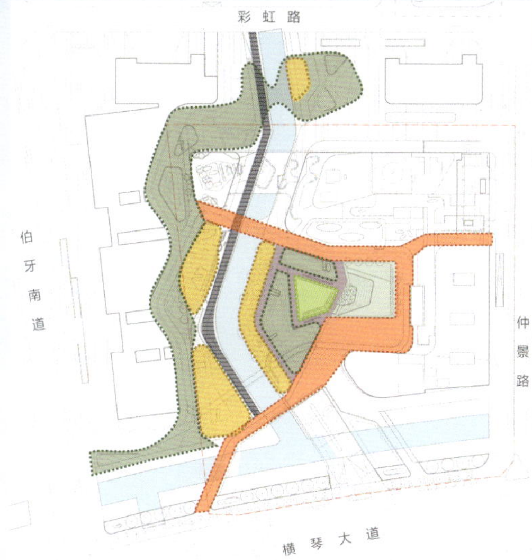

terway, pool, and accompanying ponds act as a living system, to manage water runoff. Importantly, most major public spaces, including circulation and waiting areas, face the Green Heart, providing a common visual reference to enable patients, visitors, and staff to navigate the large building. Nature acts as the wayfinding device.

The building's robust forms and simple articulation embody the importance of the institution to the city, the region, and the country. Despite the project's size and complexity, its exterior is composed of only two facade systems: horizontal ribbons at the crescent platform and glass fiber reinforced concrete vertical fins at the towers. Each of these systems morphs slightly as it is applied to different surfaces of the building, according to the particular performance requirement of each condition. The result is a strong, coherent, easily understood building, firmly anchored in the landscape, poised to serve the community for years to come.

Performance Strategy

Beginning with its siting and orientation, Hengqin Hospital is designed to be highly efficient and sustainable in its subtropical climate. All of the main building facades are oriented to the north and south, to avoid the hard-to-control morning and afternoon sun. The outpatient clinical block faces east onto a side street, but is shaded from the low morning sun by adjacent buildings. The buildings embrace a series of gardens, in which water, shade-producing trees, and other vegetation temper the hot, humid climate of the region. The building forms capture breezes, both to cool the gardens and for natural ventilation in many interior spaces. The building envelope is calibrated to maximize access to daylight while minimizing solar heat gain, mechanical systems are highly efficient, water is carefully managed, and materials are chosen to reduce environmental impact.

60% Average energy savings over typical hospital/2030 baseline

33% HVAC system size reduction compared to the 2030 baseline

44% Reduction in cooling system cost with use of sunshading fins

2,000 Houses

Energy Reduction Equivalency to annual energy usage

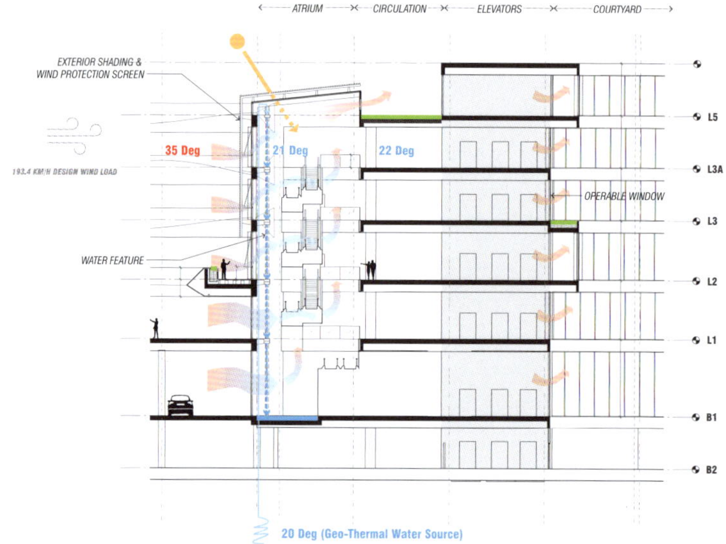

Passive Cooling at Outpatient Lobby

1 On-site Stormwater Management
2 Sunshade Protection
3 Outdoor Space Cooling Through Water Evaporation
4 Naturally Induced Ventilation In Courtyards
5 Prevailing Wind
6 Controlled Percolation
7 Outpatient Lobby

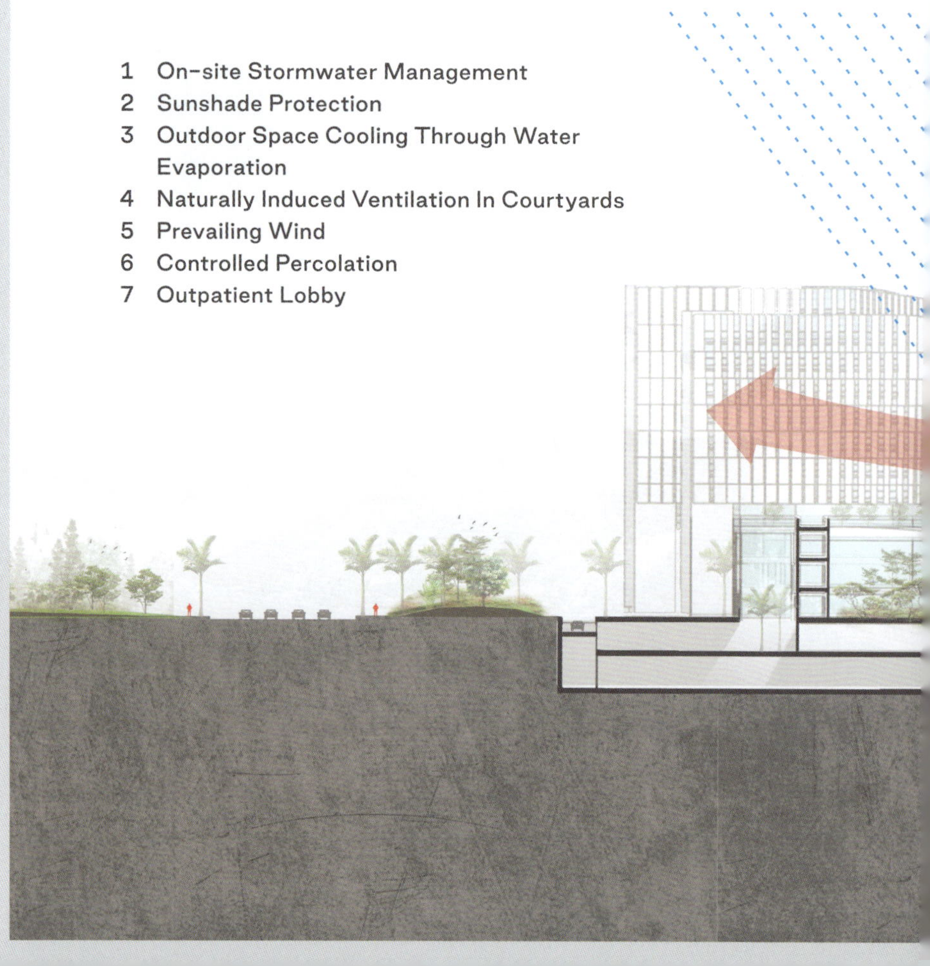

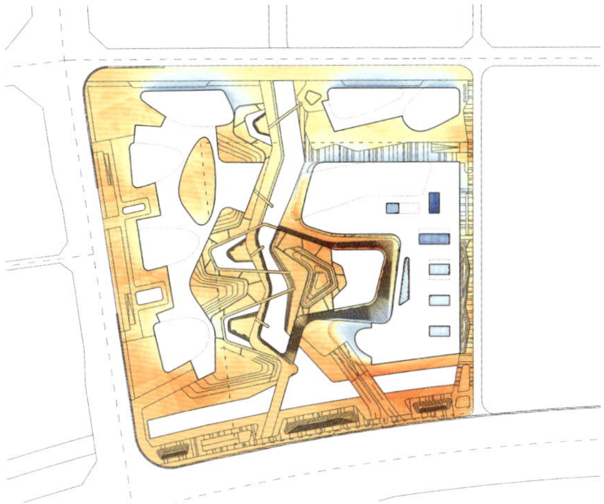

Exterior Thermal Comfort (No Planting and Water)

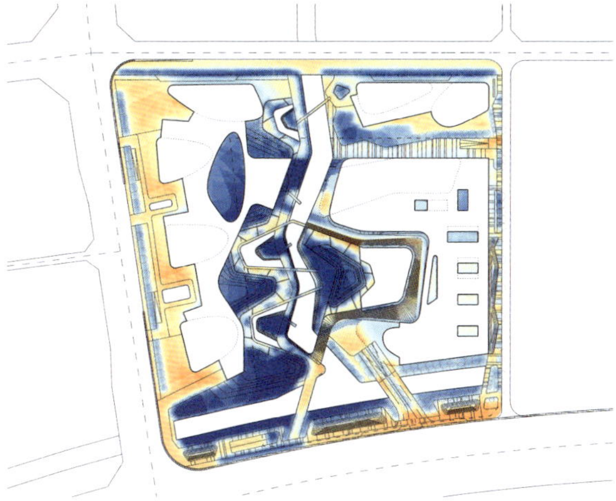

Exterior Thermal Comfort (With Planting and Water)

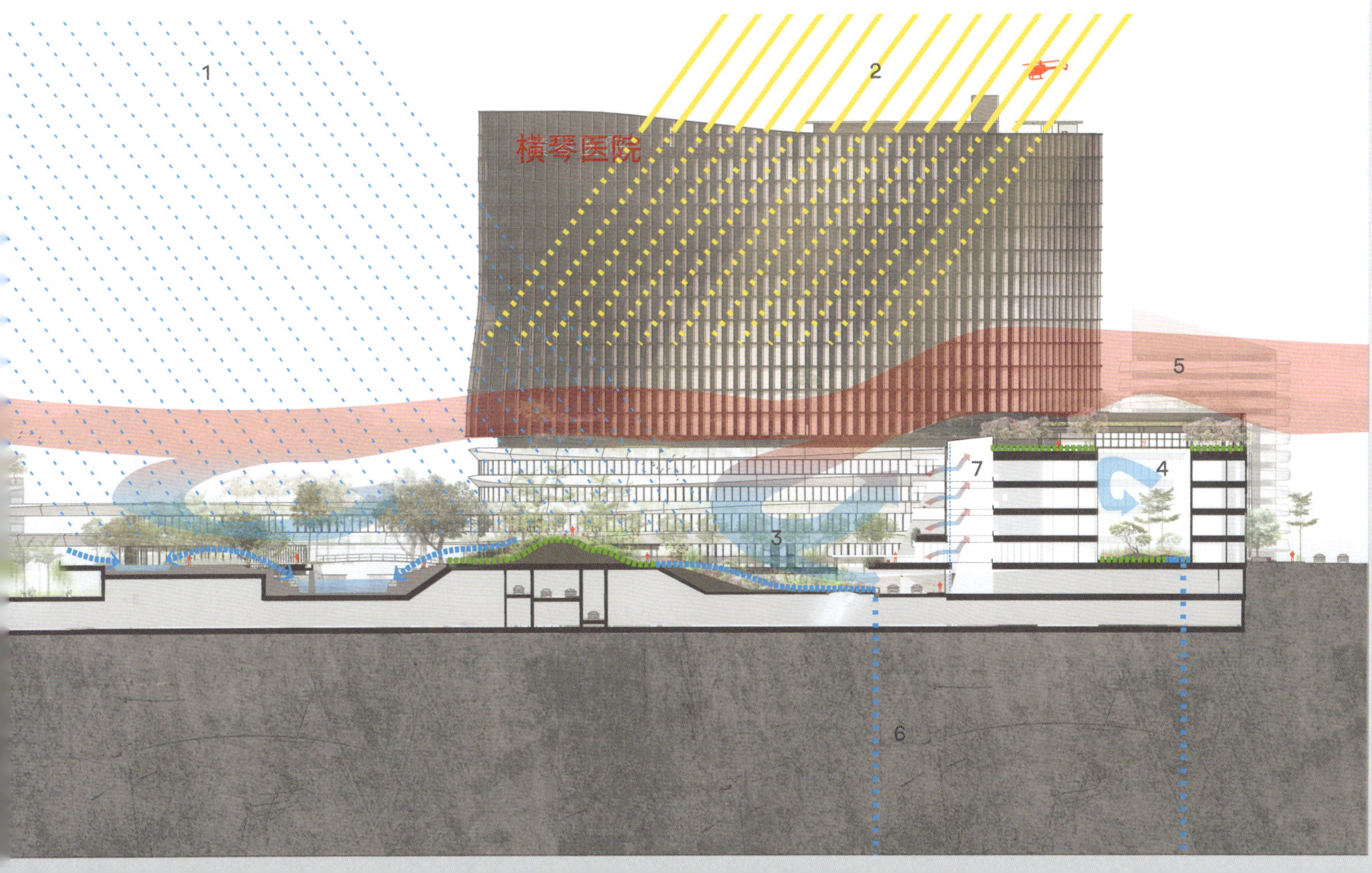

Amherst College

New Science Center

New Horizon

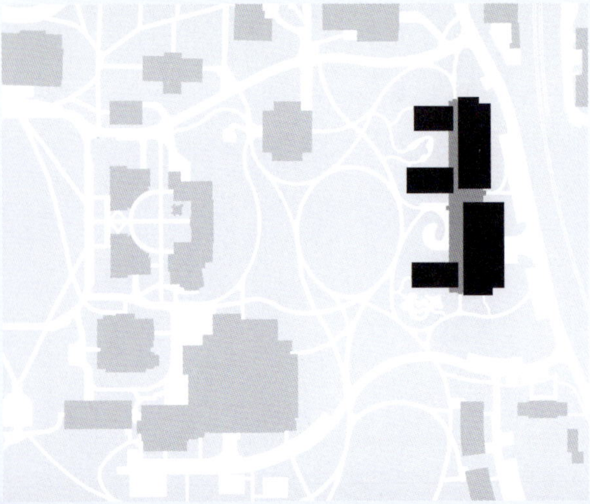

Amherst College
New Science Center

Looking east from Amherst College's Keefe Campus Center, you see through a wall of glass, over sixty feet tall, capped by a canopy of skylights. This great window frames the vibrant community of students and faculty in the sciences—studying, socializing, eating, and running up the stairs to class. It's a lively scene and a formative one for the college, which wanted to connect its science programs to the campus core. To make a central gathering place and to reveal that place vividly to the campus community were two guiding ideas for the design of this new science center.

Two ideas of many. Buildings for science are complex, both in terms of the systems required to support research and in terms of human interaction. They have many goals to accomplish, especially when they're part of a larger campus. And they're expensive—expensive to build and expensive to operate. The responsible approach to their design is to make each element do many things, solve many problems, answer many needs. It's not easy to do, but when we succeed at it, it's delightful.

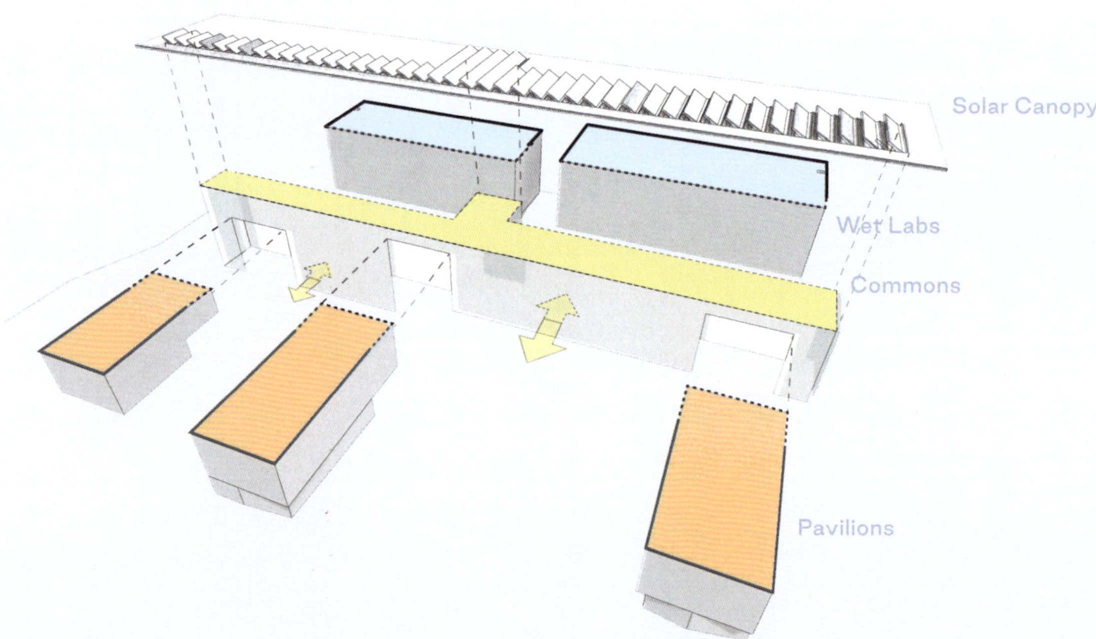
Solar Canopy
Wet Labs
Commons
Pavilions

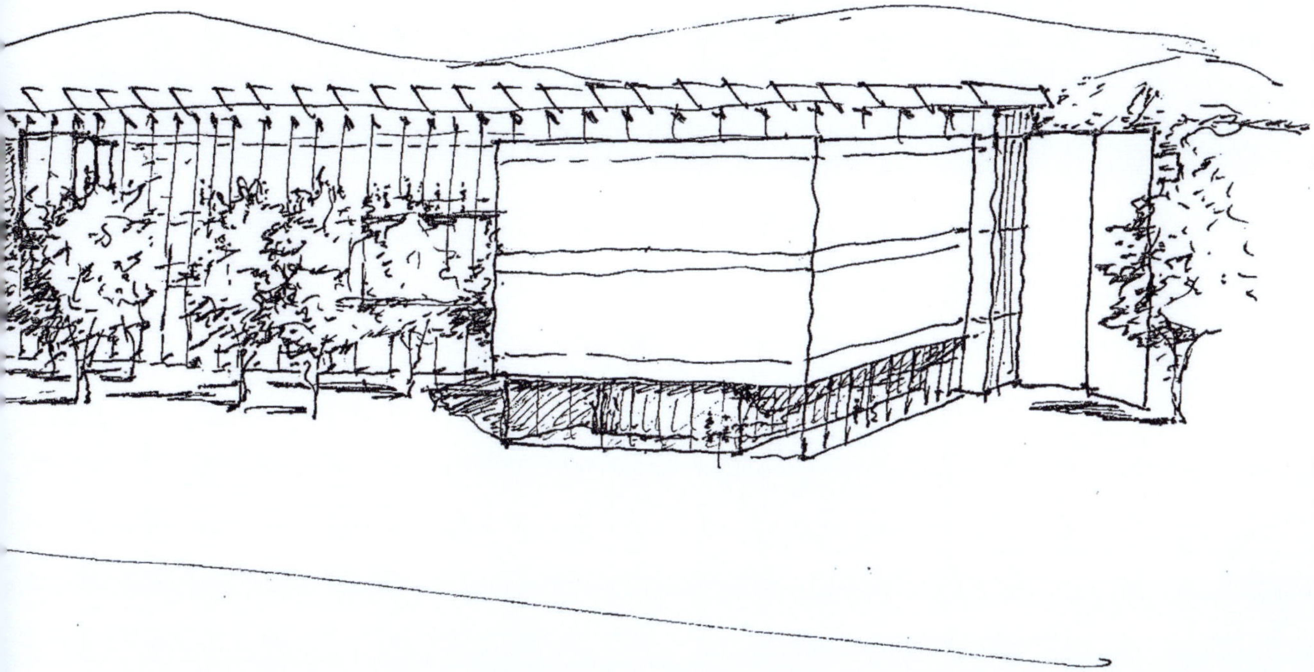

Together, this window and canopy serve many functions. At the most intimate scale, they form a commons, a place that encourages interaction among disciplines and between faculty and students. The Commons physically connects the disciplines, as well, linking together two high-energy laboratory wings tucked into the hillside to the east and three pavilions of low-intensity uses extending west toward the academic core. These pavilions, clad in russet, preweathered steel and silhouetted rhythmically against the glass curtain of the commons, mirror the traditional scale and cadence of the campus. At that scale, as we've seen, the commons highlights the role of the sciences at Amherst and invites people in to learn more. It also mends what had been a ragged campus edge and completes a new campus greenway. At the largest scale, it frames a horizon for the campus, extending the view to the distant Pelham Hills.

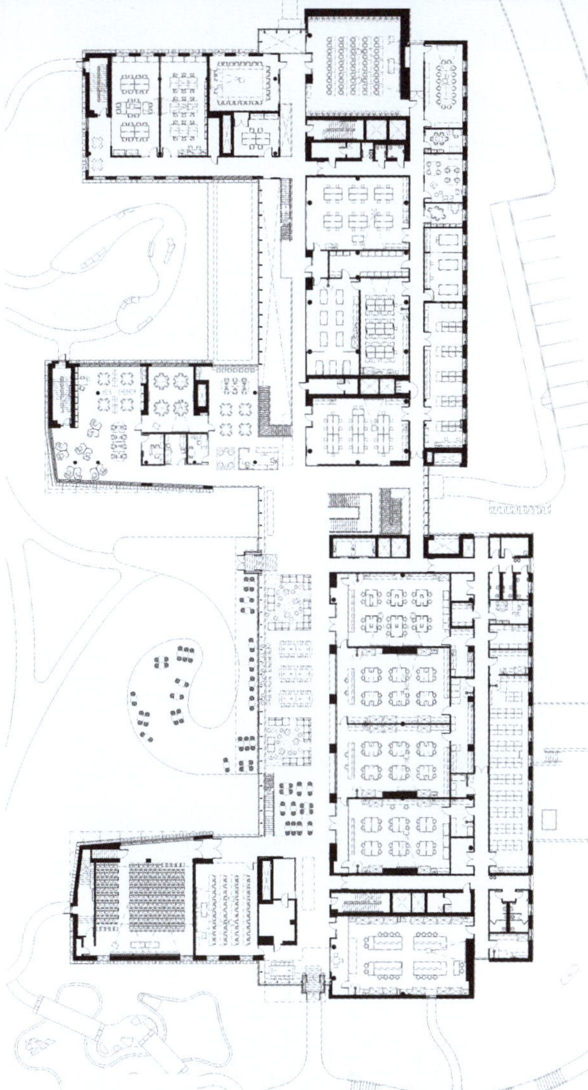

Level one

These are spatial roles, shaping how people engage with one another and with their surroundings. The window and roof canopy perform environmental roles, conditioning the commons for human comfort while dramatically conserving energy. The window is a triple-glazed curtain wall, hung on slender steel bars with only small steel plates at the base to resist wind loads. This design minimizes the consumption of materials and allows for slender brackets to hold the glass, limiting the amount of heat that passes between indoors and out. These brackets also support the automatic shading system, deployed to control glare and solar heat gain.

The array of finely crafted skylights performs many functions simultaneously. It provides both natural and artificial light, its photovoltaic panels generate electricity, its shape and materials afford acoustic control, and it radiantly heats and cools the commons.

When we first drew the long, expressive horizontal line that became the roof canopy of the New Science Center, it was a simple gesture, but even then we looked ahead to its myriad possibilities. We want every mark that we make to become part of a logical system that fuses design and performance.

Performance Strategy

The Amherst College New Science Center is a high-intensity laboratory with one of the lowest energy footprints of its type. The building employs several strategies for energy efficiency, including a high-performance envelope, abundant natural light, low-energy HVAC chilled beams, fan-coil distribution systems, optimized fume hood control strategies, demand control ventilation (including in laboratory spaces), high-performance heat recovery with indirect evaporative cooling, and freezer heat recovery for domestic hot water. Indirect/direct evaporative cooling reduces the heating and cooling needed for the ventilation system to reduce peak loads in the laboratories. Curtain wall and facade systems employ high-performance, triple-pane glazing with thermal breaks. Operable opaque panels in the faculty offices provide natural ventilation while maintaining the thermal integrity of the triple-pane windows. The Commons' roof monitors integrate elements for thermal and acoustic comfort—chilled beams, radiant slabs, and acoustic baffles—and a photovoltaic array to generate on-site power.

76% Average energy savings over typical lab/2030 baseline

91 kBtu/sq. ft.

58% Rainwater managed from a two-year, twenty-four-hour storm event

41% Predicted reduction in indoor water use compared to the LEED baseline

1,527 Houses

Energy Reduction Equivalency to annual energy usage

AIA COTE Top Ten Award

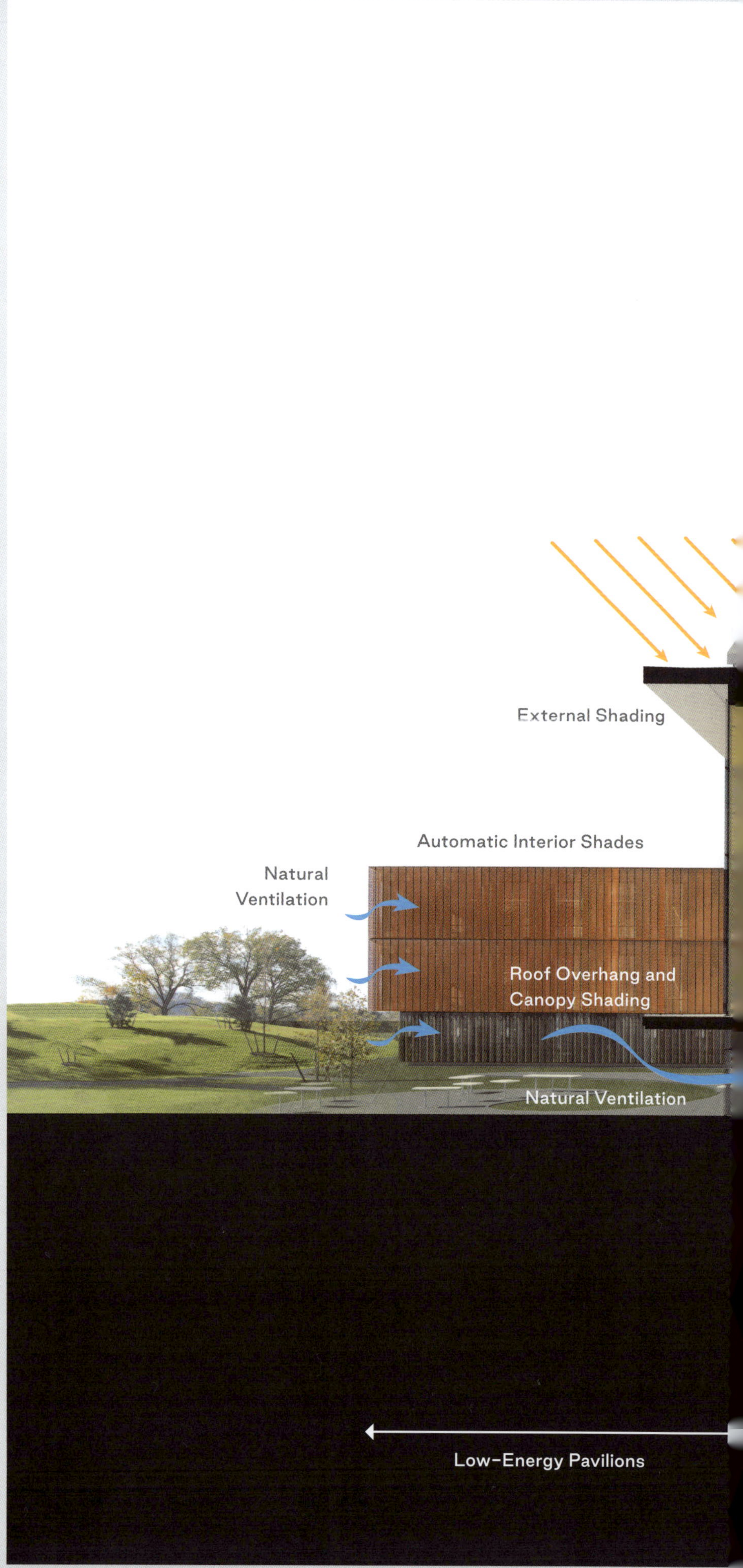

Integrated Roof Monitor Assemblies

1 Radiant Convective Cooling
2 Acoustic Sound Absorption
3 Photovoltaic Panels
4 North-Facing Daylight
5 Artificial LED Lighting
6 Concealed Structure
7 Concealed Fire Protection

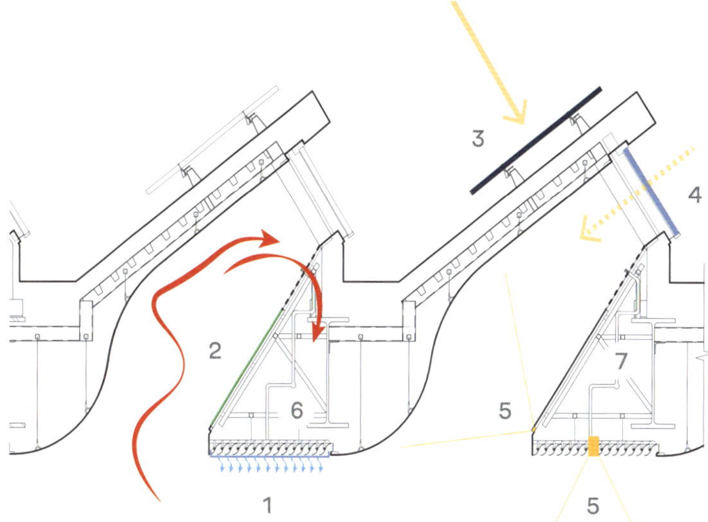

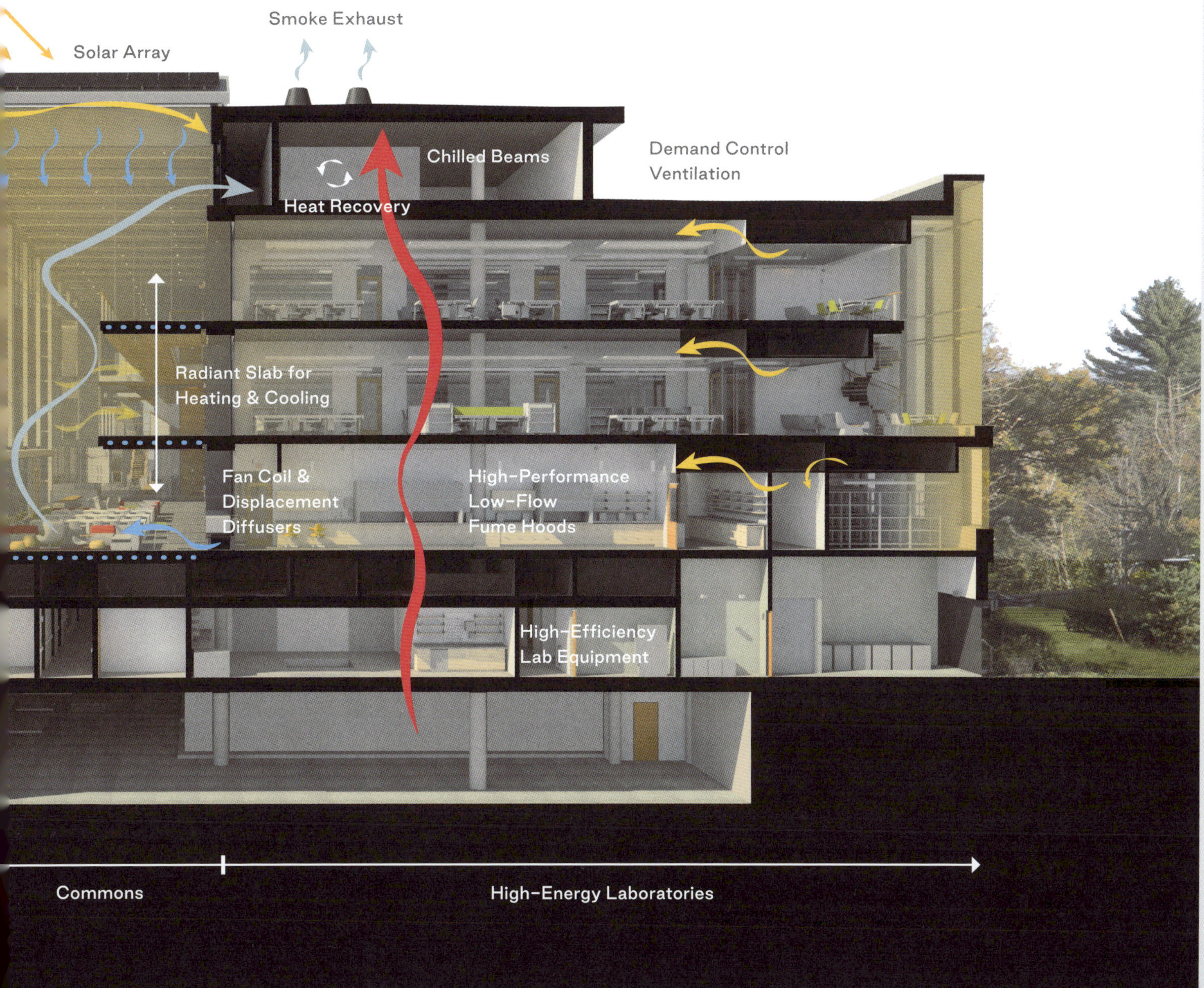

The Arc

Penn State Health

Milton S. Hershey Medical Center

PENN STATE HERSHEY CANCER INSTITUTE

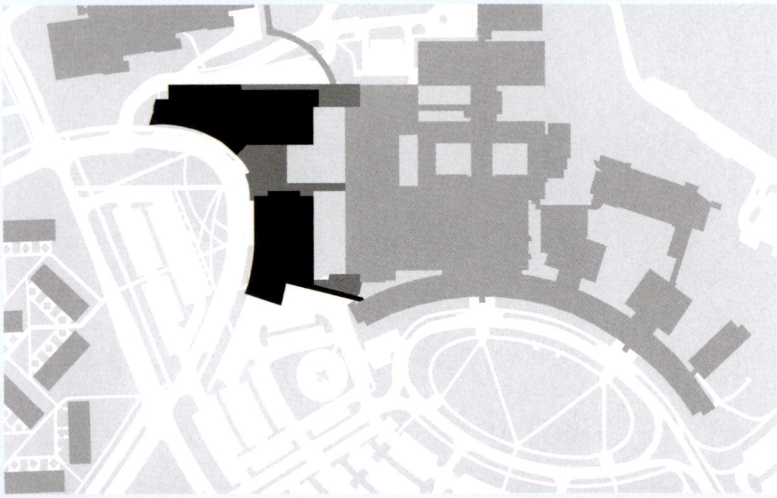

Penn State Health
Milton S. Hershey Medical Center

It is now a commonplace of hospital design that views of nature accelerate healing and reduce pain. Tom Payette perhaps intuited as much when, in 1969, he reversed the increasingly hermetic, inward turn of the building type in his design for Leonard Morse Hospital in Natick, Massachusetts—fifteen years before Roger Ulrich's landmark study first demonstrated what the sight of a tree can do. We don't, however, think it's enough to be able to see a tree. Nature isn't something just to look at; it's something to bring into the midst of things, to embed within the experience of the building. This is what we did for Penn State Health's Hershey campus, where gardens become the centerpieces around which clinical departments are organized.

The completion of the Children's Hospital in 2012 marked the culmination of a remarkable transformation of the Hershey campus, the result of a unique, decade-long integration of campus planning, landscape design, and architecture. We had been commissioned in 2003 to provide a detailed plan for the East Clinical Quadrangle of the Hershey campus, as well as the architectural design for a number of key components of the precinct—the main entry, the Cancer Institute and

PENN STATE
CANCER

Children's Hospital, the renovation and expansion of the Emergency Department, and a two thousand-car parking garage. The scale of these disparate projects, we believed, warranted a comprehensive rethinking of the precinct as a whole. Out of this rethinking emerged more than a million square feet of construction and over twenty-eight acres of site development.

Waterfall Wall and Secret Garden

Such a vast undertaking requires a unifying device. Inspired by the medical center's iconic crescent of existing buildings, we proposed a corresponding arc to link the new ones. This singular gesture operates at the scale of the landscape, redefining the main circulation axis of the campus, shifting its center of gravity to the east and allocating growth around a new campus green. It also acts as a main street, along which each significant new building—Cancer Institute, Main Hospital Lobby, and Children's Hospital—has an address. As these three buildings jointly define the Arc, they share a repertoire of materials, colors, and textures, but each maintains its individual identity through subtle changes of form and measured moments of individual expression.

The campus is conceived as a garden hospital, structured around a rich network of courtyards and gardens. These act as breathing spaces between new and existing structures, building upon the institution's heritage of internal green spaces that connect patients, clinicians, and researchers with the landscape. The gardens break down the scale of the massive institution and allow daylight deep into program spaces.

Main Hospital Entrance

The compressive and tensile forces of the Arc are embodied in the folded origami-like leg that anchors the Cancer Institute to the site.

Each garden is tailored to suit its primary users, ranging from peaceful, all-season areas of respite for patients from the infusion therapy suites, to safe and welcoming play areas for young patients and their siblings next to the dining hall of the Children's Hospital.

No one chooses to be a patient in a hospital, but that doesn't mean it shouldn't be a place worth being in, even a place you might otherwise want to be in. And it isn't, after all, the individual patient who spends the most time there. It's the doctors, the nurses, and all the hundreds of others who make the hospital possible. What a garden means to them, and what that means for the care patients receive, may not yet have been measured, but we intuit, as Tom Payette would, that it means a lot.

Children's Sky Garden

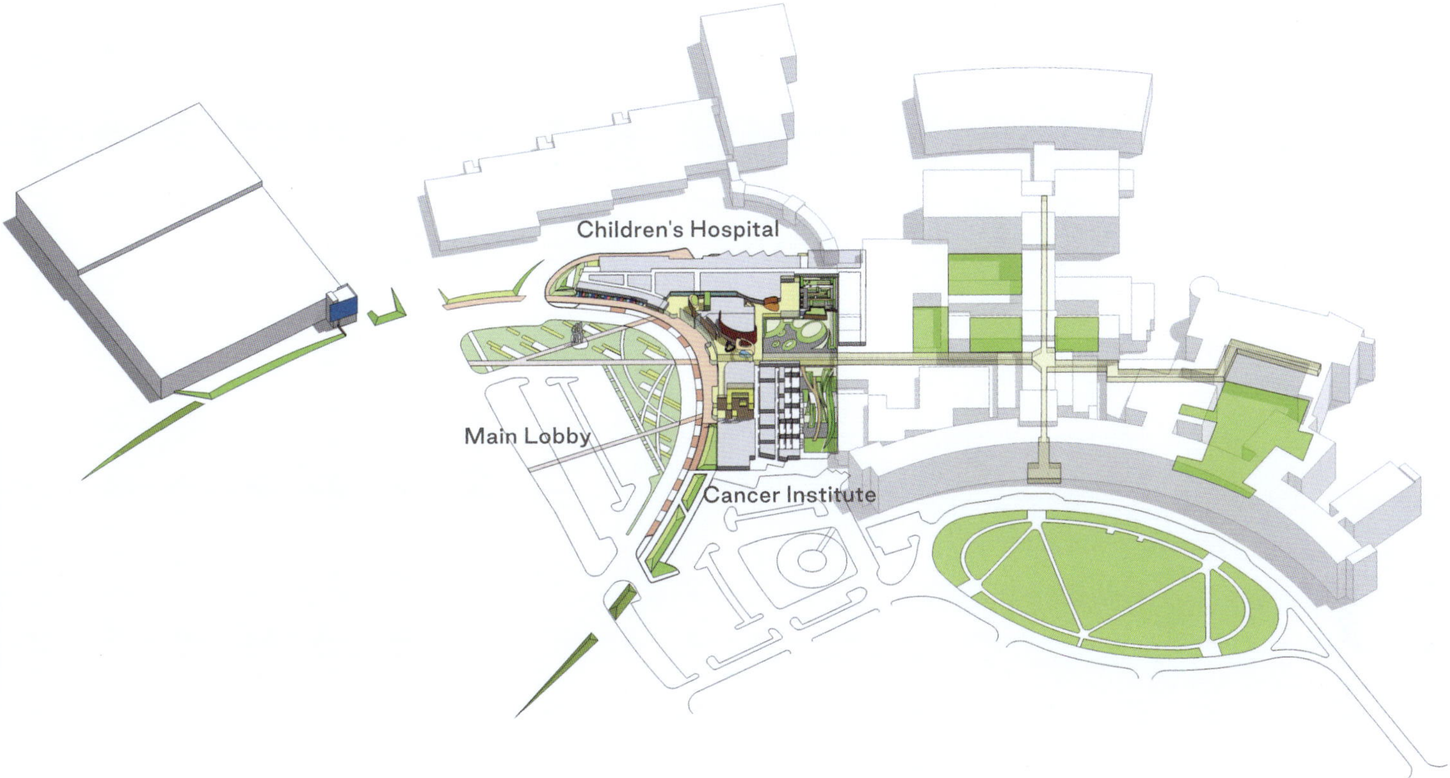

Hospital Courtyard

Winter

Early Summer

Late Summer

Spring / Fall

A Garden Hospital enhances the impact of nature on the healing process.

The Cancer Institute's Beehive Atrium organizes like typologies around vibrant, shared collaboration zones.

The design of the Children's Hospital engages children at all stages of development.

The use of a rich palette of shapes, colors and materials communicates the building's unique identity as a place for children and families.

The patient rooms include a family area with a sofa so parents can spend the night in the rooms.

Throughout the building, children and their families find a place of hope and healing.

Performance Strategy

The landscape plays a performative role in the Hershey Medical Center Campus, where embedded nature marks a significant departure from the typical monolithic hospital, detached from the natural world. Here, over an acre of fully accessible green roofs links old and new structures, forms an umbilical relationship with treatment spaces, acts as a filter for storm water run-off, decreases urban heat island effect, and creates habitat. Continuity of building systems and services is provided by a common subterranean support platform.

The landscape shapes the social geometry of the hospital. Patient treatment spaces are oriented around gardens, to hasten healing and to admit daylight, as are each of the clinical departments. A majority of spaces within the complex enjoy daylight autonomy. From the start, "learning and healing through nature" was an important theme for the project, and the Children's Hospital and main lobby are each entwined with distinct landscape features that, along with art installations, encourage learning.

41% Average energy savings over typical hospital/2030 baseline

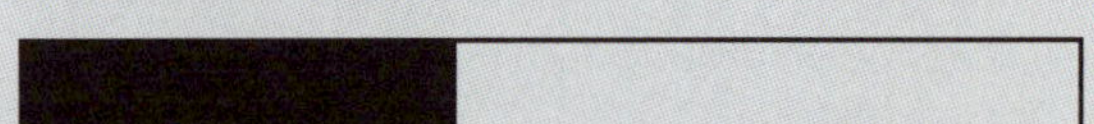

160 kBtu/sq. ft.

1 acre of green roof

12% Net floor area are green roofs

173 Houses

Energy Reduction Equivalency to annual energy usage

LEED Silver Certified

Children's Hospital

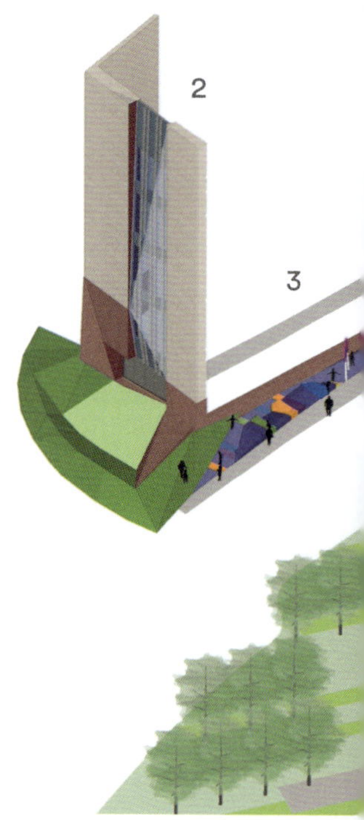

Landscape Systems

1 Secret Garden
2 Waterfall Wall
3 Light Sticks
4 Learning Wall
5 Stage
6 Cafe
7 Meditation Space
8 Sky Garden
9 Beehive
10 Leg

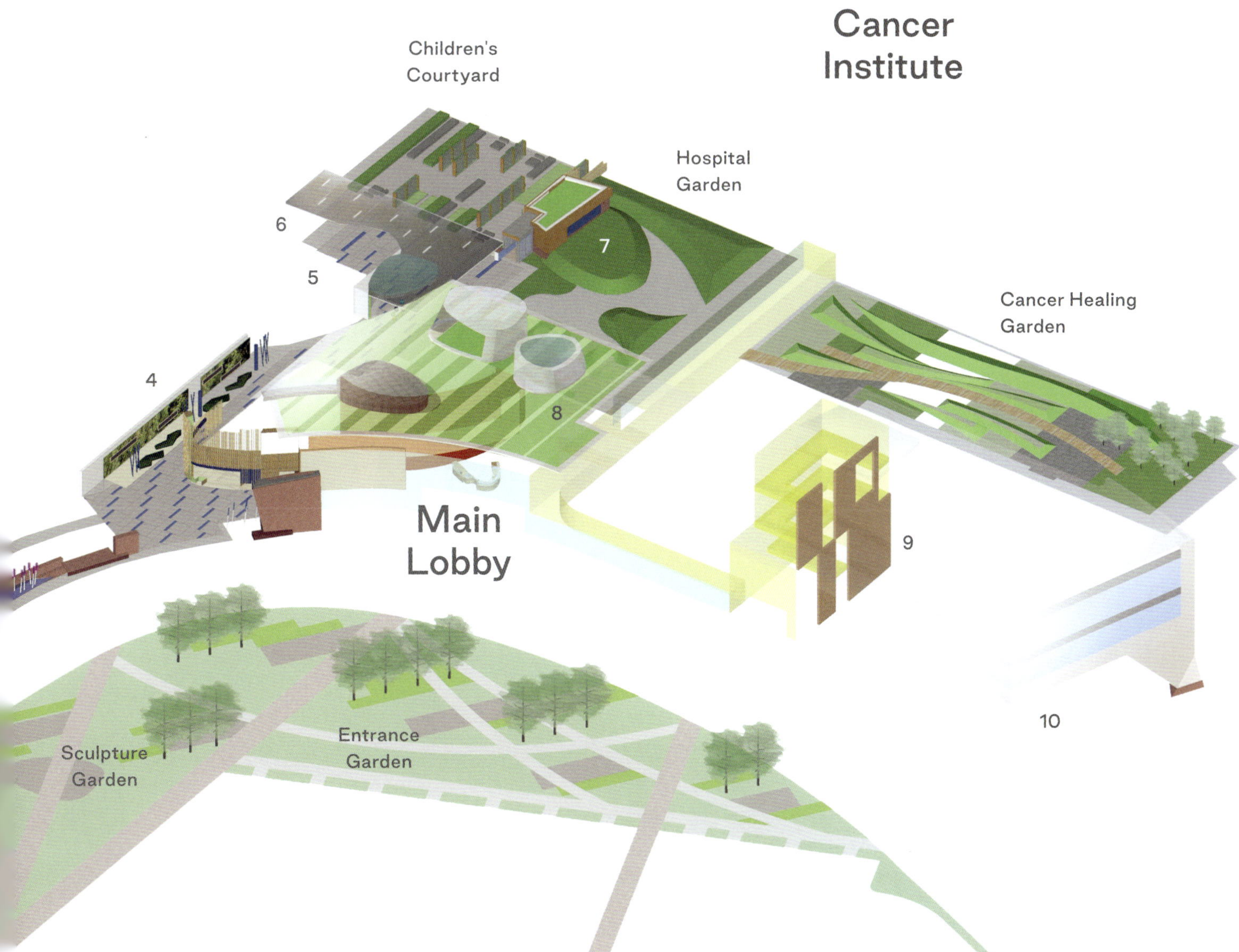

Stacked Baskets

George Washington University

Milken Institute

George Washington University
Milken Institute

What you see from the street of the Milken Institute School of Public Health hardly prepares you for what you find when you go in: an unusually narrow and irregular atrium, rising seven floors, on one side of which is an orderly block of work spaces, on the other a seemingly haphazard arrangement of curvaceous, wood-paneled volumes, floating away from the great glass wall that faces Washington Circle. Suspended on platforms between the glass and the curving volumes are small groups of people in animated conversation, students and faculty enjoying one of the most distinctive and vibrant gathering spaces of any American university.

How this space came to be is a story of an imaginative solution to a deadeningly common problem: a site with barely enough room for the program it's meant to house. And an oddly shaped site, to boot: a triangle with a corner carved away by one of the District of Columbia's busiest traffic circles. Using a conventional structural system, six floors would fit within the ninety-foot height limit, accommodating the required program, but with very little common space and, unavoidably, spaces in the center of the building without daylight or views.

The solution was an unconventional structure, which, along with highly energy- and space-efficient mechanical systems, allowed for a twelve-foot floor-to-floor height, unusually low for a classroom building. At that height, we could fit seven floors within the limit. Just on paper, that freed up 14 percent of each floor for other things, but it actually freed up more, because it allowed us to craft a plan that is both more rational and more exuberant than would have been possible with every floor fully packed.

We organized faculty offices and individual graduate student carrels in a simple bar, its long side facing west onto Twenty-Fourth Street. In the remaining triangle, we put classrooms of several different sizes and shapes, to accommodate different class sizes and modes of teaching. These classrooms float free of one another, open space flowing between and around them. With a concrete structure, it wasn't necessary for the classrooms to align floor-to-floor and we could cut away large parts of each floor, to allow daylight to fill the center of the building. These cutouts didn't have to line up with one another, either.

The upshot is an entirely new social geometry, three-dimensional rather than two-dimensional, with study and conversation spaces tucked between the classrooms and the glass wall. At the center, a surprising and engaging stair zigzags its way through the atrium, between the office bar and the stacks of classrooms. Think Hogwarts without the sudden realignments, and with a high level of contemporary craft: finely finished concrete, elegant steel and glass guardrails, and the warm bamboo skin of the classrooms.

THE GEORGE

Public health is a discipline that seeks measurable outcomes, so a year following completion we conducted a post-occupancy evaluation to assess user experience—something we do for many of our projects. More than 85 percent of respondents agreed that the building encourages movement and reinforces the school's mission of nurturing healthy lifestyles, more than other campus buildings. People use the stairs, not because the elevators are tucked away to the side (though they are) but because of the social geometry, which leads you to look up and down and across for your professor, or your study group, or someone you just might, just accidentally, want to meet.

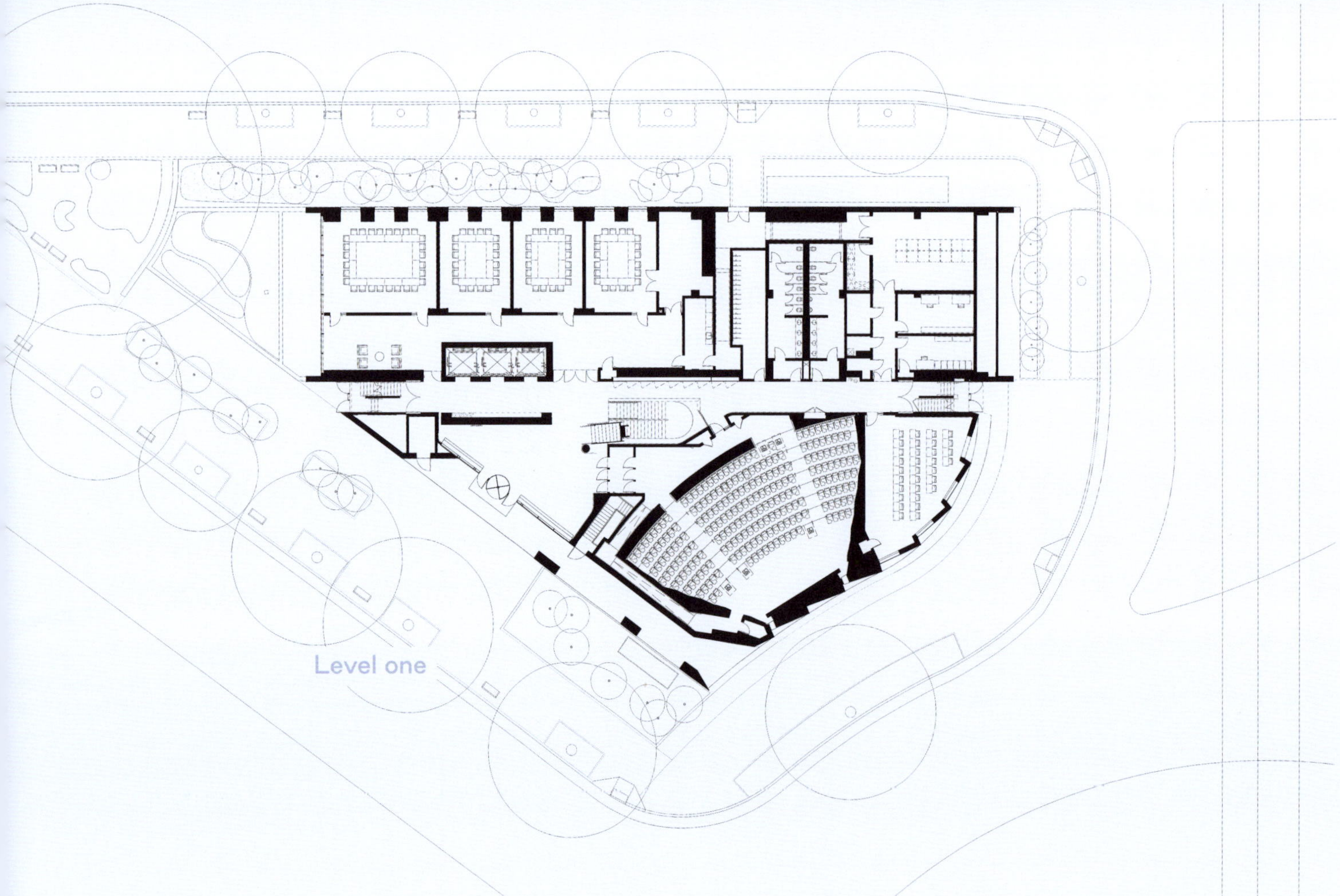

Level one

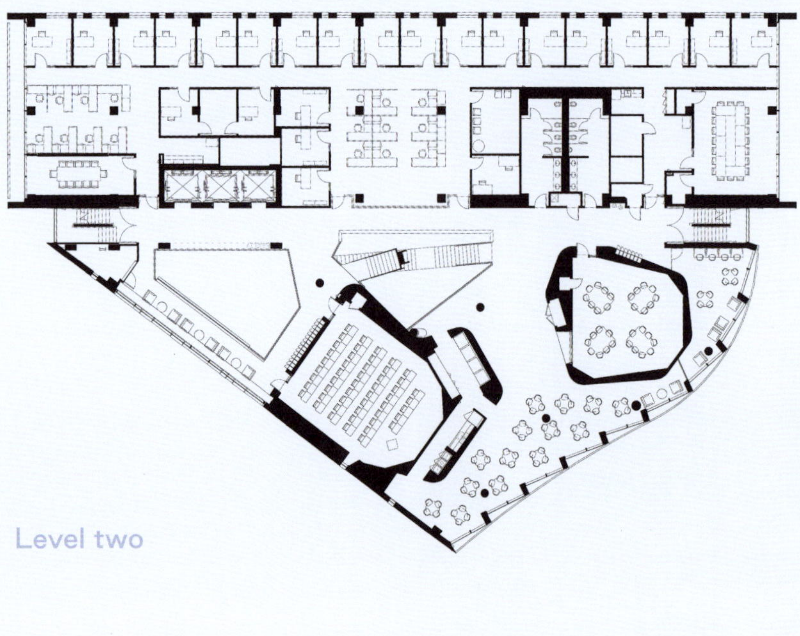

Level two

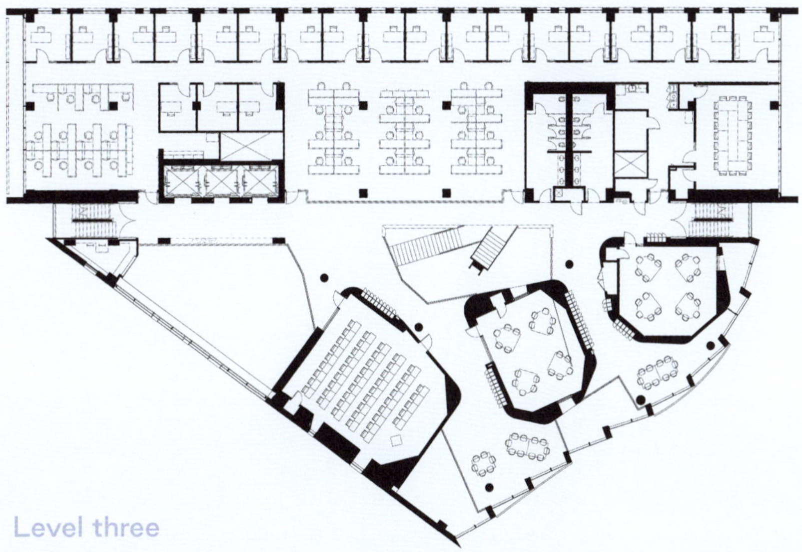

Level three

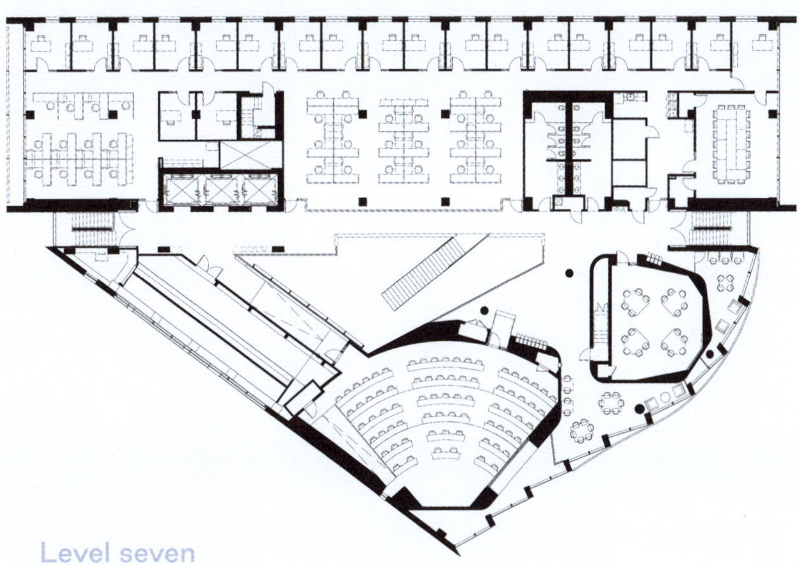

Level seven

Performance Strategy

Because light, views, and air are so associated with the core values of public health, the Milken Institute School of Public Health was conceived to maximize the degree to which these qualities infuse what could easily have been a dense urban block with little or no connection to the outdoors.

To achieve this aim, the design team pursued an unorthodox and counterintuitive strategy of reducing the building's average floor-to-floor height, in order to add an entire floor within the allowable envelope—not to increase the building's floor area, which was capped by development regulations, but rather to create a network of void spaces within the building. Instead of darker, more cramped interior spaces, what results is a building that is surprisingly open and light-filled. Wandering about the central atrium—less than twenty feet wide in most places—one encounters a rich array of views to the exterior in many directions, including upward toward a skylight punched through the mechanical penthouse. This quality of openness and airiness, so unexpected given the building's solid exterior appearance, is one of its most engaging features—and one that speaks powerfully to a public health agenda.

64% Average energy savings over typical lab/2030 baseline

67 kBtu/sq. ft.

32% of the roof area is vegetated

287 Houses

Energy Reduction Equivalency to annual energy usage

LEED Platinum Certified

AIA

COTE Top Ten Award

Conventional Six-Story Approach

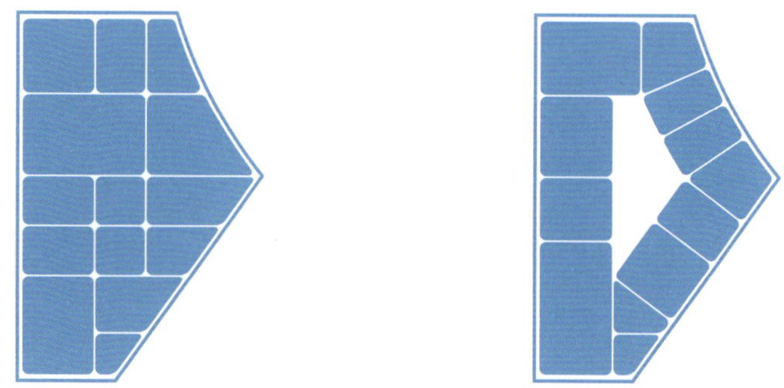

Alternative Seven-Story Approach (design)

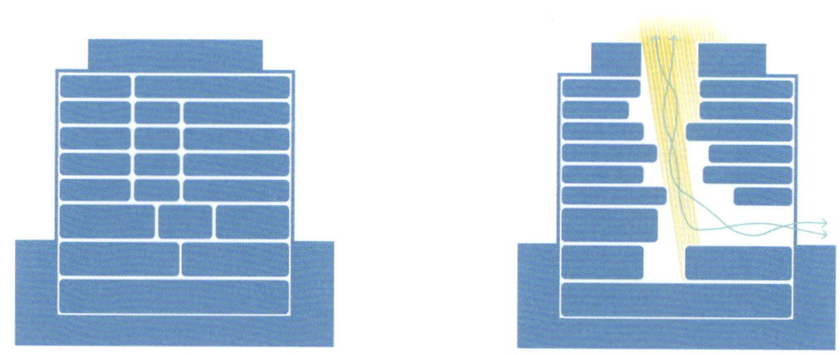

1. Rainwater Harvested for Reuse in Toilets & Cooling Tower
2. Occupancy Sensor Lighting & Ventilation
3. Climate Responsive Facades with Sun Screens and Minimized Glazing
4. Native Plantings
5. Fritted Atrium Glazing to Control Heat Gain and Glare
6. Rapidly Renewable Bamboo Wall Paneling
7. Hight Performance Glazing
8. Recycled Slag in Concrete
9. Displacement Ventilation

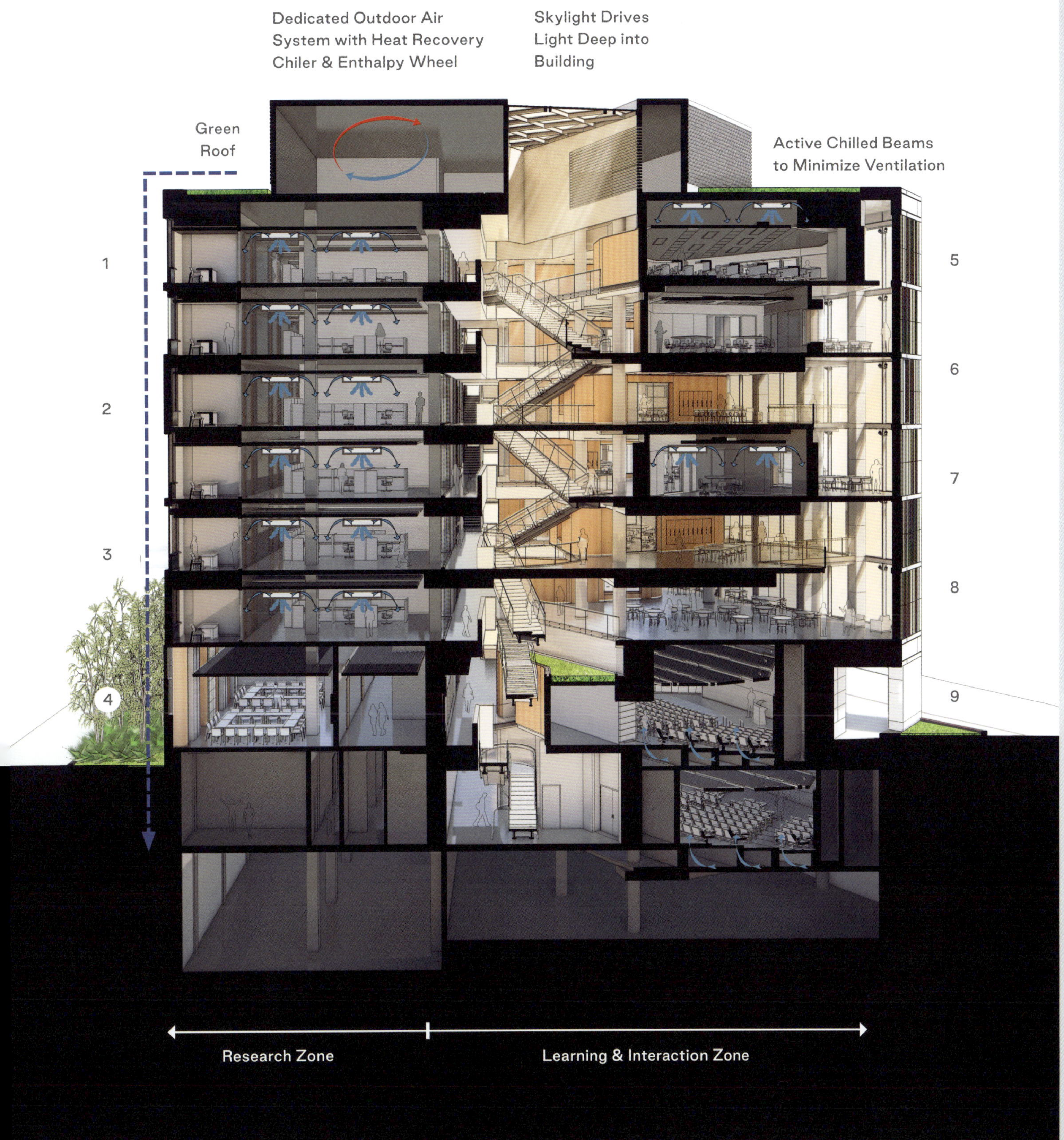

Dedicated Outdoor Air System with Heat Recovery Chiler & Enthalpy Wheel
Skylight Drives Light Deep into Building
Green Roof
Active Chilled Beams to Minimize Ventilation
1
2
3
4
5
6
7
8
9
Research Zone
Learning & Interaction Zone

Opaque Crystalli

Boston University

Kilachand Center

&

ne

PRUDENTIAL

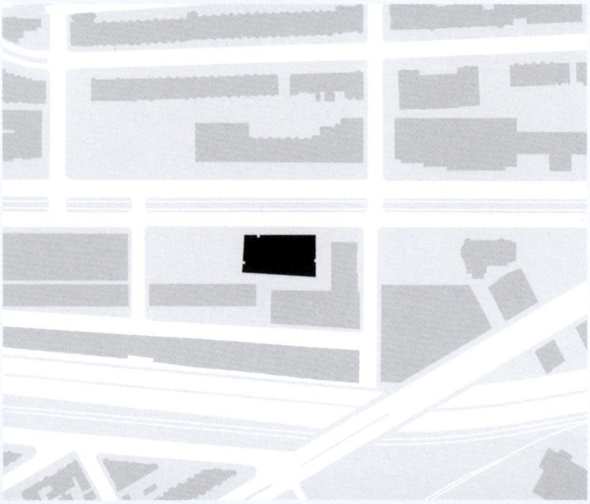

Boston University
Kilachand Center

Sometimes a building should stand out, distinctive and iconic, to represent a community or an institution. In other situations, it might better recede quietly into the background, to give a sense of continuity to a place. Whether a building should be perceived as icon or background is a choice the architect is often asked to make. For a building on a busy thoroughfare, there's a related question: Is it to be seen primarily by people cruising along in cars or by people strolling down the sidewalk? Faced with such either-or questions, we wonder: Why not both?

That's what we asked of the Rajen Kilachand Center for Integrated Life Sciences and Engineering, on a prominent site on storied Commonwealth Avenue. We found the answer, a way to resolve both oppositions—background versus icon, and pedestrian versus car—in the crafting of the building's skin. It employs large, glass fiber reinforced concrete (GFRC) fins and panels to dramatic effect.

From a distance, the building's simple volume appears solid. Approached obliquely, the gaps between the fins progressively increase until the fins all but disappear,

ALFRED L. MORSE
AUDITORIUM

SILBER WAY
BUS

momentarily rendering the skin almost entirely reflective, before the phenomenon reverses and the building's solidity reasserts itself. It is both intangibly crystalline and impassively opaque. This interplay of opposing qualities gives the otherwise quiet building a surprising presence, enabling it to stand forth as an emblem of the sciences at Boston University. At the same time, it echoes the rhythm and verticality of the neighboring neo-Gothic buildings by Ralph Adams Cram that first gave identity to the Charles River Campus, falling in step with them to form a coherent street wall for the avenue.

The back-and-forth of visual qualities enlivens the sides of the building that open onto the avenue and adjoining park. The sides facing adjacent buildings are stiller. Here, the same materials lie side-by-side in a common plane, the projecting fins becoming flat panels between the sheets of glass, deferring to pedestrians passing through the tall, narrow spaces flanked by the buildings. The transition at the corner, from fin to panel, is one of the more magical moments of the building, a seemingly effortless resolution of the distinct personalities of the two facades. It is an instance

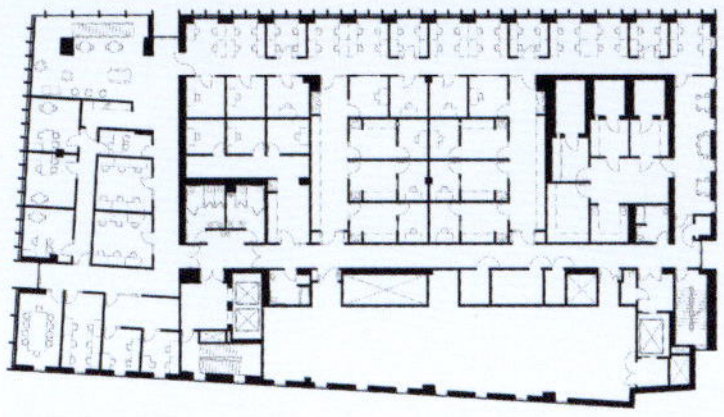

Level nine

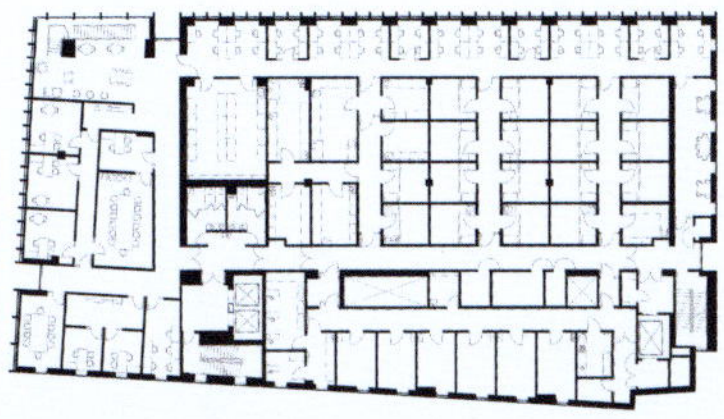

Level seven

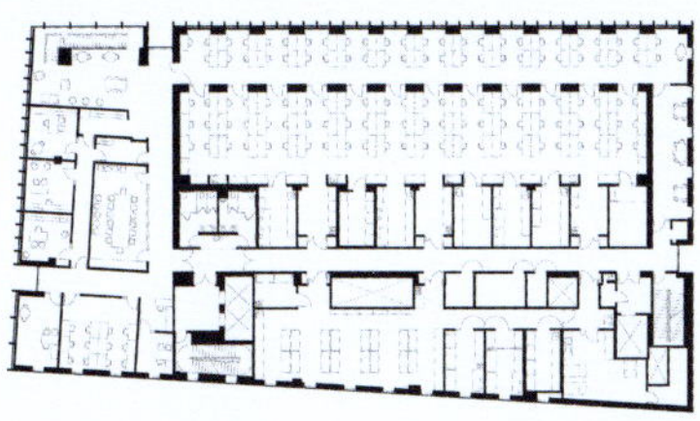

Level four

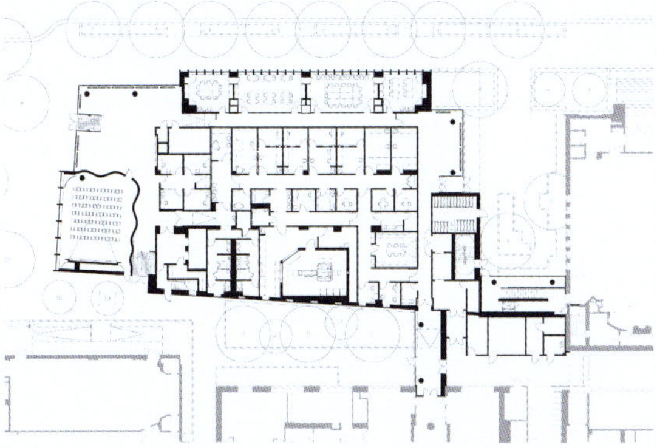

Level one

of what architect and theorist Marco Frascari called the "tell-the-tale detail," a key to the logic of the building.

The vertical pattern of panels and fins also helped us to introduce gracefully a basic rethinking of the building's mechanical infrastructure. Conventionally, big mechanical equipment goes either in the basement or on the roof, to "get it out of the way;" that's just how things are done. If, however, you stop to think—and we like to stop and think—neither of those placements would make much sense here. Why put sophisticated equipment (the single biggest capital expense of the project) underground, where you have to contend with groundwater and perhaps, increasingly, outright flooding? And why in the world would you give the heat exchangers the best view in the place?

Mechanical systems aren't, in any case, something to "get out of the way." They are vital elements of architecture that need to be integrated. So we came up with an altogether new idea: we put the equipment on the second and third floors. From there, services are distributed efficiently to the laboratory floors above, which, now being higher than the roofs of adjacent buildings, enjoy wide views of the city and the river.

Two floors of mechanical equipment between the entrance level and the labs could appear pretty clunky, but in fact you barely notice them. Here, again, the crafting of the building's skin is the key. Across the middle two-thirds of the street-front facade, the vertical fins carry the eye smoothly past the interruption. The corners are stepped back, with the second floor forming a canopy over the entries, while the third floor acts as a base for the labs above. In these roles, scaled to the building as a whole, neither seems like a floor at all.

AUDITORIUM

Performance Strategy

With the increasing interdependency of data collection and computational analysis, it is more important than ever for laboratories and office/group work areas to be close to one another. In this neuroscience research laboratory, we applied a Layered Lab concept, in which computational research is immediately adjacent to the open laboratory, separated only by a tempered glass partition. This layering allows separate mechanical systems for the low-energy computational space and the medium-energy open lab, which reduces energy use and, at the same time, makes the laboratories more flexible. A high-intensity lab zone—an area of enhanced capabilities to support unusually demanding research—forms a third layer, with access to twice the air handling, cooling, and power capacity of the basic lab, as well as improved vibration isolation. Like the basic laboratory zone, this area is designed to allow for uninterrupted open spaces, but it is envisioned primarily for specialized environments such as imaging suites, clean rooms, and those functions that require very tight control of temperature and humidity.

Layered Laboratory Prototype

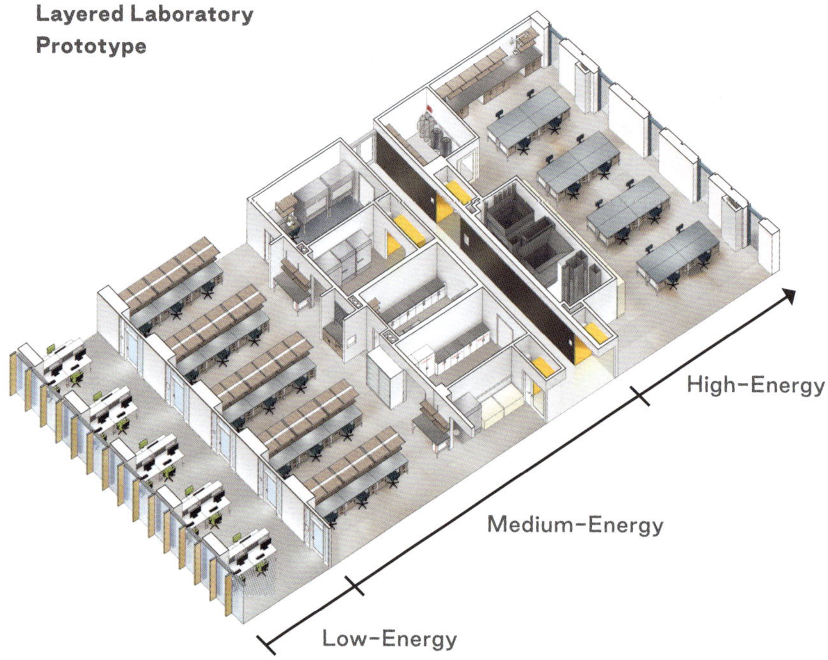

72% Average energy savings over typical lab/2030 baseline

134 kBtu/sq. ft.

45% Reduction in building water use compared to the LEED baseline

27% Reduction in stormwater runoff compared to the LEED baseline

647 Houses

Energy Reduction Equivalency to annual energy usage

LEED Gold Certified

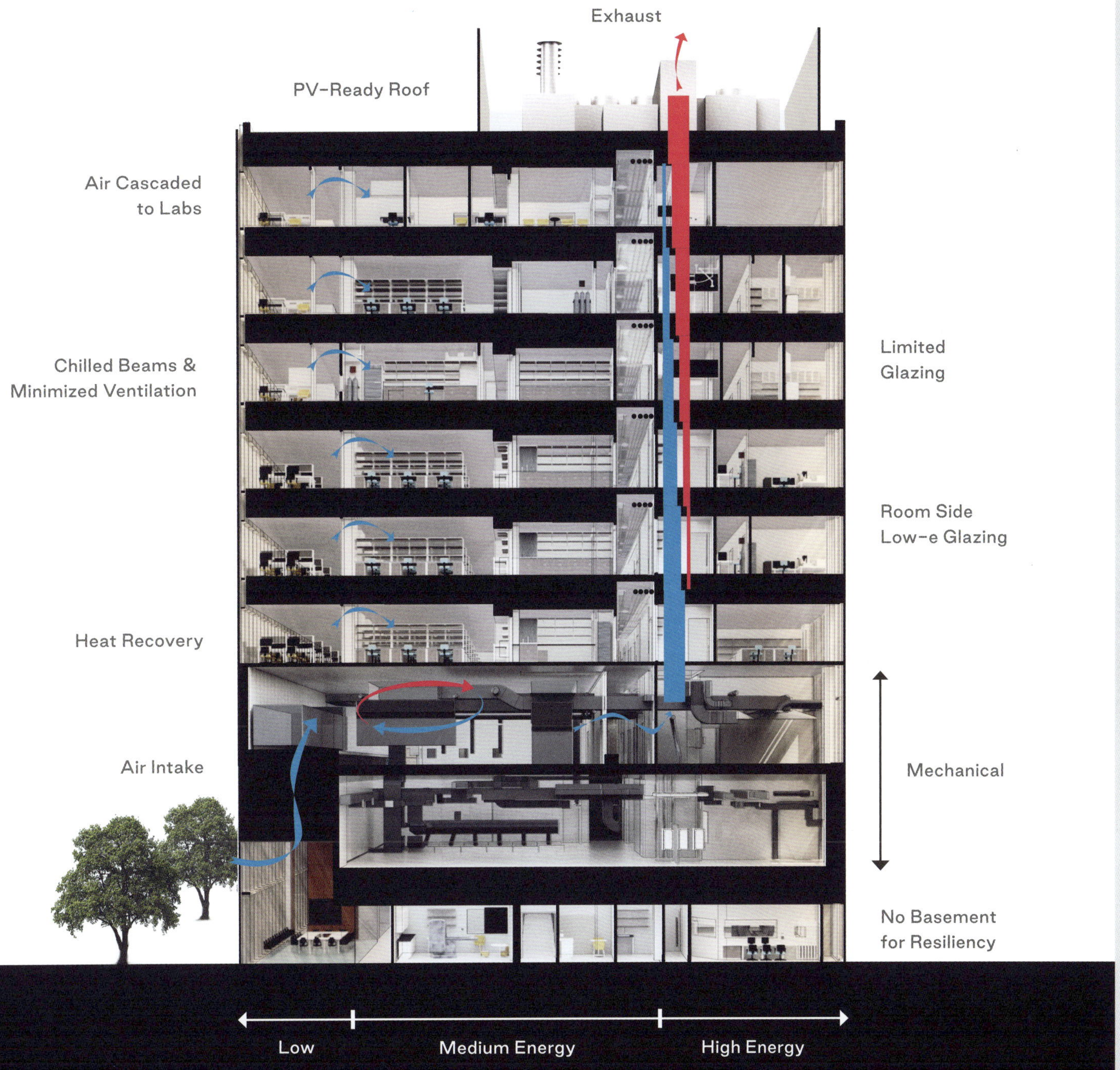
Exhaust
PV-Ready Roof
Air Cascaded to Labs
Chilled Beams & Minimized Ventilation
Heat Recovery
Air Intake
Limited Glazing
Room Side Low-e Glazing
Mechanical
No Basement for Resiliency
Low
Medium Energy
High Energy

SPANDREL

Values

Our work is grounded in a deep reading of program as an essential subtext of architecture, the key to the project's unique story. Our goal is to understand and make a home for that story, a place to carry it forward. Many factors shape place, and each asks us to articulate a value. For us, the most fundamental are:

→ Craft
We believe that the material qualities of a building are just as meaningful as its form and programmatic inventiveness.

→ Embedded Nature
We think of nature not as something existing outside the building but as something to be embedded within it.

→ Identity and Transformation
The landscape defines the true context for our work. A good background building, asked to adhere to or reinforce an established campus character, can be as important as a building that invents a new place, radically transforms a sector of the campus, or introduces a new formal or aesthetic direction.

→ Measuring Performance and Energy Efficiency
A single healthcare or science building can consume as much energy as a small town. It is our responsibility to tame that consumption.

→ Complexity
We seek elegant solutions to the challenges of extremely complex typologies.

Our buildings perform at a high level technically, programmatically, and environmentally. At the same time, they foster rich social relationships, and they're a delight to experience. We're confident of their performance, because we model it throughout the design process, and we measure it in the field. We cherish facts, and numbers are our friends. We formed our Building Science Group to focus our research and modeling, and in signing onto the 2030 Commitment we pledged ourselves to a rigorous standard. But not everything can be measured, nor do we want the measurable things to outweigh the others. Light is energy, but it is also ambiance. The elegant solution optimizes both. It fuses design and performance.

In the following pages, we discuss each of our values—Craft, Embedded Nature, Identity, and Transformation, Measuring Performance, and Complexity — to illustrate them through moments in our work and to assist in an understanding of our collective goals, providing a snapshot of the multitude of powerful voices that define our practice.

Taming Complexity

Kevin B. Sullivan

Payette is dedicated to incredibly complicated building types. We strive for elegant solutions to complex problems. To create the graceful, calming environments that we value, we must tame these complexities in ways that seem effortless. We embrace the challenge of taming complexity because it often leads us to unexpected places.

A deep understanding of science and healthcare typologies, honed through decades of practice, guides our work. Unlike some architects, who cast their buildings in self-referential styles, we explore typology as an integrative, systematic logic. We don't solve individual problems—of massing, geometry, program, performance, and so on—one-by-one. We explore multidimensional solutions, transcending particulars to create places experienced as complex organisms, each with a life force of its own.

The programmatic intensity of hospitals and laboratories is one source of complexity; another is the frequently peculiar nature of their sites, which can add an interesting twist. The intersection of type and place is always unique, so no two of our projects are alike. They are linked in spirit by how they feel, how they reflect the culture of place, and how their apparent simplicity belies their enormous complexity. They share a similar quietness.

The search for an effortless architecture brings clarity and focus to our work. We don't employ complexity as a compositional element on its own to set up contrasting oppositions. Instead, we apply the concept of *Fusion* to bring disparate elements into an integrated whole. There is always a key, unifying idea, sometimes visible, sometimes not. We reveal the complexities of social geometry and performalistic rigor subtly, through nuanced detail, just enough to make our intentions clear, without exaggeration. Often, the more complex a design problem is, the more confidently quiet our response will be.

We've assembled several projects to demonstrate how we tame complexity. They range from a building on an impossible site, to an invisible building that provides an engine for renewal, to architecture entwined with industrial design, to an enormously large project with a singular prototypical design element, and to a very small project with mind-blowing mechanical complexity. In program and scale, the projects are complex on many different levels, but they are not visually complex and, in fact, they are relatively easy to understand, elegant, and effortless.

The Impossible Site

Impossible sites pose a particularly rich challenge because they so often take us to unexpected places. The conditions themselves provoke inventive solutions.

The James Mandell Building at Boston Children's Hospital is built on an incredibly small site. To make the project possible required a tortuous array of structural and mechanical solutions, and yet the Mandell Building sits, confidently and quietly, without revealing these challenges.

Nicknamed "Skinny Binney" due to its tight urban site and its slender silhouette along Binney Street, its delicate presence hovers above the urban cacophony. Largely hidden from view, the building is a complex form that grows upward and spreads outward like a tree from its trunk to fill a very small triangular void in a dense urban bock. The building's apparent simplicity belies the complexity of its construction. A dramatic, sixty-foot cantilever carries eight floors of the building mass, including a suspended exterior courtyard, allowing the existing operating rooms and ambulance drop-off below to function continuously throughout construction.

The footprint of the site is half that of the building above, the massing of which comes from filling in the holes on the site like a jigsaw puzzle and pushing the limits of the zoning envelope both horizontally and vertically. The result is an odd triangular floor plate that gives form to the new bed tower and shapes a courtyard oasis at its core, a shared amenity for both new and existing patient rooms.

The "hanging garden," a quiet urban oasis suspended six floors above grade, is a hidden jewel that embeds nature into the core of the complex. Carved from the center of the dense urban block, it is a vital piece of urban design that brings abundant natural light into the heart of the medical center to create a vibrant sense of place for patients, families, and staff.

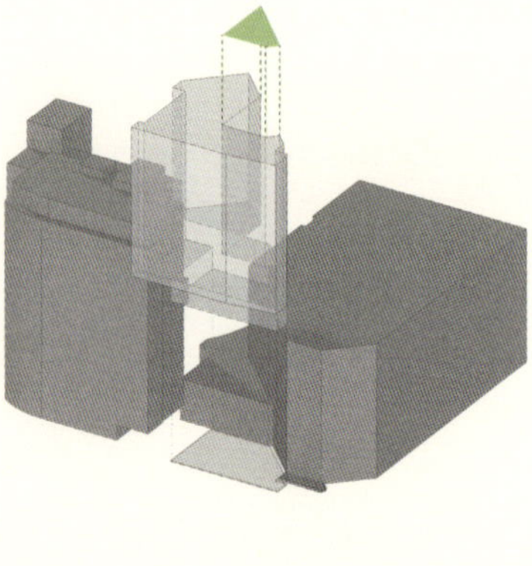

The narrow footprint accommodates all the complexities that come with an urban streetscape—loading docks, drop-offs—as well as critical programs for an academic medical center. To refine the visual complexity of the streetscape, we applied an architectural language of simplicity and quiet elegance to the patient tower. A minimalist, reflective curtain wall frames a pedestrian arcade and Panelite art wall along its base. The art wall provides camouflage for the hectic emergency treatment cubicles and radiology apparatus behind it and forms an urban canvas, alluding to nature, energy, and life.

The panelite art wall acts as camouflage, concealing the sensitive activities of the ED and Radiology Department located directly behind.

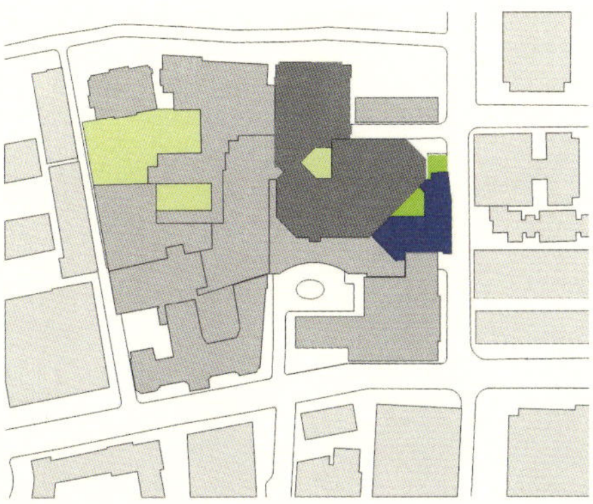

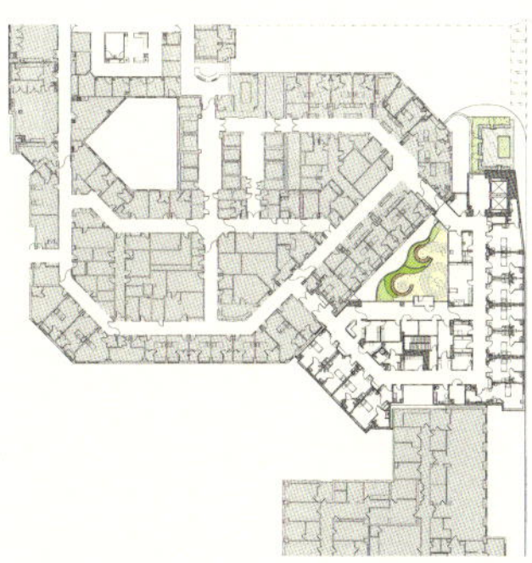

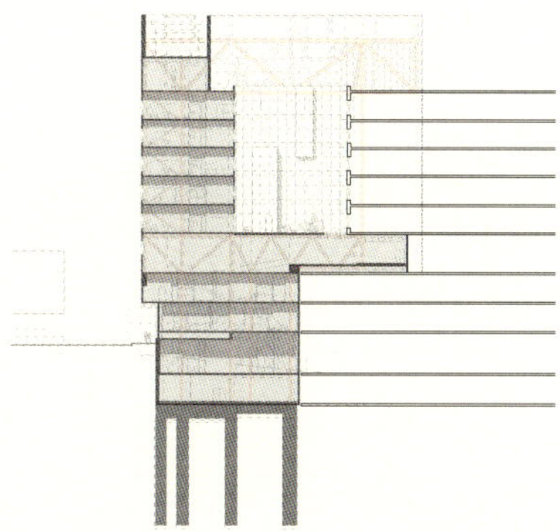

Architecture as Industrial Design

We are often challenged to use our expertise to span between industrial design and architecture to develop new prototypes that revolutionize the industry.

The Advanced Multi-Modality Image Guided Operating (AMIGO) Suite is the result of a decade-long research, planning, and design process to develop a new prototype for surgical care and a new paradigm for translational medicine. In this groundbreaking clinical research facility, an operating room is linked to adjacent imaging suites, enabling the patient to stay in place while the machines—including a 33,000-pound MRI—move from one chamber to another during a surgical procedure. We used extensive physical mock-ups and simulations to design the equipment, test and refine the choreography of the moving parts during surgical procedures, and design the space itself.

In the AMIGO Suite, the patient remains on the table as an MRI, angiography, or PET/CT scanner moves into place. Once the images have been completed and reviewed, the scanner glides out, the ceiling booms rotate back into place, the shielded door slides shut,

Moving ceiling-hung equipment allows the room to transform from an operating room into an imaging suite where the patient remains stationary on the table.

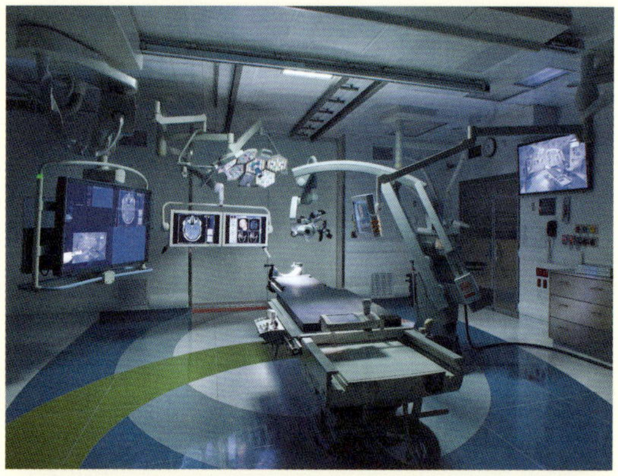

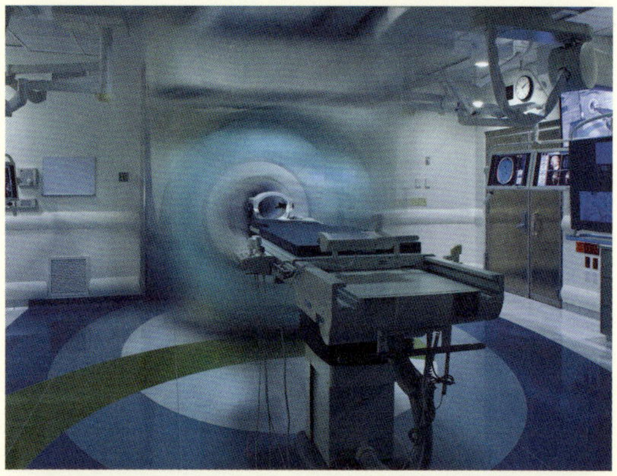

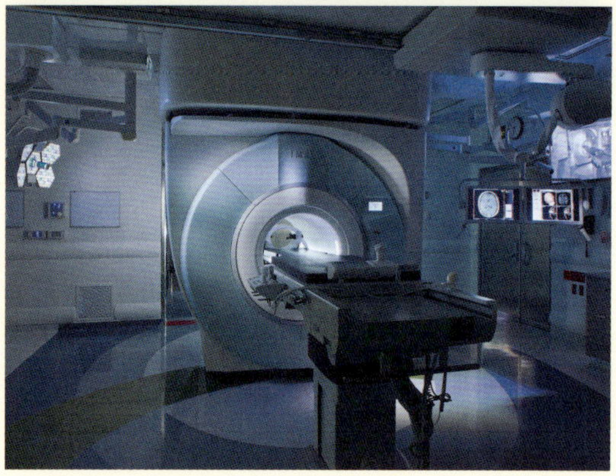

1 Positron emission tomography
2 Operating room
3 Magnetic resonance imaging

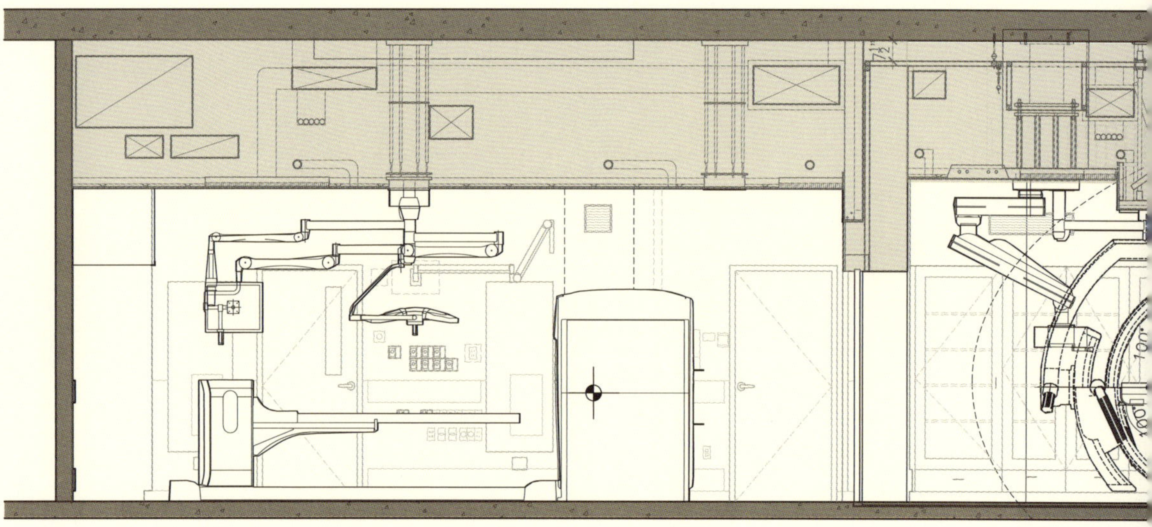

1

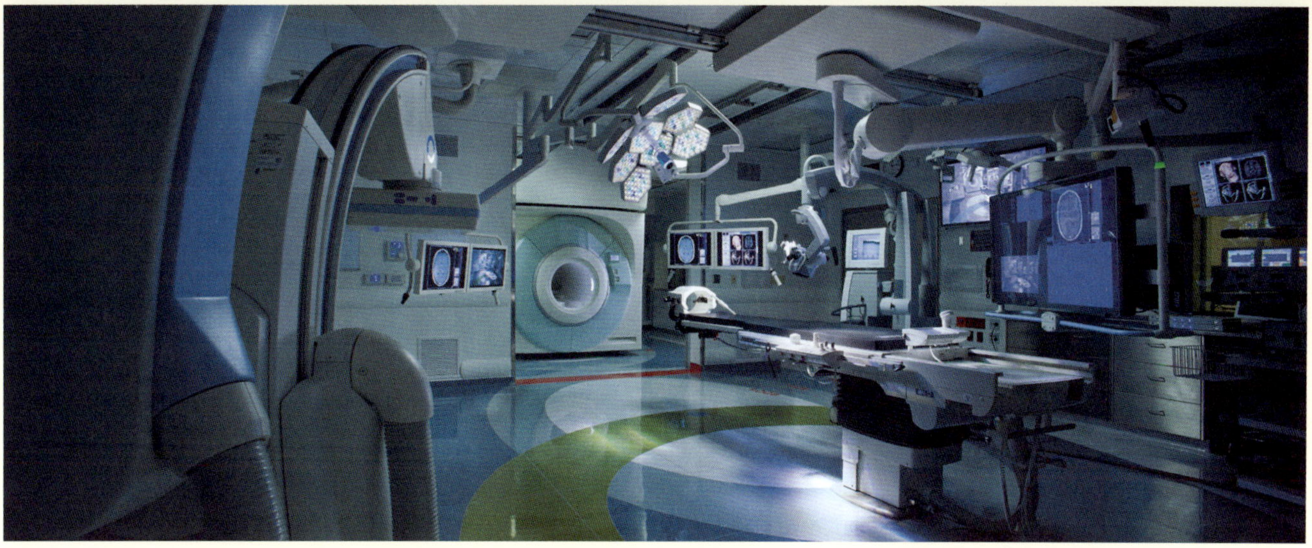

The AMIGO Suite seeks to directly improve patient care by creating a lab wherein surgical procedures and innovations can be tried, tested, and refined.

and surgery can continue.

While the attributes of the project are overwhelmingly technological, the space is comfortable and uplifting, simple and clear. Neutral walls and ceilings do not compete with critical displays. The kinetic qualities of the suite are, instead, captured on the floor, where the arc of the operating table's rotation and the limits of the magnet's Gaussian surfaces are colorfully inscribed. The remarkable sense of openness created by the "en suite" configuration of the spaces and the large viewing windows makes the AMIGO project uniquely different from a typical opaque and cellular operating room.

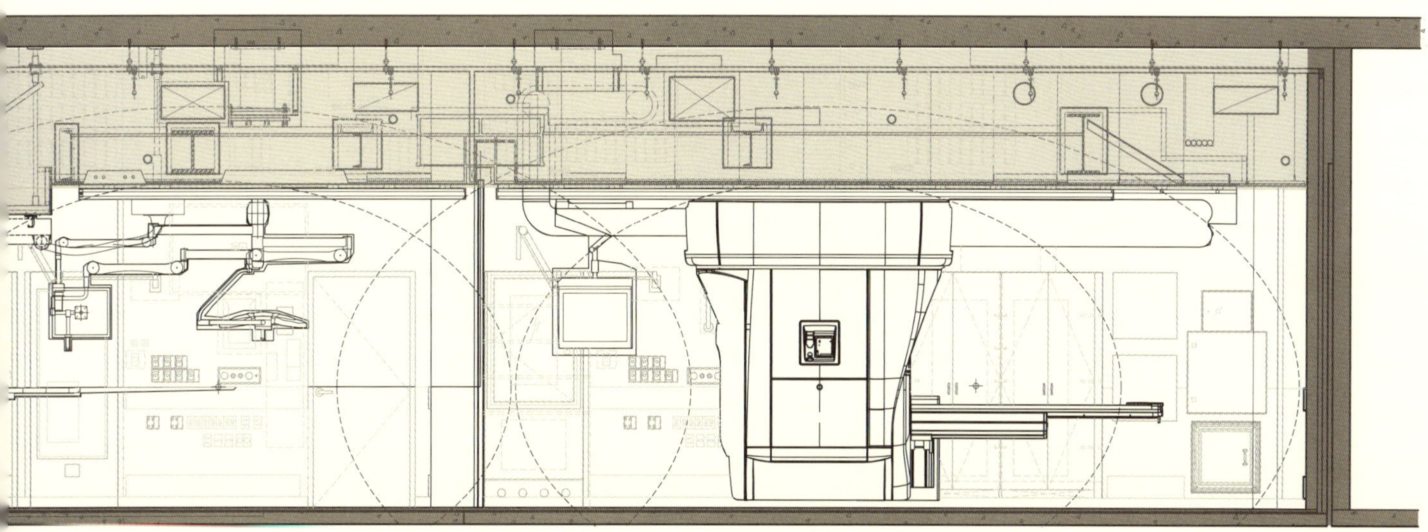

2

3

Family Nest

In China, new hospitals vitalize and catalyze entire cities. Their sheer size is the root of the challenge: to provide a sense of place and humanity.

The Fifth Xiangya Hospital in Changsha is a 5,600,000-square-foot, high-tech megastructure with 2,500 patient beds and over 100,000 patient visits per day. It is big and complicated.

The hospital's vast complexity is softened by its relationship to the landscape and the presence it assumes within it. Two inpatient bed towers, floating above a diagnostic and treatment podium, zigzag to optimize solar performance and site vistas, forming iconic, easily understood "Twin Dragons." A unified landscape strategy extends the adjacent Xianguling Park through the center of the complex, embedding nature in the hospital in the form of gardens, courtyards, and roof terraces. Light monitors and generous windows provide abundant natural light and frame views of the natural surroundings.

Design concept and building organization

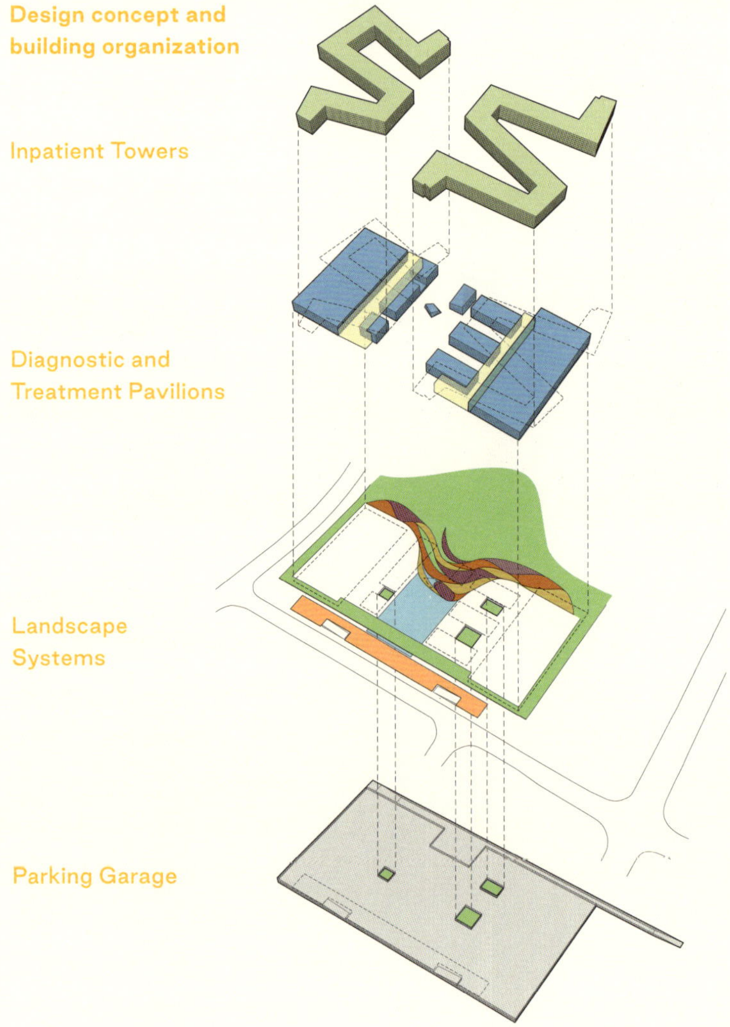

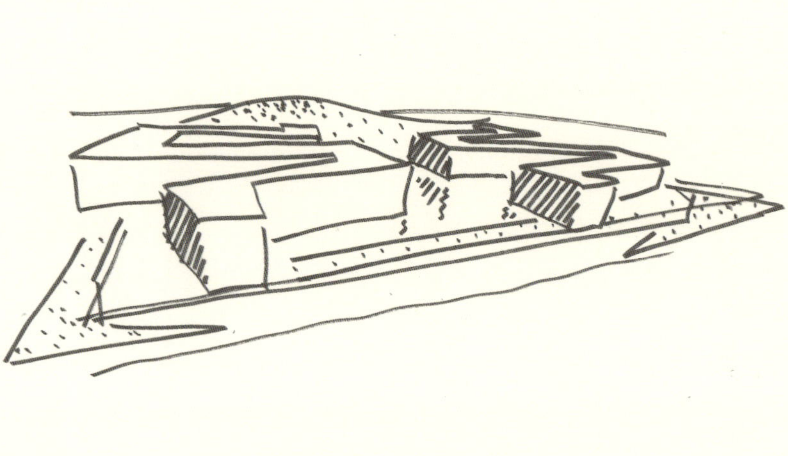

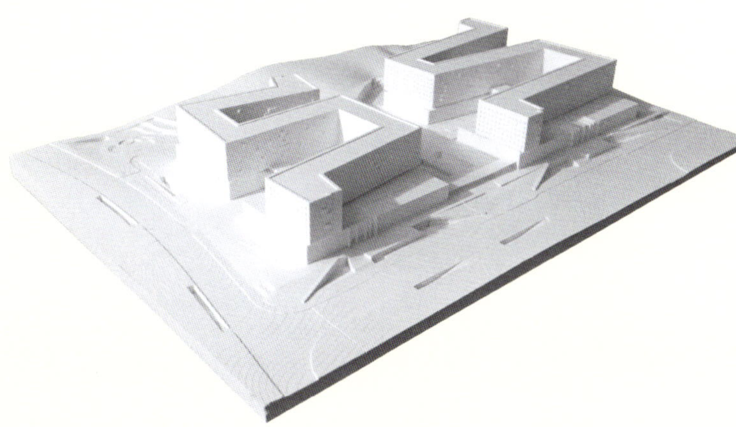

The Family Nest provides a place of respite for patients and visitors.

The enormity of the megastructure is suppressed through the relationship of the typical patient room window to the whole. We conceived this window as a Family Nest, delicately scaled to the patient and the patient's family. The Family Nest symbolizes the hospital's commitment to creating a healing environment, focused on the individual and promoting a strong sense of respite. Inside, it is the focus of the patient room, a space for many different uses—a niche for individual meditation and relaxation, an alcove for a parent and child to relax together, or simply a picture window overlooking the garden. From outside, it is a metaphor for the patient room and the key building block of the facade, mitigating the enormous difference in scale between the hospital and the individual patient and family.

The Fifth Xiangya Hospital features over 2,500 patient rooms, each with a carefully calibrated window box. Leveraging the resources of our FabLab, we augment conventional design process with full-scale prototyping and material exploration. We use our ability to build things as both an internal design tool and a means of communicating architectural intent to clients and builders.

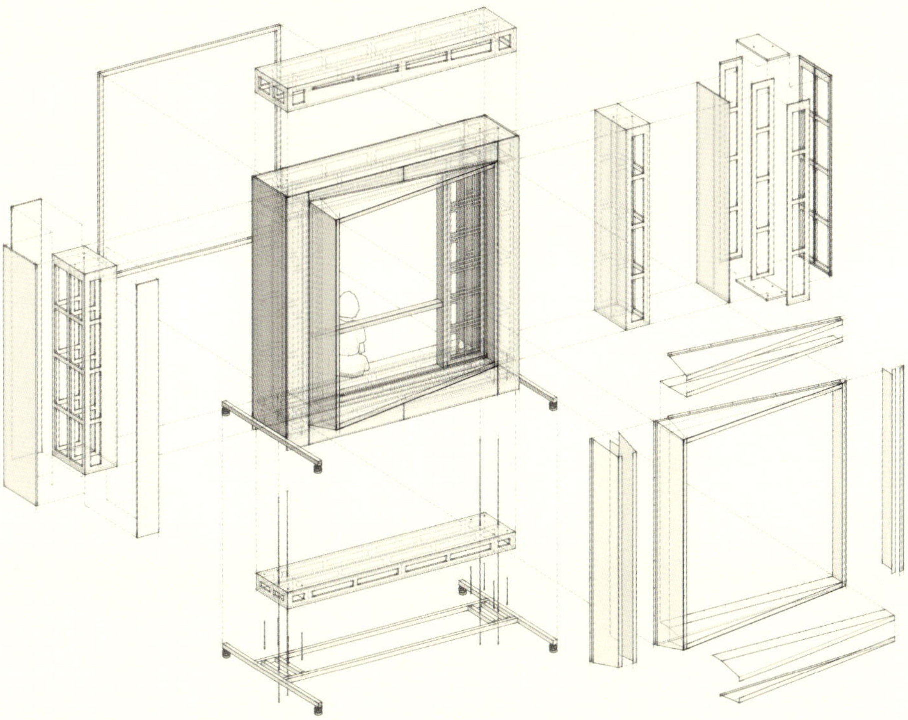

Invisible Architecture

Sometimes a building has to be invisible for it to have the most impact once it is discovered.

For over a century, the Main Group at MIT—the university's original complex of buildings, linked by the famed Infinite Corridor—has served as its primary, iconic image. The Physics, Department of Material Science, Spectroscopy and Infrastructure (PDSI) project renews these historic structures and extends their viability for the next hundred years, without changing their historic exterior appearance.

Inside, the transformation is complete. PDSI breathes new life and much-needed infrastructure into the historic core. On one level, it is a simple infill addition, inserted into an underutilized service courtyard, to provide an intimate academic oasis just off the Infinite Corridor. On another, it is a technical engine and social connector, weaving together pathways for people and systems, enabling the hundred-year-old complex to remain a vital home for high-technology research.

The project provides new distribution routes for twenty-first-century infrastructure and a new social geometry for teaching and research. Largely invisible itself, it connects the surrounding spaces in rich ways, creating opportunities for chance encounters and collaboration that extend well beyond its footprint to affect all of the neighboring wings of the Main Group. It has fostered an interactive environment that quietly permeates the historic fabric without undermining its heritage. The taming of complexity is at the core of the design, which solves multiple problems simultaneously and effortlessly.

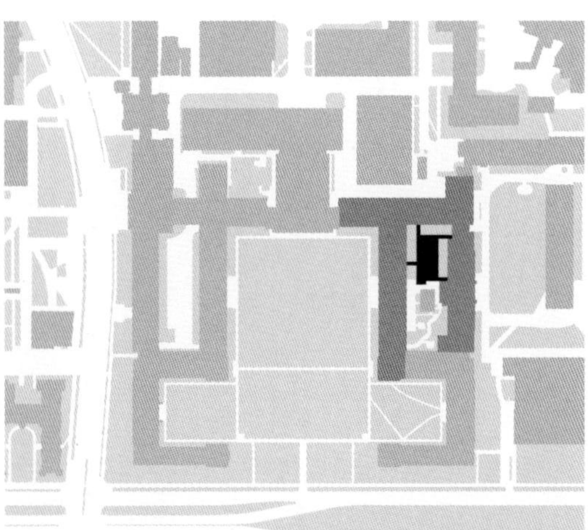

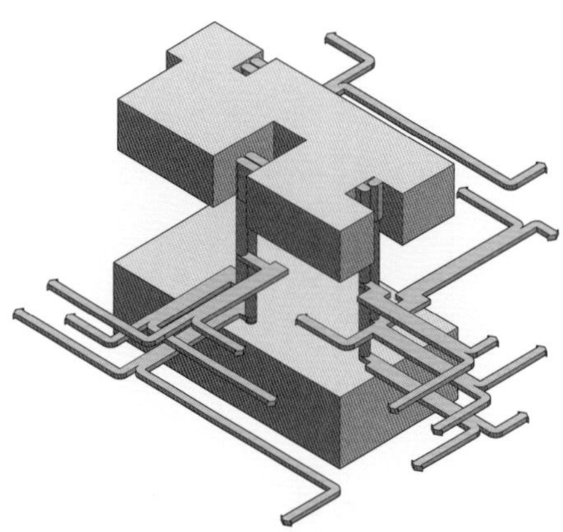

To maximize natural lighting and preserve a sense of the original courtyard, the new addition was held back from the face of the existing buildings and detailed as a series of hovering planes with dematerialized walls. Programs connect back to the historic Main Group structures with a network of delicate pedestrian bridges and utility ductwork. The facades were detailed as frameless glass, outfitted with operable windows and sliding translucent screens. While the overall effect is light and diaphanous, the construction still supports privacy and personalization.

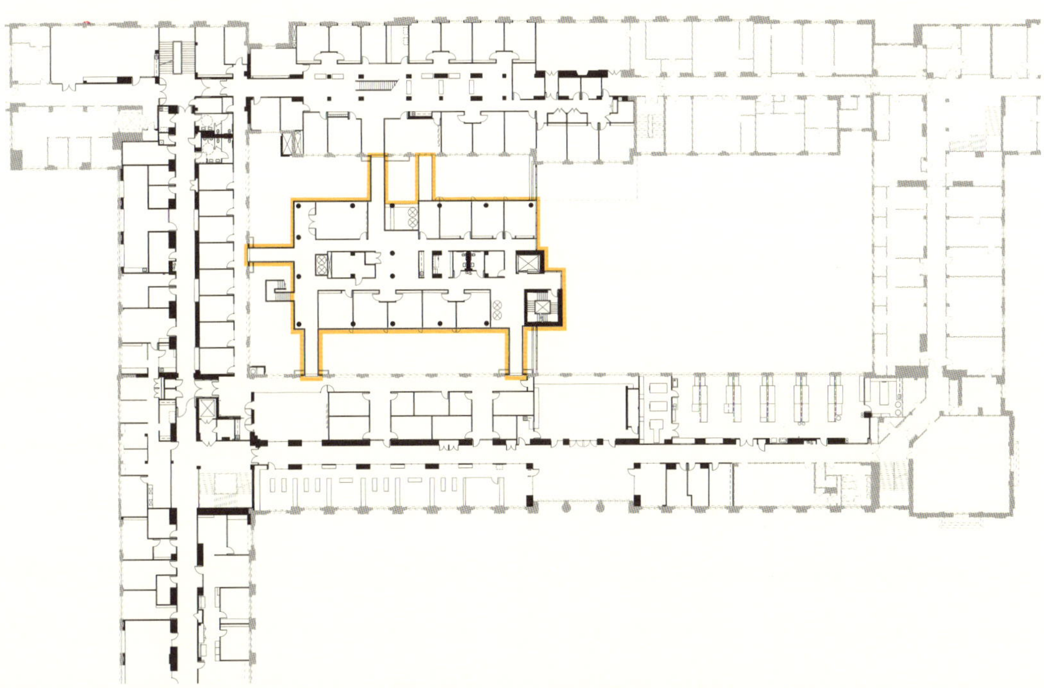

BioBARN

The outward appearance of the BioBARN can be deceiving. It emulates its neighboring buildings with its agrarian structure, but inside is a cutting-edge infectious disease research program.

The program of the Pell Laboratory is complex and intense. It houses some of the most pioneering infectious disease research in the world in a "BSL-3 Enhanced" biocontainment facility, where scientists study aerosol- and insect-transmitted diseases such as avian influenza, plague, tuberculosis, West Nile virus, and tularemia in a safe and secure environment.

Biocontainment laboratories are typically windowless bunkers, buried deep within the core or basement of a larger building. The stand-alone Pell Laboratory challenged this approach by bringing natural light and transparency into the facility, without compromising research requirements. Great care was taken to provide access to the natural environment for workers who spend most of their day in cumbersome Tyvek suits and respirators. Scientists can see one another across the biocontainment barrier, enhancing biosafety as well as security by allowing instant visual connections within most spaces in the laboratory.

The Pell Lab is sited on the College of Agricultural Sciences campus of Pennsylvania State University, set within the rolling agrarian landscape of central Pennsylvania. The surrounding vernacular landscape contains several simple rectangular barns capped by zinc-clad roofs and silos that frame the horizon. The barns are utilitarian wood or cinderblock structures that often step in section down the side of a hill. The Pell Laboratory builds on these traditions, but with an attitude that reflects its cutting-edge program.

The laboratory's most distinctive feature is its undulating roof, which connects the twin bars of concrete block laboratories that straddle a central spine, framing dramatic landscape views at each end. The zinc-clad roof form houses a complex array of mechanical systems and provides a dynamic silhouette against the tree-lined horizon.

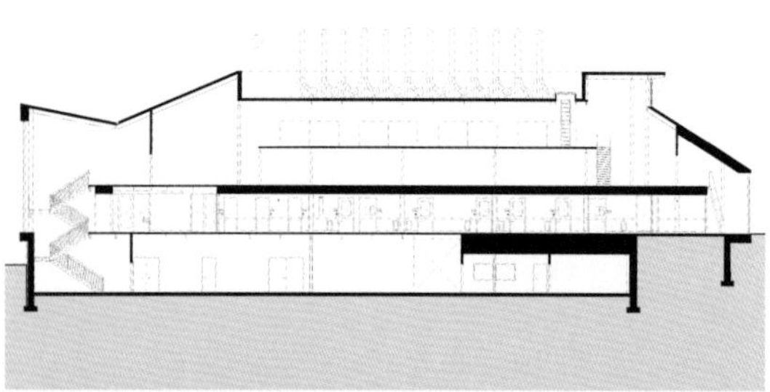

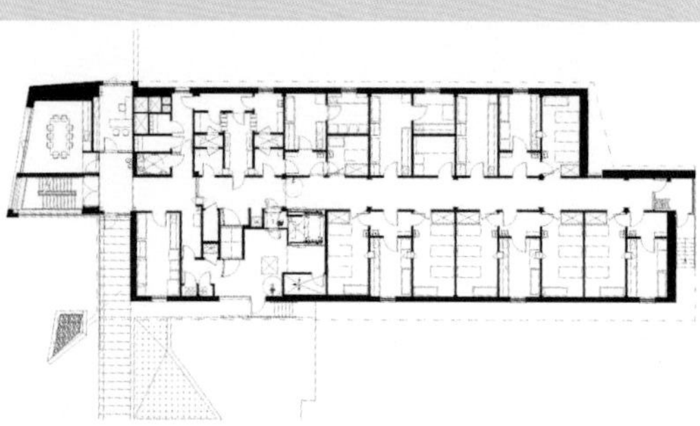

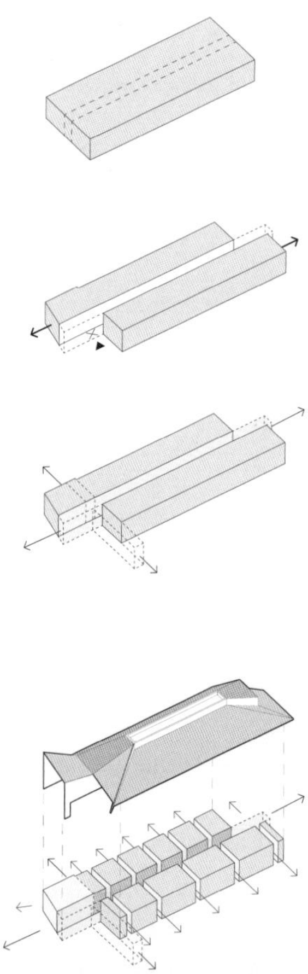

Because of the mechanical intensity required for a BSL-3 Enhanced environment, roughly two thirds of the building's square footage is required for mechanical systems. To keep these systems from dominating the experience of the building, a stepped section conceals below-grade mechanical, and the highly expressive roof form conceals the rooftop equipment.

Building Campus: Identity and Transformation

Leon W. Drachman

Campus in motion: A campus is a complex place, a long-term enterprise in constant flow. At any given time, it is at once the result of decades—or centuries—of earlier activities, and a place inexorably awaiting the next activity. Building on a campus is, therefore, an act not only in a specific place, but also at a particular point in time. We tend to think of the current project as "completing the past." Yet, in fact, today's project will both join—and modify—the existing context and, in its turn, become "existing conditions" for the inevitable next project. A project is, by definition, an act of continuity. We are always building context.

With this understanding in mind, we may ask: How do we see the role of the current project within this ever-changing process? How should the project deal with the identity of the place, which is constantly evolving?

At Payette, we believe that positive transformation is found in adding value to an existing asset and projecting it toward new possibilities. It follows that excellence is a function not of scale, but of maximizing the range of action of each project and amplifying its positive effect, both on the immediate campus realm and beyond. We believe that this is not only the natural role of large projects, but it is also the latent potential of every project. Whether injecting new life into an underperforming campus space, enabling an aging building to perform at a higher standard, or inserting a small addition into an underutilized courtyard, we must ask projects of any size to contribute to the continuous improvement of the larger campus environment. A good background building, asked to adhere to or reinforce an established campus character, can be as important as a building that invents a new place, radically transforms a sector of the campus, or introduces a new formal or aesthetic direction. By simply restoring the clarity of the plan or broadening the visual connection to the outdoors, a small-scale project can make a profound, if incremental, improvement in the way a facility works or how it is experienced.

The Role of Landscape

Since the beginning of our practice, Payette has relied on landscape design to embed a building within its site and to embed nature within the building, always focusing on the creation of place. In campus settings, the embrace of landscape has created opportunities to extend the project's area of influence beyond the reach of the buildings themselves. This integrated way of thinking has transformed campus environments in profound ways.

For example, at Penn State's University Park campus, Payette combined the design of two separate, concurrent building commissions: the Chemistry Research Building and the Life Sciences Building. The team took advantage of the new emergent scale by assembling a prominent complex of buildings and open spaces that amounted to more than the sum of its parts, including the creation of a new pedestrian promenade, now known as Shortlidge Mall. While respecting the character of the adjacent architecture and landscape, the project nonetheless relied heavily on landscape to transform the precinct, creating a signature new place on campus, enabled by closing Shortlidge Road.

Identity in Flux

Projects for campuses possessing a strong physical and institutional identity are typically expected to adhere to the dominant campus character. At Connecticut College, the New London Hall addition and renovation responded to a consistent and well-established architectural context by adding a quiet but impactful wing to the existing building. Intended to densify the core of the campus, the renovated and expanded science building shapes, with adjacent buildings, a new exterior space called Centennial Plaza, which has become the outdoor heart of the science precinct. The added wing respects the prevailing campus architecture—in particular the historic building to which it is attached—through continuity of massing and proportions, form and general texture. Upon closer examination, however, the building reveals a measured departure in language, reflecting a subtle hint of contemporary spirit.

The exterior materials reflect a crisp, modern palette that complements the heavy, yet elegant, granite exterior of the existing building.

The addition and renovation to Connecticut College's science building preserves and revitalizes the existing historic building.

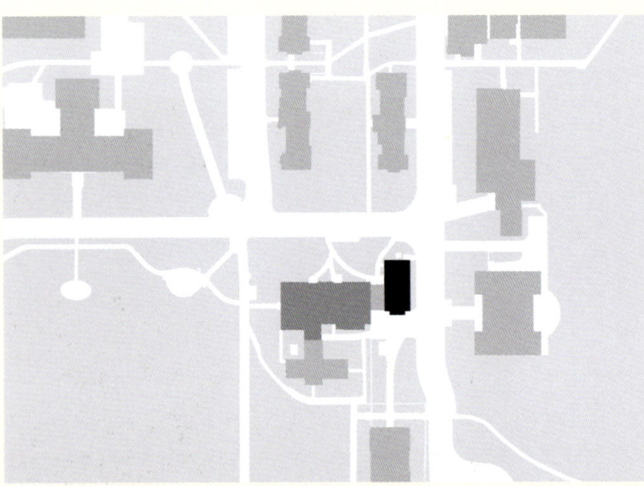

The Mohler-Faria Science and Mathematics Center at Bridgewater State University revitalizes the heart of the main campus.

On the other hand, campuses with weak characters—or institutions looking to create new precincts or establish new campuses—can be either open to modifications or transformation of their present identity or to the creation of a new identity altogether. At Bridgewater State University, the new Dana Mohler-Faria Science and Mathematics Center employs a strategic ensemble of operations: demolishing one wing of the existing L-shaped building, gut renovating the remaining wing, and creating a major addition. The resulting assembly forms a three-wing Y that departs from the surrounding architectural character as it introduces a strong and clear new expression, while at the same time addressing very different surrounding contexts through subtle shifts in vocabulary and materials. The building thus draws together existing structures and spaces that lacked coherence of language or consistent quality, bringing new life to existing buildings at the heart of the campus.

A New Identity

Buildings and major open spaces are the physical means by which campus identity is shaped. Large capital campaigns often represent the best—or only—practical opportunity for an institution to implement a significant shift in identity. Over the years, Payette has had the opportunity to explore this issue of campus identity in a variety of contexts. In the extreme, identity can be established from scratch through a single building project, what we call "campus-in-a-building," where a new campus is created through the execution of a building or group of buildings, integrated through landscape. This is the case in two large hospital projects currently under development in China.

The Fifth Xiangya Hospital in Changsha creates and completes a new megahospital in only two phases. A series of interconnected buildings and gardens forms the new campus, covering an undisturbed site of almost thirty acres. Two patient towers float above a shared four-story diagnostic and treatment podium. Unifying this array of building volumes is the ubiquitous presence of nature. The hospital is planted in the topography of the site, facing Xianguling Park and the surrounding mountains.

Fifth Xiangya Hospital aerial rendering

Nature is further embedded into the superstructure through gardens, courtyards, roof terraces, light monitors, and generous windows that provide abundant natural light and frame views of the natural setting.

The Hengqin Hospital in Zhuhai, will inaugurate—and anchor—a new medical campus after the completion of the single-phase megastructure project. Nature also plays a critical role in defining the character of this medical campus: a network of gardens, promenades, terraces, courtyards, and parks organizes the site and provides the structure for the entire complex. In both cases, a strong architectural character is established through clear massing, simple and legible allocation of exterior expressions, and the unifying power of the landscape.

Fifth Xiangya Hospital rendered landscape plan and aerial rendering

Hengqin Hospital rendered landscape plan

Hengqin Hospital model

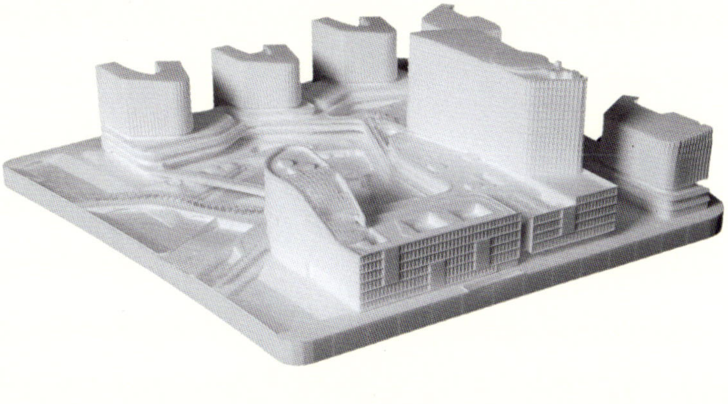

Evolving Character

More common are cases where institutions rely on new building projects to tweak or refresh the identity of their campus. Doing so often requires delicate calibration, finding the right position along a contextual spectrum, with blending in at one end and full disruption at the other. At the National University of Ireland in Galway, the Hardiman Research Building (HRB) was conceived as a modest addition to the existing 1970s-era James Hardiman Library. By laminating the addition onto the west side of the library, we introduced a new front door to the entire library complex. Despite the modest scale of the building, it has had a profound impact on the configuration and spatial structure of the core campus. Along the west side, the building frames a new plaza that negotiates a change in grade by creating sitting steps for students facing the afternoon sun. This plaza also establishes a new circulation node that reorganizes the confluence of pedestrian pathways coming from different directions. The building underscores this functional prominence by breaking with the aesthetic language of the existing library to provide a distinct ceremonial backdrop for the new green space it frames. The floating volume is gently angled to pick up the geometry of the approaching campus paths and to define a sense of place at the entry to the amphitheater and the library complex. Together with the Hardiman Library to which it is attached, the HRB established a new signature place on campus, while transforming the experience of entering the campus from Newcastle Road.

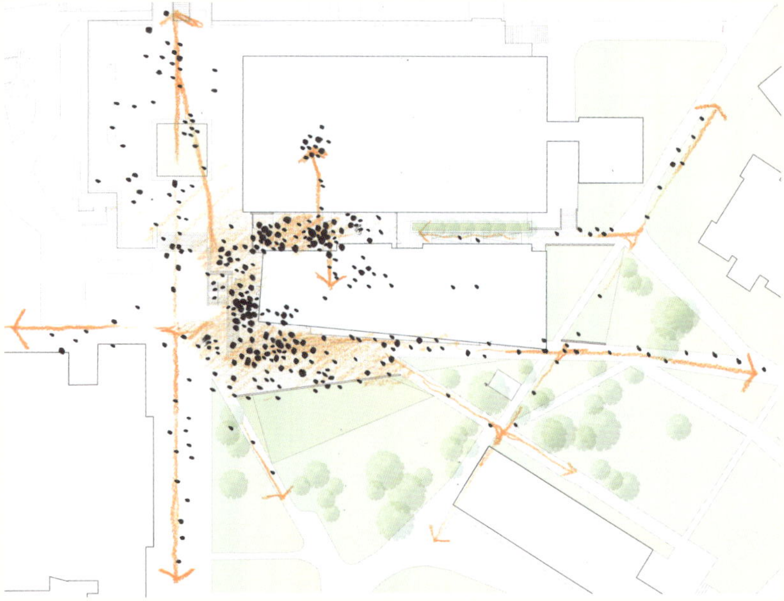

Situated at a critical campus location, the new library responds to multiple pedestrian approaches and establishes a new face for the university.

The exterior space on the lower levels of the building extends the public space of the campus walk and lawn through a pair of amphitheaters.

Measuring Performance

Andrea Love

Architecture is an art and a science. It both sparks inspiration and joy in a well-crafted space and has a myriad of measurable environmental and human impacts. Great architecture cannot sacrifice one for the other, but must do both to succeed. A building that does not spark joy in its inhabitants is a failure to those who pass through or by it, but likewise a building that neglects its environmental impact is a failure to our world and all who inhabit it. The design process must seek to integrate the unmeasurable and measurable of buildings.

Integrating performance information throughout the entire course of the design process is critical to delivering high-performance buildings. For this reason, in 2011 Payette started the Building Science Group to integrate research into the practice and bring rigor to our designs. The group's backgrounds straddle architecture and engineering, so we bring both technical thinking and an understanding of the design process and how to most productively influence it. We design not by the numbers, but with the numbers, leveraging them to strengthen both design and performance, simultaneously.

From the onset of design, before pen is put to paper, the Building Science Group is an integral part of our design discussions, allowing them to both influence early design decisions and to understand the drivers and evolution of the design. By focusing primarily on early stage, quick performance models—often "shoebox" models of a typical building space—we can learn what the performance drivers are and which design decisions most affect performance. Determining the questions the team is trying answer, be they impact on energy usage, the quality of daylight, or the comfort of the occupants, is the fundamental starting point of any analysis. It determines the metric that will best gauge success and the tools that are most effective in answering questions that arise. As our computational abilities continue to grow, we are able to leverage parametric analysis and utilize a growing range of tools in new ways to better influence our projects.

There are, however, still many gaps in our knowledge of the interrelation of building performance and architectural design. The swift pace of projects and the always-looming deadlines often make it a challenge to delve deeply into these unknown areas. For this reason, when the Building Science Group was started, it was also charged with developing internal research programs that would enable us to tackle reoccurring questions that we were seeing in the design process. Stepping outside of the project's time constraints, we can study questions more thoroughly, knowing that to understand them will pay dividends for our future projects. So, while the research we do at Payette may take place for the most part outside of a specific design project, it is born of our past projects with the intention of informing our future work. Its mission is to elevate the practice's expertise by studying how buildings perform and how people use them.

Crowdsourced Research

Practice-based research within design firms varies widely in structure and approach, so it is worth understanding in greater detail how we do it at Payette. Our research is not undertaken solely by the Building Science Group, but crowdsourced across the entire firm, leveraging the greater manpower and more diverse skill sets.

Though facilitated and guided by the Building Science Group, the research is conducted by small teams comprising junior staff, who frequently have more time and enthusiasm for taking on a research question, paired with more senior staff, who can lend their experience and knowledge to the endeavor. In addition to creating mentorship opportunities, this distributed model of research serves as a feedback loop, embedding its findings directly within projects, and thus works to advance the practice in immediate and concrete ways.

Those participating in research spend on average a few hours a week on it amidst their regular projects. They may spend no time at all on it in the weeks leading up to a major project deadline or devote several full days to it during a slow period in their project work, filling in gaps in their billable time and directing their overhead efforts to better understand a research question. Setting internal and external deadlines along with regular meetings helps to hold everyone accountable and keep research projects moving forward.

Since most of our research work is project-independent, the questions we study are broadly applicable to both our practice and the industry at large. We share the results of our work widely and openly, believing we can all advance if we learn from one another's discoveries. This open exchange of information promotes an evolutionary spirit in our studio and drives a culture committed to perpetual learning. Our research addresses both technical and behavioral aspects of architecture. It takes the form of white papers, funded grant reports, conference presentations and independent studies that we make available on our website. Though research topics vary, the research that has had the biggest reach outside of the firm has been around high-performance building envelopes.

In 2012, Payette was awarded an AIA Upjohn Research Grant to better

The examples below from Penn State Health Hershey Medical Center show how the simulation tools are used to optimize the comfort of occupants during the design phase.

Occupant thermal experience in the winter in a patient room.

Mean Radiant Temperature

Downdraft Speed

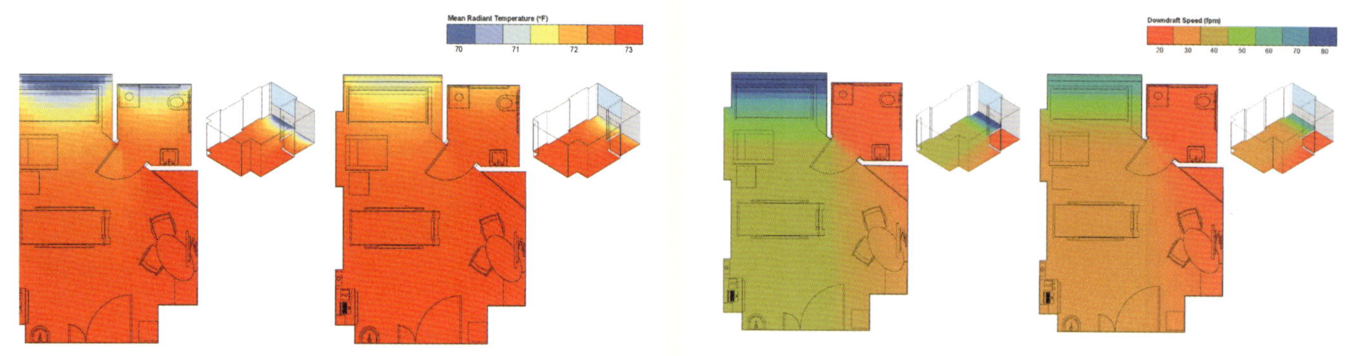

Typical Construction

Proposed Construction

Typical Construction

Proposed Construction

understand thermal bridging and the performance of facades. The research team used thermal images to measure the performance of a range of facade types in the field, to understand the actual thermal performance of building envelopes. These field studies allowed us to quantify discrepancies between design intentions and actual R-value performance. Using heat-transfer simulations, the researchers developed models that allow us to understand the sources of thermal bridging and arrive at improved detailing of facade systems, as well as to propose alternatives to industry standards to enhance thermal performance. This research has been implemented on most of Payette's projects and has become a regular part of how we deliver designs.

Because of the many ways that glazing affects occupant comfort, we applied our research to develop the free and publicly available Glazing and Winter Comfort Tool, which offers designers a simplified method for analyzing the comfort achieved by their glazing designs. The tool was developed by an interdisciplinary team of building scientists, designers, and software developers. We are currently developing a Glazing and Summer Comfort Tool as a complement to it. We have employed the Winter Comfort Tool extensively, and it has allowed us to demonstrate the value of investing in high-performance, triple glazing. Since the tool's release, the majority of Payette's projects have utilized triple glazing.

Our practice is rooted in problem solving. Whether in project-based inquiries or deep dives outside of a project, the Building Science Group works across our practice to better understand what the problems actually are and how best to solve them. As the following projects demonstrate, we do so in ways that are integral to design, advancing rather than constraining it.

Percentage of People Dissatisfied (Predicted Mean Vote)

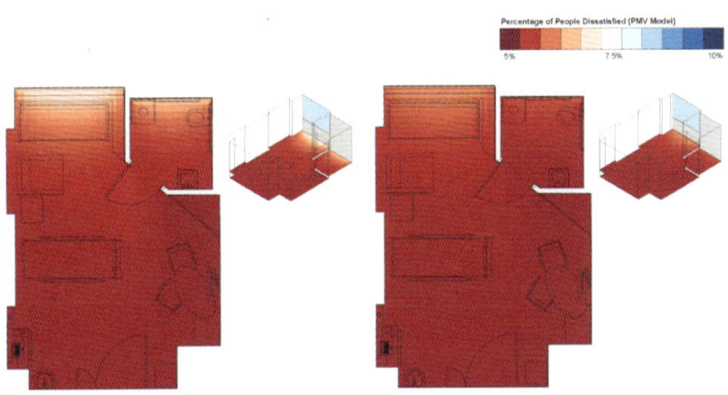

Typical Construction

Proposed Construction

Percentage of People Dissatisfied (Ankle Draft)

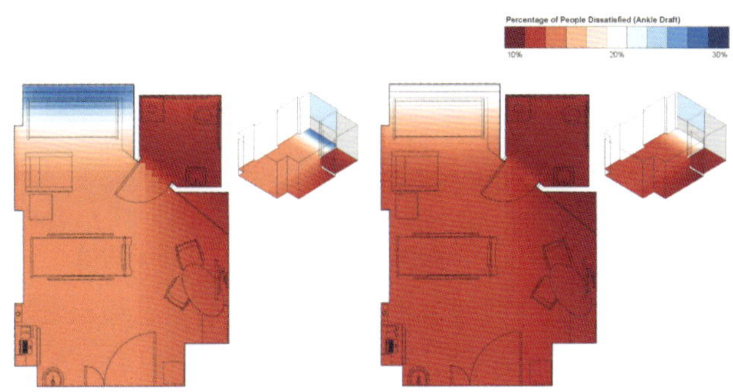

Typical Construction

Proposed Construction

Columbia University, Gary C. Comer Geochemistry Building

The plan of the Gary C. Comer Geochemistry Building at Columbia University is born out of a focused effort to minimize the building's environmental impact. It is one of our first examples of high-low energy massing. Departing from the recommendation of the campus master plan, we sited the building on an existing parking lot, downhill from the center of campus, to minimize land disturbance and preserve trees. Seizing on the imbalance between required office and laboratory spaces as an opportunity to create a highly sustainable massing strategy, we coupled a three-story wing of offices (ten feet in height) with a two-story wing of laboratories (fifteen feet in height) of approximately equal length. The resultant "skip stop" arrangement has a 19 percent smaller footprint and takes up 13 percent less volume than the two-story building first envisioned, significantly reducing the quantity of materials used. The lab side is a high-energy environment with complex technical systems; the office side is a low-tech structure with operable windows and individually controlled heating and cooling, resulting in a building that is over 90 percent daylit and uses 28 percent less energy.

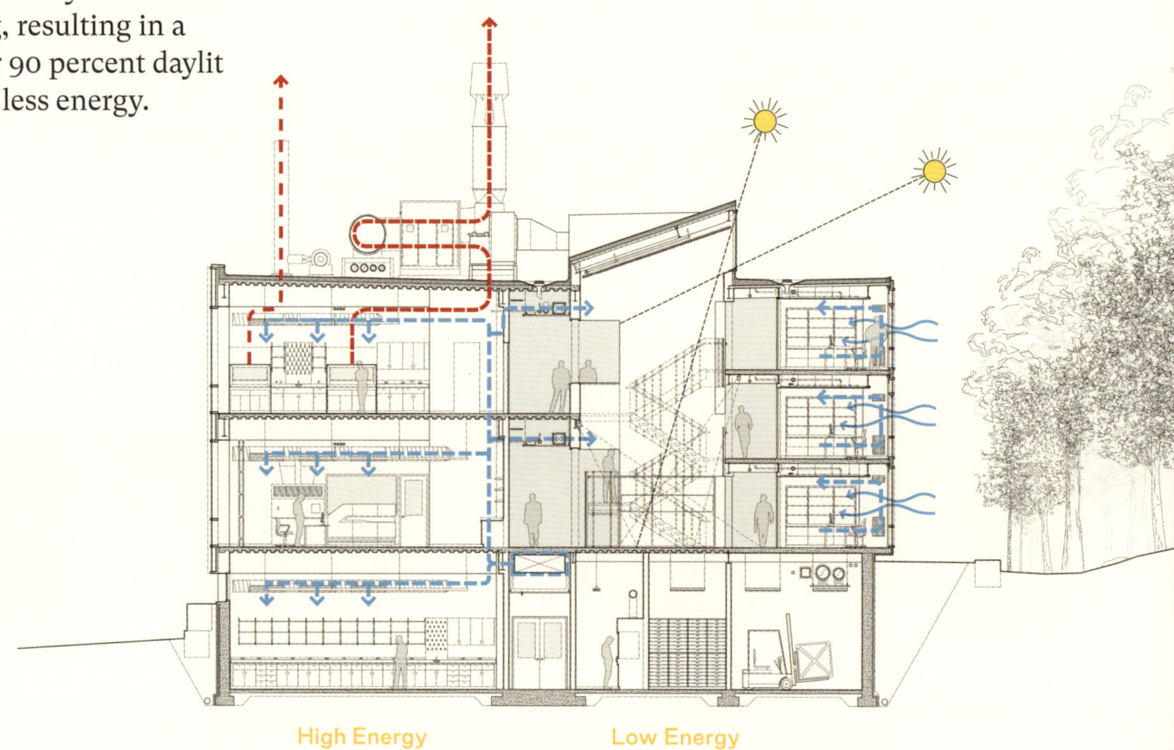

Recognizing that floor-to-ceiling height requirements differ between lab and office programs, the design coupled a three-story wing of offices (ten feet in height) with a two-story wing of labs (fifteen feet in height) of approximately equivalent length.

National University of Ireland Galway, Biosciences Research Building

The Biosciences Research Building for the National University of Ireland Galway is one of the most energy-efficient research laboratories in the world and is our first built example of the layered lab concept. The laboratory environment is separated into high- and low-energy zones. The most mechanically intensive spaces are consolidated into distinct areas adjacent to the larger open lab space; less energy-intensive spaces, such as writing carrels, offices, and interaction spaces, surround the highly energy-intensive lab spaces along the building's perimeter.

Embracing the moderate climate of Ireland, the less energy-intensive spaces create a "thermal sweater" for the climate-controlled research spaces and utilize passive strategies over active systems. This approach enables 80 percent of the floor area to be daylit and 45 percent to be naturally ventilated, requiring mechanical heating or cooling in those areas for less than 10 percent of the year. Interior glass partitions allow natural light to filter into the open labs, creating daylight and views for all of the occupied areas. This innovative design for a research building led to its recognition with an AIA COTE Top Ten Award in 2016.

Operable windows articulate the facade much like gills, allowing the facade to breathe and bringing with it a dynamic presence as temperatures fluctuate throughout the day.

High-Low-Energy Lab Module

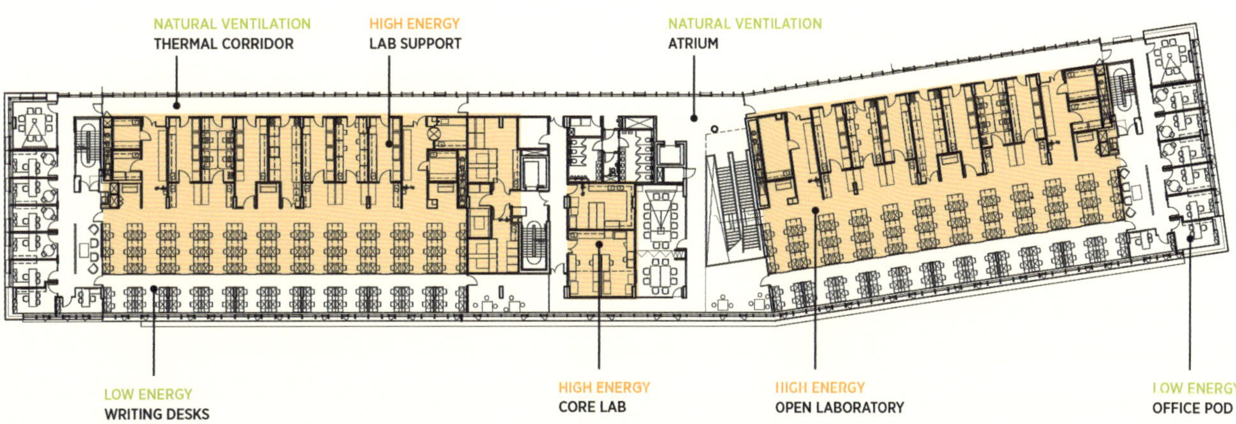

Beth Israel Deaconess Medical Center

Beth Israel Deaconess Medical Center's new inpatient bed tower incorporates the expansion of hospital departments in the adjacent Rosenberg Building, while allowing it to remain in operation throughout construction. A major challenge of the project was coordinating the clinical requirements with the structural complexity that results from the site's location, geometry, and topography. This lot-line-to-lot-line building is set on a site that is skewed approximately forty-five degrees from the cardinal orientation. Drawing on early radiation analysis, we designed serrated facades for the harshest solar exposures, so that the glazing faces true north and south, in order to minimize heat gain and occupant discomfort, and to give the building an elegantly scaled and textured appearance.

Early energy analysis demonstrated that the use of chilled beams would be one of the best ways to reduce building energy use. Decoupling cooling from ventilation led to a smaller mechanical system, allowing us to reduce the floor-to-floor heights and the size of the penthouse, saving first costs as well as operational costs. For this strategy to work, however, the peak thermal loads of the facades could not exceed the capacity of the chilled beams. To align the performance and aesthetic goals, the Building Science Group worked back and forth with the design team, conducting iterative analyses of the facade design as it was developed.

Beth Israel Deaconess Medical Center's New Inpatient Building utilizes a serrated facade to precisely tune solar exposure for each patient room.

Conventional Flat Facade

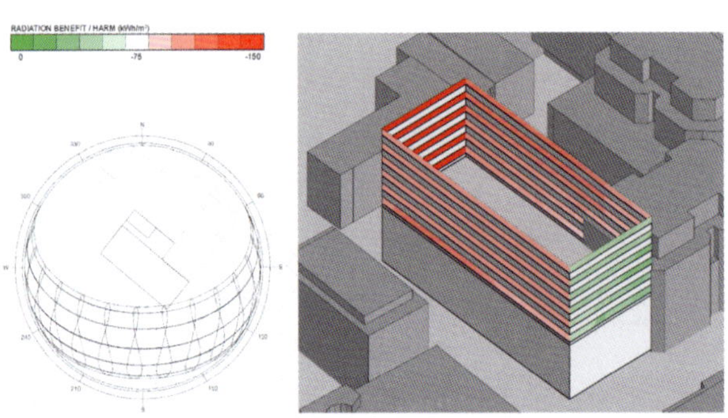

Serrated Facade

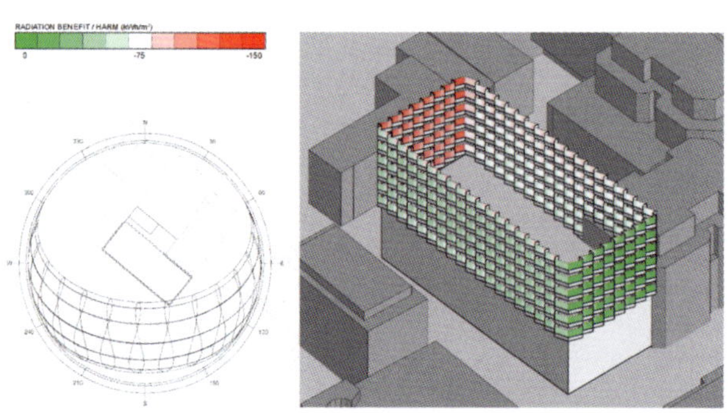

Chelsea Soldiers' Home

Perched on Powder Horn Hill in Chelsea, Massachusetts, and capped by an iconic solar canopy, this model of long-term care for veterans targets a goal of net zero energy, while making the most of natural light. Designed to harness panoramic views of downtown Boston and the harbor, the transformative new facility will have 154 private rooms organized around shared community spaces and surrounded by generous courtyards.

The new Soldiers' Home is not only a model for dignified long-term care; it will also be a cutting-edge example of resilience and sustainability. Extensive shoebox modeling guided development of the typical patient room, and Payette's net zero goal was the driver for key design decisions. The combination of geothermal heating and cooling, a heat recovery system, a high-performance building envelope, a 0.7 megawatt rooftop-mounted solar array, and natural ventilation in all resident spaces yields a building that uses 71 percent less energy than allowed by code and eliminates the use of fossil fuels during typical operation. Through the purchasing of off-site renewable energy, this project is anticipated to achieve net zero. The result is a forward-looking building that not only meets the Commonwealth's energy reduction goals but also provides a healthy, comfortable, and inspirational environment for residents and staff.

Targeting net zero, Chelsea Soldiers' Home uses geothermal cooling and heating, solar collection, green roofs, and stormwater management, integrating landscape and building to create a wonderful healing environment.

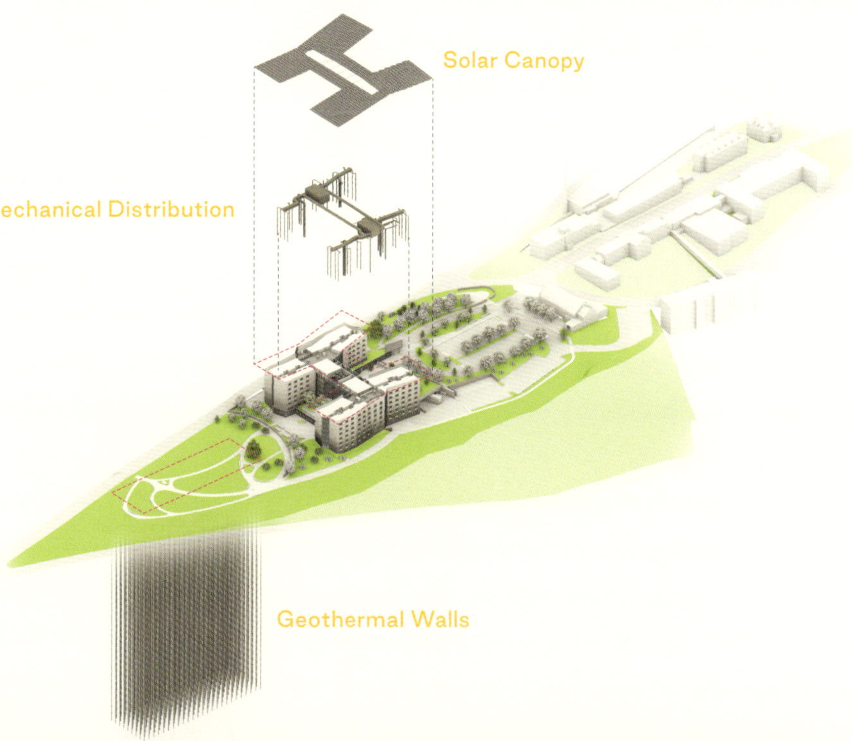

Diagram of energy systems.

Materiality and Craft

Peter F. Vieira, Jr.

We believe that the details of construction convey ideas, that material qualities are just as meaningful as form and programmatic inventiveness and should be integral to them. Materials and details may reinforce a larger notion, but just as often they may contradict it, allowing the building to be understood in different ways—as both solid and ephemeral, heavy and light, respectful and fresh. Such complexity of character allows us to weave together disparate circumstances: divergent scales, new buildings and old.

Materials help us to forge strong connections to place. These connections can be overt or subtle; contrast and juxtaposition can be as powerful as camouflage. It depends on the place, on the qualities of the existing architecture or the character of the vernacular landscape.

Ours is an ethos of diligent attention to craft, working from underlying ideas through to highly tailored responses. We mock up, experiment, observe, refine; sometimes we start over. Throughout, we imagine what it's like to use our buildings, day after day. While most become unassuming settings for life events, both profound and profane, they deserve care. We are driven to make them as physically and visually engaging as we can.

Ceiling

Columbia's engineering school occupies a densely packed complex of buildings at the northeast corner of the university's iconic Morningside Heights campus. A small project to redesign its main entry and adjacent student lounge turned on an unexpected discovery: a fire stair no longer served its original purpose, and eliminating it would open a nearly unobstructed space across the width of the building. Its boundaries, however, lacked spatial definition, and a cacophony of structural members and mechanical systems overhead thwarted any obvious means of organization.

A taut metal ceiling that is crisply folded, like sailcloth, across a filigree of battens posted down from the floor above, resolves the old plan irregularities, tying the space together with economy and simplicity. Fabricated using customized CNC milling technology, the ceiling is perforated throughout with small round holes in a nuanced pattern of varying density. The holes are smaller in areas where there was more ceiling infrastructure to hide and imperceptibly increase in size where we could afford greater transparency.

Lighting, in short strips emanating from the support members across which the ceiling is stretched, is effective yet unobtrusive. And while the ceiling could have remained entirely aloft, curiously it doesn't; in a quick succession of sharp creases, the metal surface darts down the wall, Spider Man-like, to lightly touch the floor in two places.

The attention-grabbing ceiling obviated the need to organize the space in more conventional—and rigid—ways. Fixed space-defining elements, like walls and windows, were ultimately rendered unimportant here, allowing the program—a vibrant and busy student lounge catering to contemporary ways of interacting socially—to be accommodated as flexibly as possible.

Interspersing offices between large desk rooms creates a connected series of intimate neighborhoods.

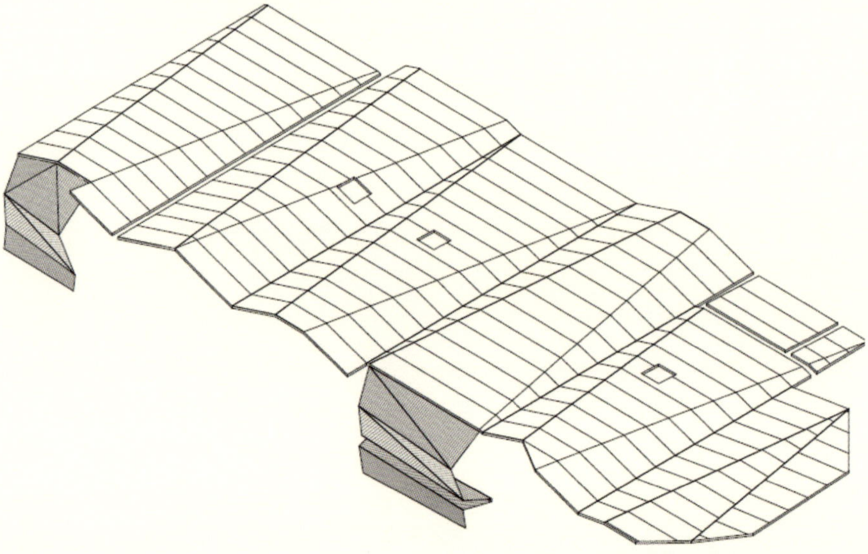

The perforated metal ceiling provides a strong signature element to unify the space and preserves the feeling of verticality and lightness.

Scale

Occupying a city block, this built-to-suit research laboratory for Alexandria Real Estate Equities is located at a juncture between the dense urban fabric of Kendall Square and the residential neighborhoods of East Cambridge. It is articulated as two separate buildings connected by a transparent, five-story high public atrium, where a network of gardens, terraces, bridges, and balconies weave public and private space together. Tenant lobbies, conference rooms, and breakout spaces adjoin the atrium, creating a hub of activity. Larger-scale laboratory programs are placed along Binney Street, and smaller-scale offices face the neighborhoods and adjacent Rogers Street Park.

The building's facades respond to a desire to reduce its scale. Eschewing the all-glass facades that predominate in Kendall Square, the building is clad in tall, ultra-high-performance concrete (UHPC) panels, a full story in height, that appear to move freely along horizontal rails at the building's floor lines, alternately concealing and revealing a dark grid of windows beyond. Periodically, deep voids are carved out of the building's inner volume, generating balconies and multistory overlooks within the narrow layer of space behind the rows of staggered panels. At the time of the building's construction, the UHPC panels were the largest yet manufactured in the US.

Distinct from the pervasive glass box buildings in Kendall Square, the building's facades are composed of large windows between staggered panels along the length of each floor.

The surface of each panel features a pattern of vertical ripples, cast directly into the concrete, that is deep enough to be legible from a considerable distance. Coupled with their provisional placement, the undulating texture contributes to an impression of weightlessness. The undulations stand in marked contrast to the clean lines of the gridded outer facade and heighten the sense that the panels are in motion. Instead of being edged in the same material, each panel incorporates a brightly colored side return that brings the facade further to life when viewed obliquely.

Brick

For Lafayette College's Rockwell Integrated Sciences Center, our challenge was how to build the largest academic building on campus without upsetting the intimate scale and sense of place. The key was topography: while the project is experienced as a contextually appropriate three-story building from the main quad, it cascades down a hillside in a network of sunken courtyards that welcome daylight yet conceal its five stories, visible only from a seldom-visited service drive. Spatially, the project is organized around a continuous open stair that links an array of academic and community spaces within.

Seen as a contextually appropriate three story building from campus, the building cascades down the hill using covered landscape and sunken courtyards to maximize daylight.

Materially, the building is highly contextual. The red brick of the main facades is nearly identical in color to that of the surrounding buildings. Windows are centered in repetitive structural bays and are within deep openings, with pitched sills that render the exterior wall thick and heavy. Like their classically ordered, load-bearing neighbors, window proportions "correctly" change between floors.

Yet, closer inspection reveals a deft contemporary handling of this traditional material that savors its visual and tactile qualities, while conveying that it does not actually bear the weight of the structure. The brick has a higher iron content than that of neighboring buildings and thus reflects more light, making it difficult to distinguish wall from glass. The windows fluctuate in width, according to a pattern that belies an obvious load path to the ground. Window openings take up a larger proportion of wall area than they ought to. They come very close to corners, obfuscating the thickness of the exterior wall. A brick cornice runs continuously around the top of the wall, but it is, improbably, only eight inches high—even when spanning a twenty-foot-wide window opening. And many of the building's facades are creased; brick surfaces that first appear to be coplanar break into individual surfaces that move in divergent directions.

ROCKWELL INTEGRATED SCIENCES CENTER

Form

Our first concept for this small project treated its two elemental parts—a research greenhouse and a botany research laboratory—as separate design entities, each responsive to its own nature: the greenhouse is more akin to a machine disguised as a building, with little room for architectural deviation, whereas the essential form of a small research lab is a scaled-down version of its larger siblings. We quickly realized this was a marriage doomed to failure, an unhappy assemblage of disparate parts that would do little to bring architectural cohesion to the complex of agricultural laboratories at the campus's northwest corner.

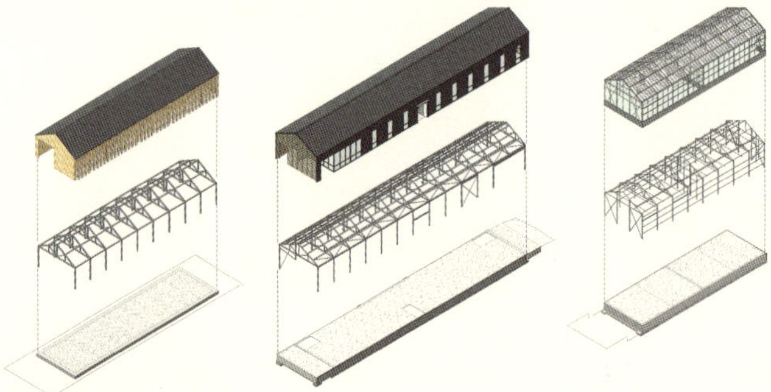

Our solution instead embraced the vocabulary of one of the two: the research greenhouse, whose idealized shape is a pragmatic response to its functional needs. Its gabled roof recalls the archetypal form of the New England barn. In its modest scale, its construction system and its spare finishes, the greenhouse proved highly adaptable to the spatial, material, and technological requirements of the small research laboratory.

The greenhouse and lab share a trussed structural skeleton, exposed mechanical systems, and a concrete floor. While the greenhouse is sheathed in insulating glass and aluminum fittings, the lab is clad in standing-seam zinc panels. The design emphasizes raw simplicity of form, finish and detailing, eschewing paints, stains, trim, and other applied finishes in favor of materials that weather in their natural state. Reconceived in the spirit of a conservatory, the lab sits perpendicularly at the head of four greenhouses, connecting and organizing them into a single coherent structure. The sum of the parts is much greater than the whole.

We draw inspiration from the greenhouse "machine" and from the historic barns of western Massachusetts to give shape to the laboratory.

Surface

McKim, Mead and White's Fayerweather Hall, constructed in 1893, is one of the most distinctive buildings at Amherst College. Its redbrick facades, accented with ornamental terra-cotta belt courses, water tables, window moldings, and other decorative trim, give it extraordinary detail and texture. Our project, the Beneski Earth Sciences Building and Museum of Natural History, sits adjacent to Fayerweather and is similar to it in height and footprint.

From a distance, the building is deliberately uncomplicated—a gabled masonry box quietly at home with the historic campus structures that surround it on all sides. Clad in red brick and terra-cotta, the building takes its basic material cues from Fayerweather. Up close, however, these two materials are experienced quite differently; their contemporary handling gives the building's simple rectilinear surfaces unexpected depth and definition.

Projecting terra-cotta bands, in courses alternating with the running brick bond, extend uninterrupted across window openings, functioning simultaneously as louvers to control daylight and as textured fields that animate taut masonry planes. While the individual terra-cotta baguettes are improbably delicate when viewed up close, when applied in veil-like screens they permit even large expanses of glazing to read first as masonry surfaces.

Molded terracotta accents recall the campuses historic brick architecture

Inside Out Upside Down: Form as Performance

Mark Lee

If the spirit of invention, freedom, and an enthusiasm in the face of challenges have thus far defined American architecture, the future of American architecture will necessarily embrace the challenges of our time with the same characteristic qualities. In this vein of inventive and ambitious design, Payette's practice embodies some of the best in American architecture today.

Payette is the leader of a generation of architects using building performance as a guiding design principle, enlisting performance-based criteria and priorities as an integral part of their decision-making process. The firm employs a holistic approach that synthesizes form and performance, utilizing digital technologies and simulations to offer a comprehensive approach to the design of the built environment. Inaki Ábalos and Renata Sentkiewicz, in their *Essays on Thermodynamics, Architecture and Beauty*, refer to this new and innovative architecture as *thermodynamic materialism*. As Ábalos writes, "[A]ir in motion now demands to be studied in its different manifestations, revealing its different descriptions, and to become the object of meticulous analysis to experience its powers, name them and proceed to construct what we have termed a new idea of thermodynamic beauty, which, without renouncing tectonic tradition, completes it, offering new and unsuspected directions to the work of the architect."[1] This concept opens up a novel aesthetic category that places performance on par with form-making, distilling a building's programmatic and performance objectives as a way of determining the formal qualities of the project. Throughout their work, Payette consistently unites these two objectives to create dynamic buildings in which form and function are harmoniously blended to achieve a natural flow that is palpable.

At its most basic level, performance-based design involves the optimization of the technical components of a building, including structural, thermal, and acoustical systems. At the Interdisciplinary Science and Engineering Complex at Northeastern University, Payette uses the light-filled, central atrium as a climatic buffer zone between the laboratories and the office space, allowing for the economization of mechanical systems in the lab areas while achieving a layered visual transparency between all three program bars. At the New Science Center at Amherst College, Payette's performance-based design results in skylights running the length of the building that integrate structural, mechanical, and lighting functions while simultaneously improving daylight quality on the interior and providing a strong design aesthetic on the exterior. In both buildings, natural ventilation works in tandem with shading and radiant heating and cooling strategies to conserve energy and relieve the necessity for more advanced, costly mechanical systems.

These strategic design decisions are similarly reinforced by Payette's careful calibration and detailing of the facade at Northeastern. The form, profile, and performance of the curved solar veil on the Interdisci-

1 Ábalos+Sentkiewicz, *Essays on Thermodynamics, Architecture and Beauty* (New York: Actar, 2015), 221.

plinary Science and Engineering Complex's office pod has been optimized through iterative simulations that target its solar performance. The specific orientation, layering, and offset between the screen fins defines a sculptural, three-dimensional outer layer that gives the building a continuously changing appearance based on the light and viewing position. Similarly, Payette's Biosciences Research Building at the National University of Ireland Galway, has a tailored exterior envelope fine-tuned in terms of its orientation, materiality, and depth in order to eliminate solar heat gain and the supplemental cooling system that would have otherwise been required in the low-energy zones. In each of these projects, the design of the facade is carefully engineered to protect the interior from direct sunshine and ensure that the occupants are provided with generous views outside.

Performance-based design can also be defined much more broadly—beyond the purely technical components of the building—to include multiple realms from social and cultural to economic and urbanistic processes. One example of this is Payette's characteristic optimization of the internal spatial and programmatic organization of its projects. The Interdisciplinary Science and Engineering Complex at Northeastern is defined by its transparency, incorporating glazed walls that provide unobstructed views through the research spaces and that separate high- and low-energy use zones. This strategy reduces the volume of ventilated research space and thereby decreases the overall building energy use. The building's spiral stair provides a prominent visual and sculptural object that also functionally organizes the spaces of the atrium around it, fostering interaction through the openness of the central void.

At Payette's Tufts University Science and Engineering Complex, interior and exterior spaces are strategically nested, creating warm, inviting spaces for congregation and informal meetings. Here the interior is designed as a series of interactive, collaborative spaces that engender communication and interaction while at the same time respecting the needs of users to concentrate on their work by providing different scaled spaces where they can withdraw. Payette's designs are based on the idea that the lab, classroom, and other learning spaces must be flexible in their design to accommodate new discoveries, tools, and approaches. Its architecture affirms that the built environment can enhance the creativity and success of scientists, students and all others who spend time within.

Beyond the quantifiable performative aspects of building design, Payette's architecture embodies a shift to processes of form generation based on performative strategies grounded in larger-scale issues of cultural and urbanistic functionality. The arrangement of the volumes of the project at Northeastern University acts as a thread that extends the campus across the railroad tracks and frames the surrounding neighborhood. The massing celebrates the intersection of Boston's civic life and the scientific community on campus. A strategic layering of materials, floor patterns, and openings serves to connect the exterior of the new building with its surroundings, while at the same time highlighting the activities taking place within the building.

Payette's thoughtful application of bridges and buffers emblematizes an architecture that trends towards the empathetic. In every possible instance, walls are left transparent and are treated as buffers rather than stark divisions, and barriers are mitigated by bridges and pathways that intuit ways to usher visitors into a building with the sense of a warm welcome. At Northeastern, the paths in the central courtyard extend the open feeling of the interior to the outside. Extending across to the broader campus, a pedestrian bridge unites the building with the rest of campus—its design serving to guide pedestrians across in a symbolic empathetic embrace.

Payette's performance-based principles signal a shift towards a different notion of aesthetic, one that is intrinsically linked to a clarity of purpose and an honest recognition of a building's connection with natural and cultural ecosystems. This shift, an energizing development in the field, embodies an effective response to Ábalos and Sentkiewicz's call for a type of design that surpasses the limitations and burdens of modern hierarchical architecture. Unburdened by preoccupations with status-based materiality and traditionally divisive hierarchy, Payette has effectively broken away from constructing artifice as a division from nature and society in order to move towards a more inclusive, considerate architecture; one that embraces and bolsters community and environment, and is in turn embraced and bolstered by its environment and community. It is an architecture that, in Ábalos and Sentkiewicz's terms, "recover[s] the capacity for intervention in the reality of contemporary societies and their forms, crystallized in the metropolis and its buildings." Such, they say, "is a primary aim, but so too is the creation of new forms and material conceptions that address the twofold need for technical innovation and aesthetic renovation." Their summation of this emerging attitude aptly describes Payette's agenda:

2 Ábalos+Sentkiewicz, "Thermodynamic Materialism," in *Essays on Thermodynamics, Architecture, and Beauty*, 247.

With the introduction of a new field of definition of architecture based on modeling phenomena and materials that used to be invisible, these new ways of understanding relations between form, material, space and program provided unbounded scope for architectural speculation: a new idea of beauty emerged and, with it, the hope of a coming together of society, technology and aesthetics.[2]

Payette's characteristic capacity to synthesize sustainability with programmatic goals and performance stems from an unusually honest approach to design. The firm's design sensibility, which is allowed to emerge rather than being arbitrarily decided or imposed, results in high-performing structures with an elevated aesthetic that bring value to the institutions and communities around them. While the sum total of the accumulating benefits of Payette's departure from confining architecture is impossible to quantify, the enhanced atmosphere is tangible within their buildings, where it impacts the experience on an individual level before resonating throughout the surrounding communities and broader urban areas.

Fingerpri

nts

Science

1 Northeastern University, Interdisciplinary Science and Engineering Complex, Pedestrian Crossing and EXP
2 Tufts University, Science and Engineering Complex
3 Boston University, Rajen Kilachand Center for Integrated Life Sciences & Engineering
4 George Washington University, Milken Institute School of Public Health
5 Amherst College, New Science Center

1

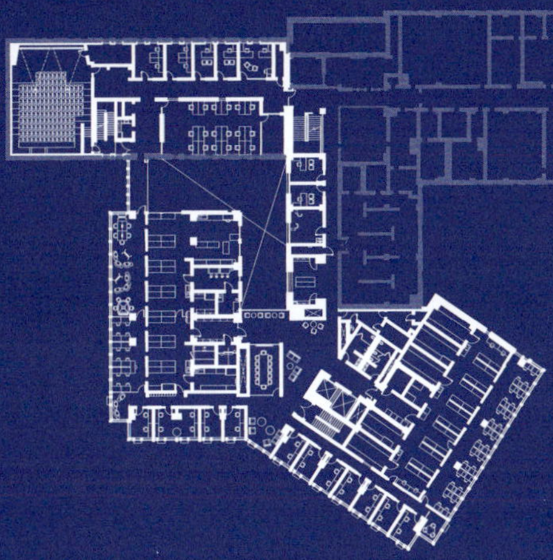

2

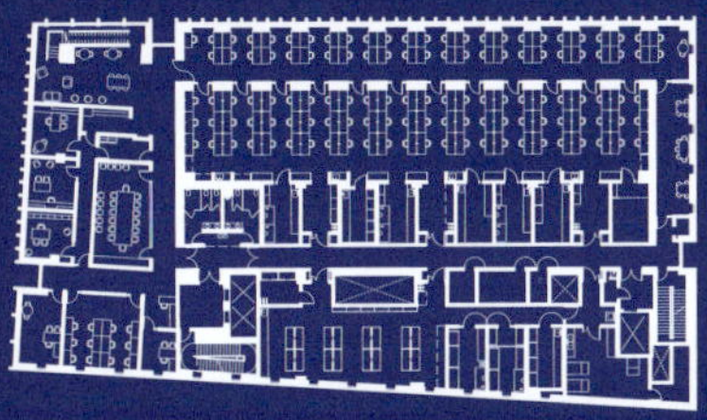

3

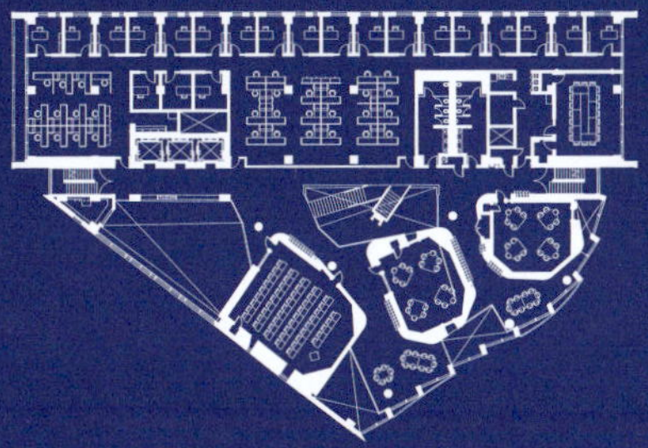

4

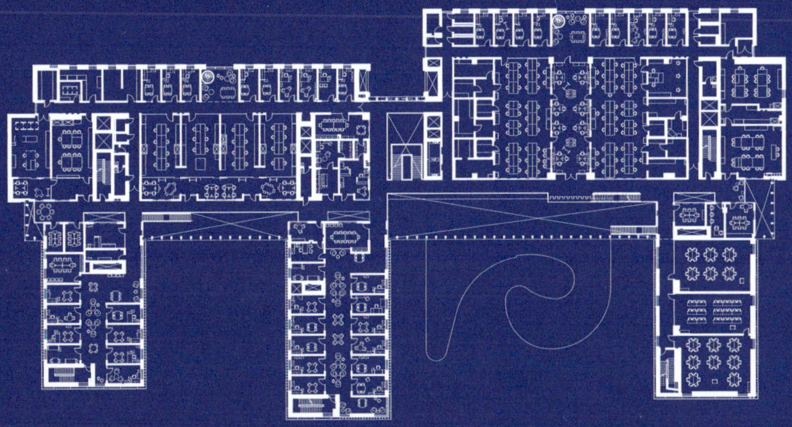

5

6 The Pennsylvania State University, Chemistry Research and Life Sciences Buildings

7 The Pennsylvania State University, College of Engineering, West 1 and West 2 Buildings

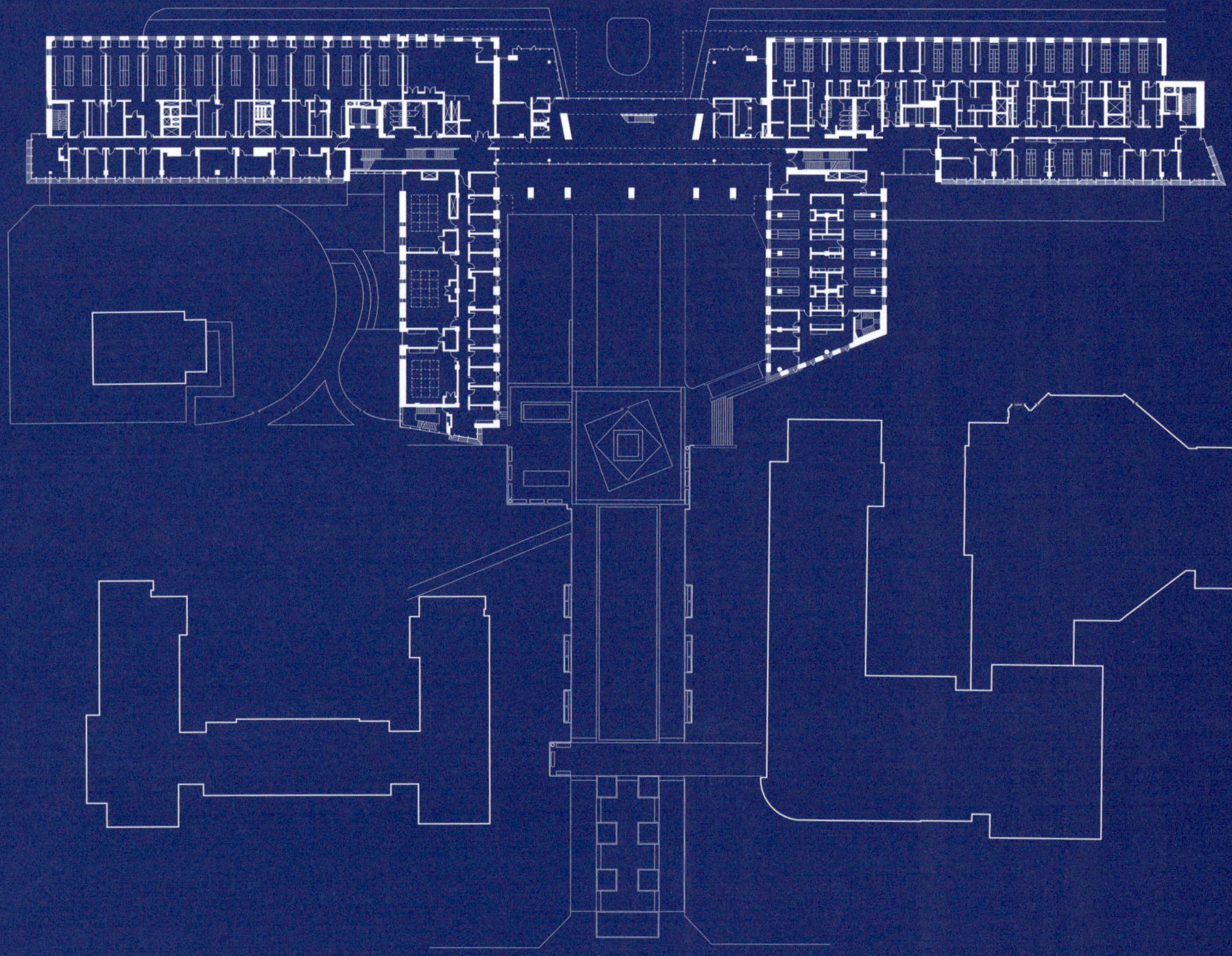

6

7

8 University of Rhode Island, College of Pharmacy and Center for Biotechnology and Life Sciences

9 Tulane University, Environmental Sciences Building and School of Science and Engineering District Space Study

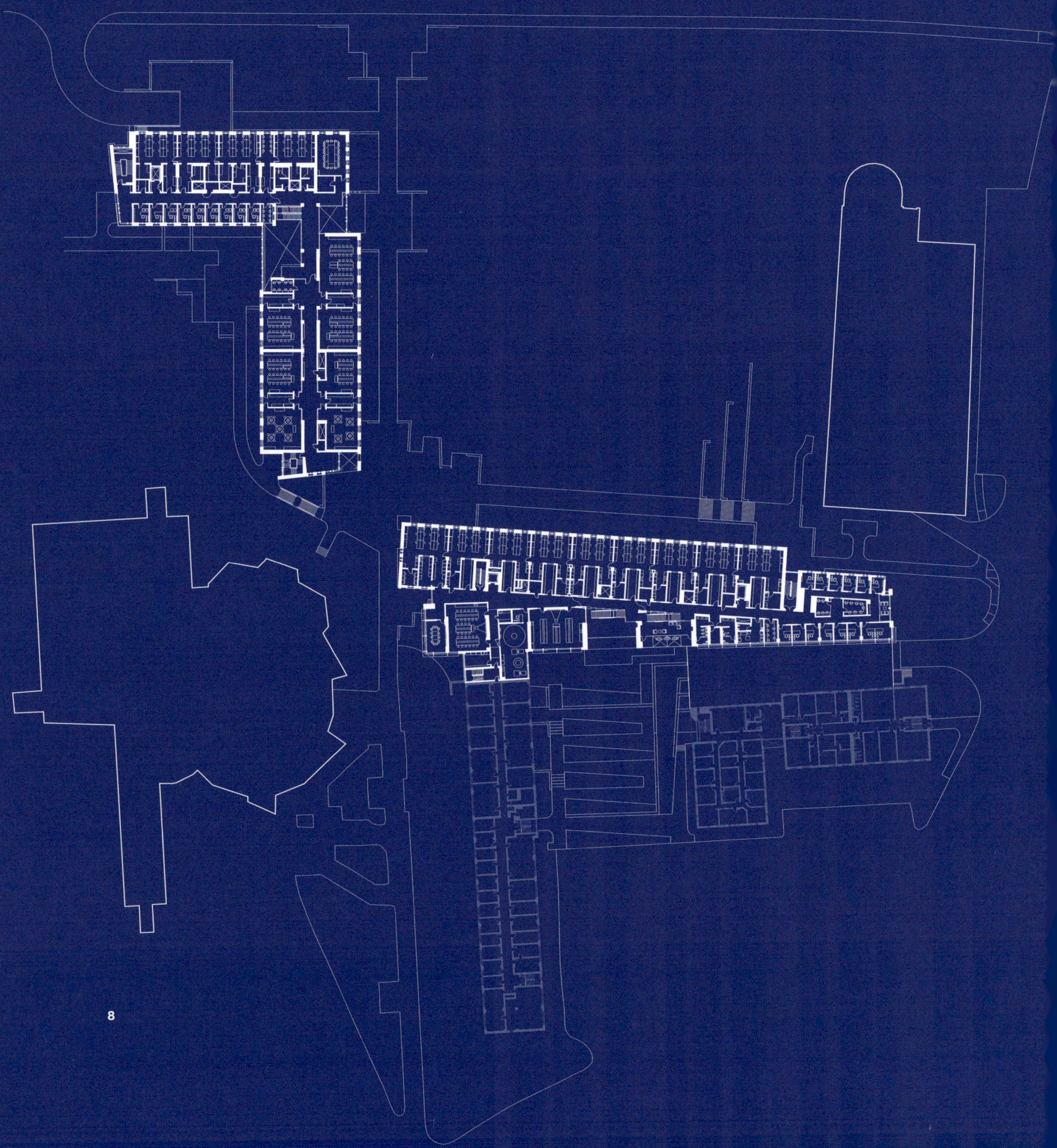

8

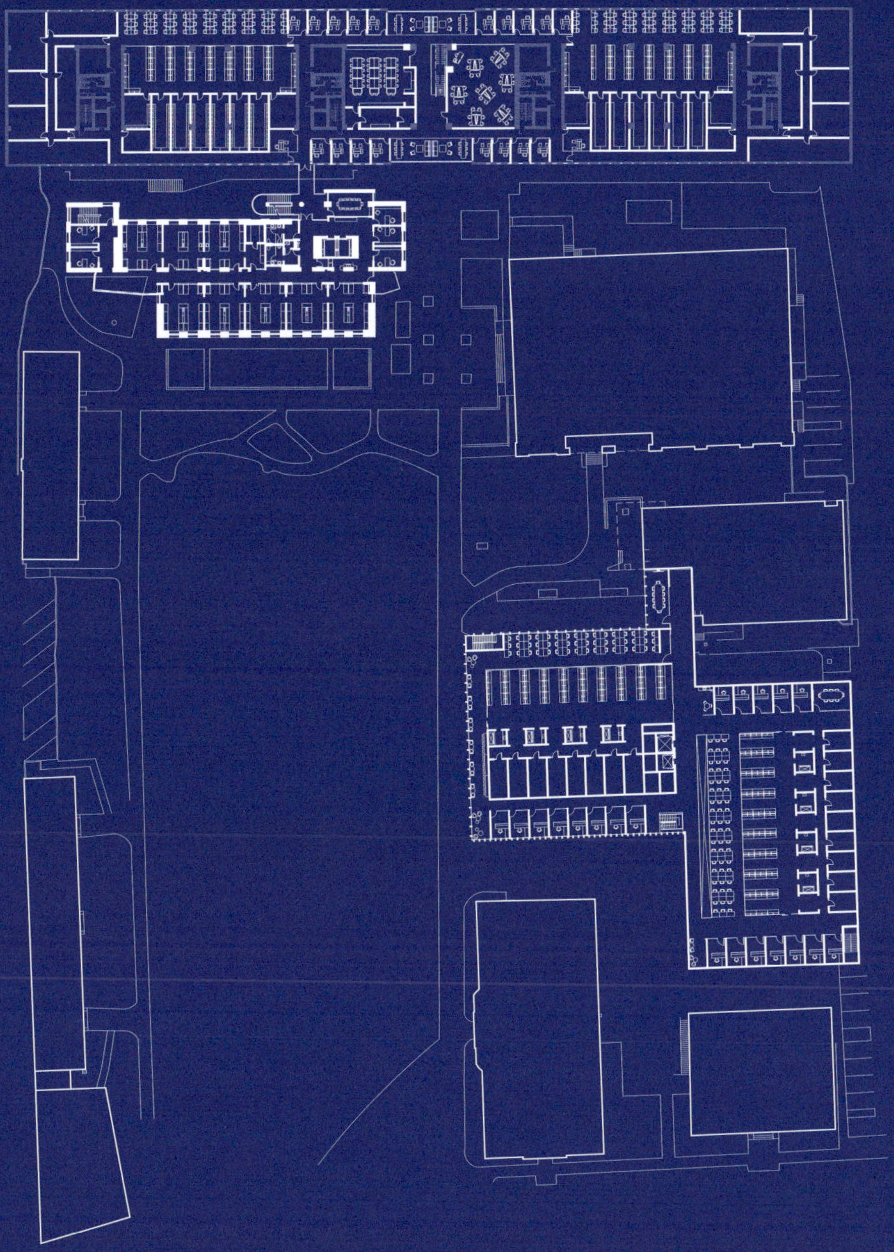

9

10 Duke University, Levine Science Research Center and Grainger Hall: Nicholas School of the Environment
11 Duke University Medical Center, Medical Sciences Research Building
12 Princeton University, Guyot Hall Renovation and Lewis Thomas Laboratory
13 Princeton University, Frick Chemistry Laboratory

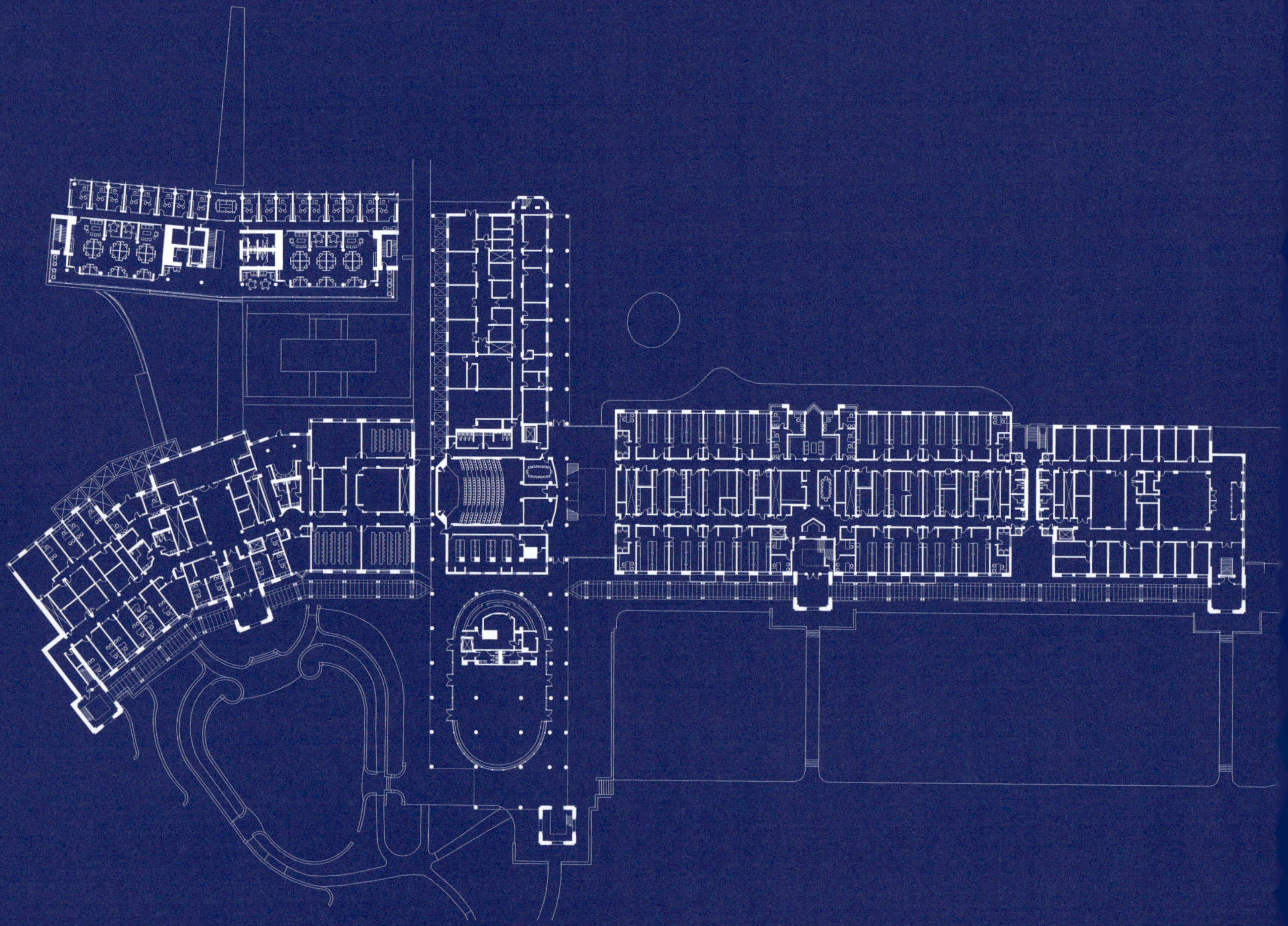

10

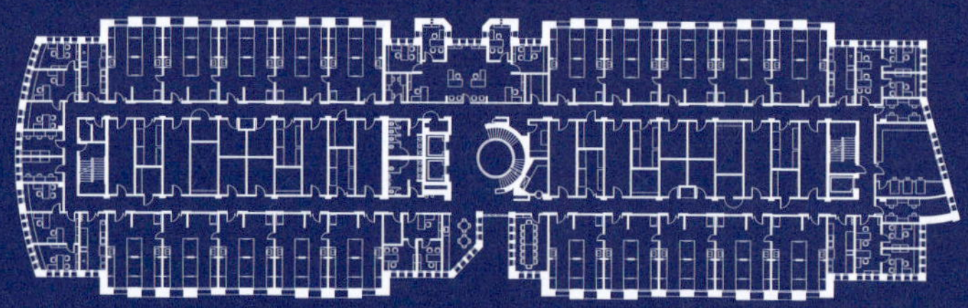

11

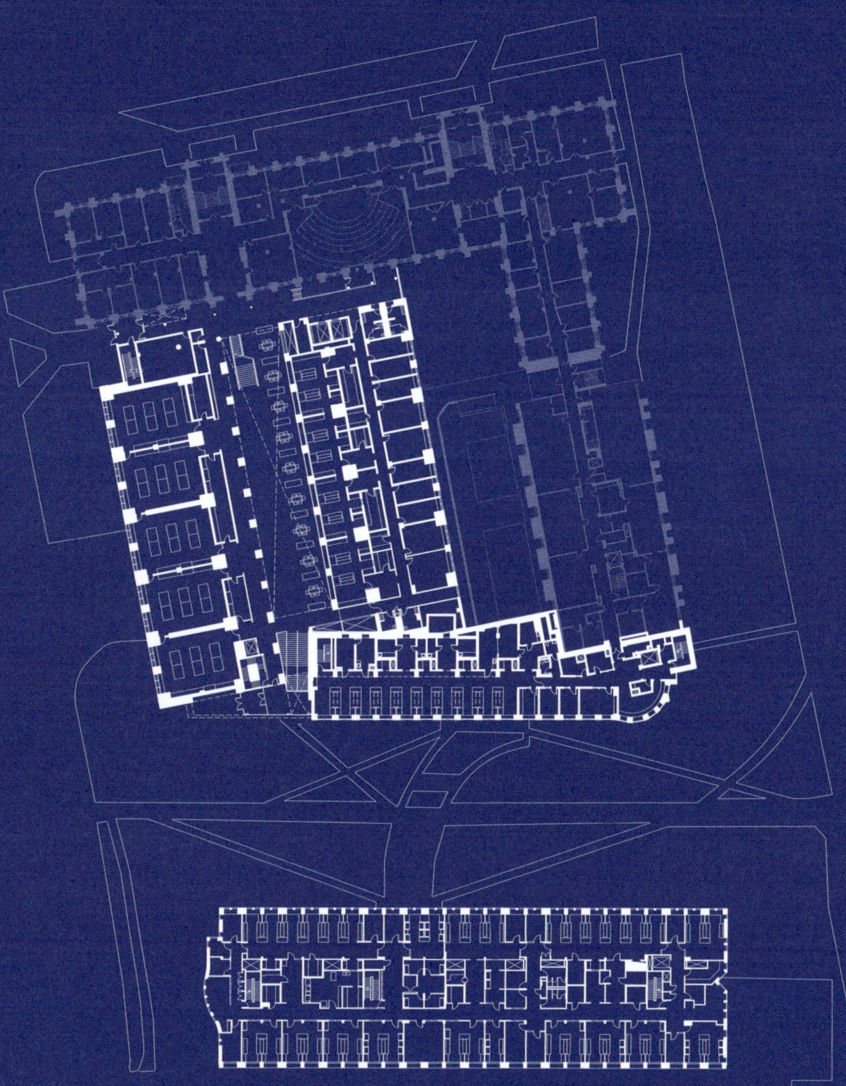

12

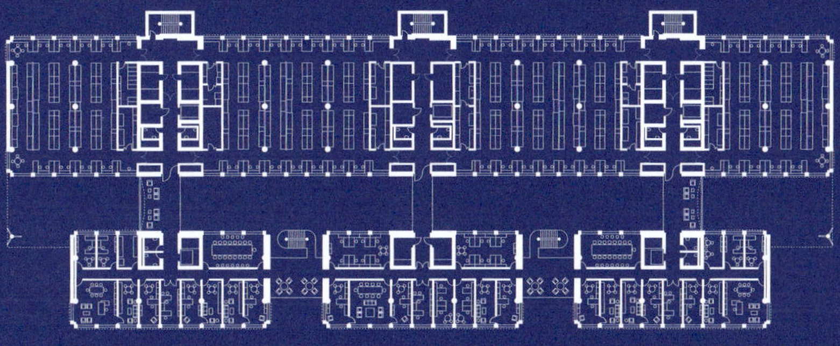

13

14 Brandeis University, Carl J. Shapiro Science Center
15 Williams College, Science Center Expansion

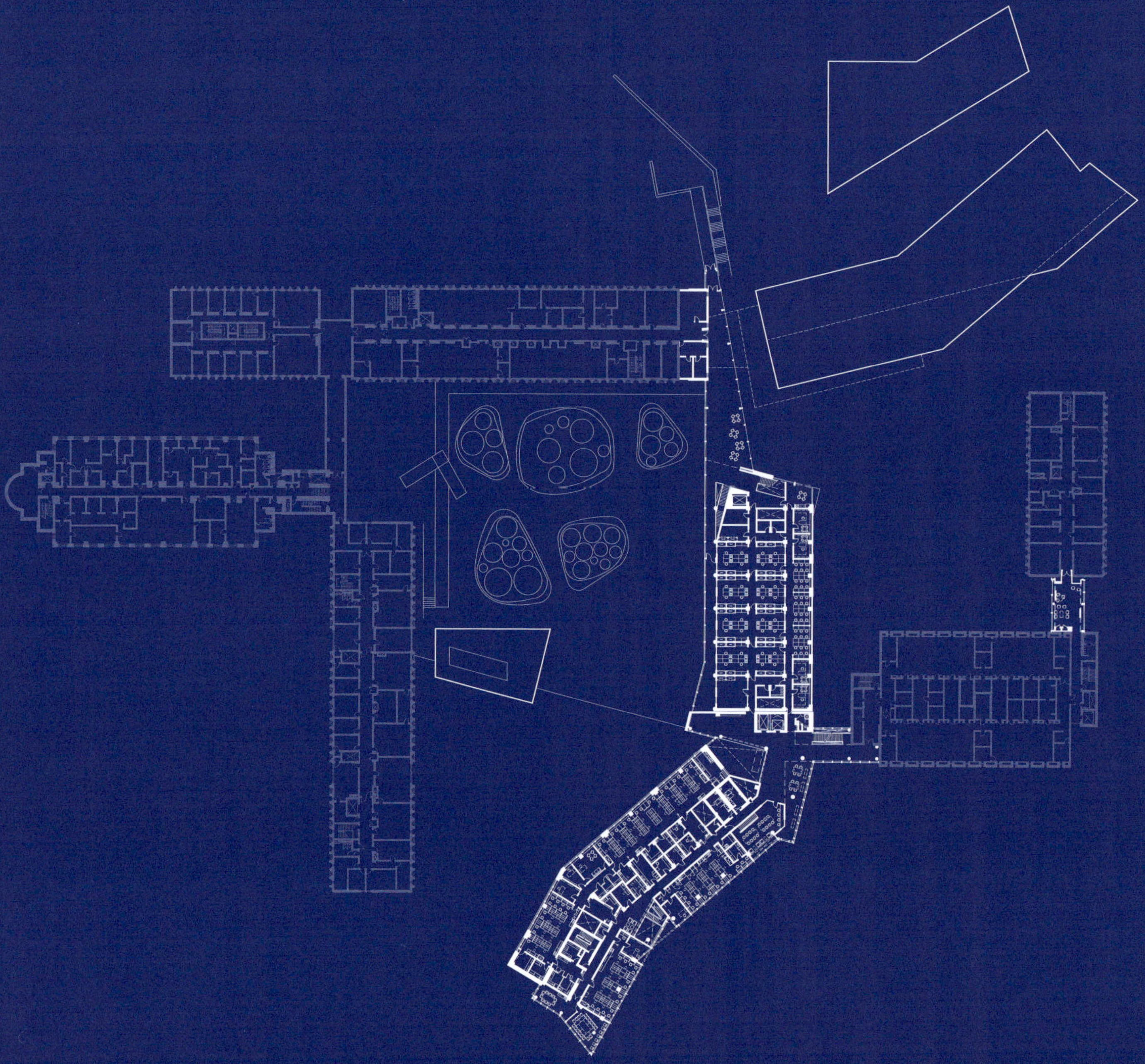

14

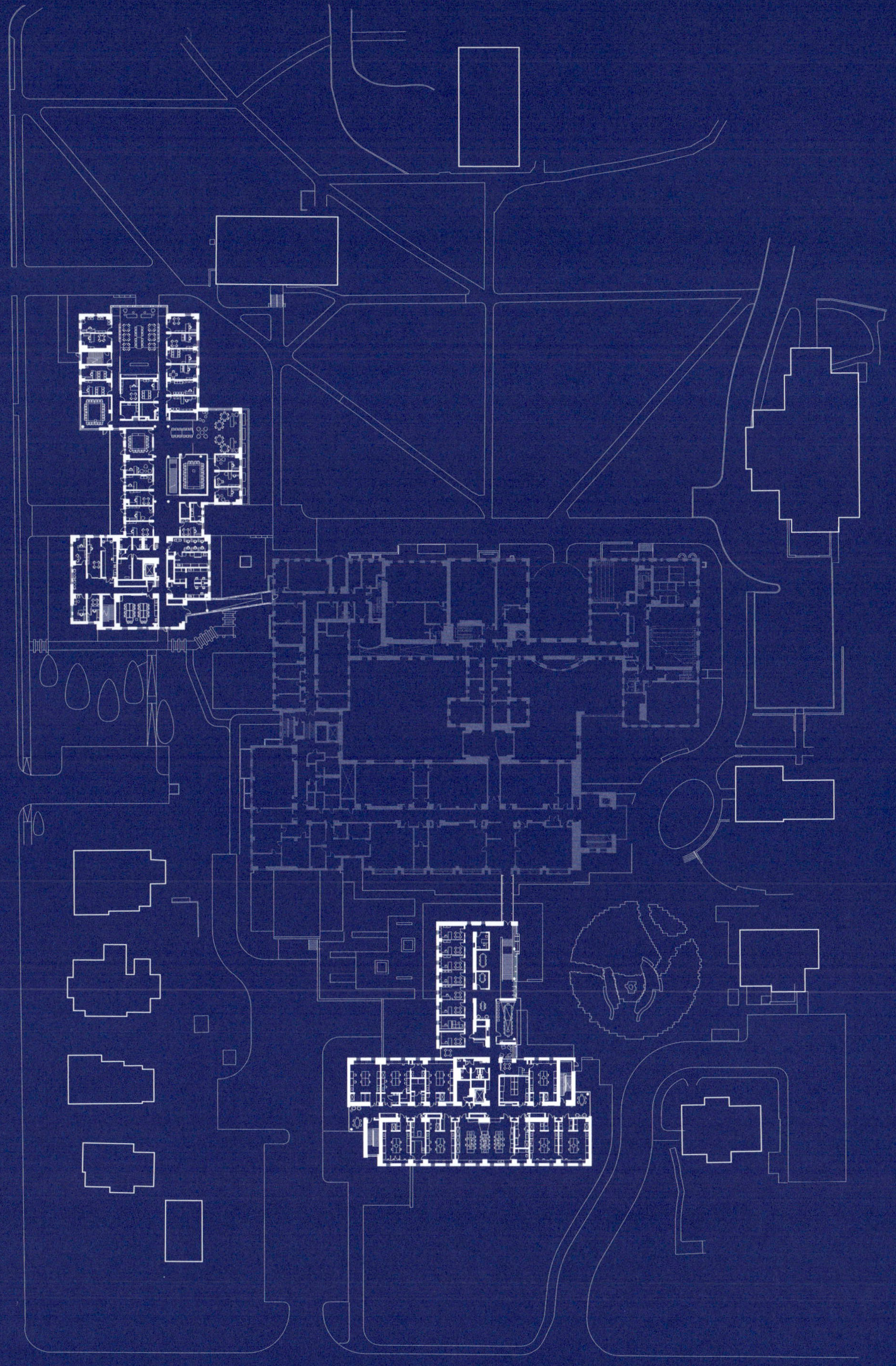

15

16 National University of Ireland Galway, Hardiman Research Building
17 National University of Ireland Galway, Biosciences Research Building
18 National University of Ireland Galway, Clinical/Translational Research Facility
19 Cape Cod Community College, Science and Engineering Building
20 University of Hartford, New Academic Building: Health Sciences, Engineering and Nursing
21 Clemson University, Materials Science and Engineering Building and Civil Engineering Building
22 Hudson Valley Community College, New Science Building

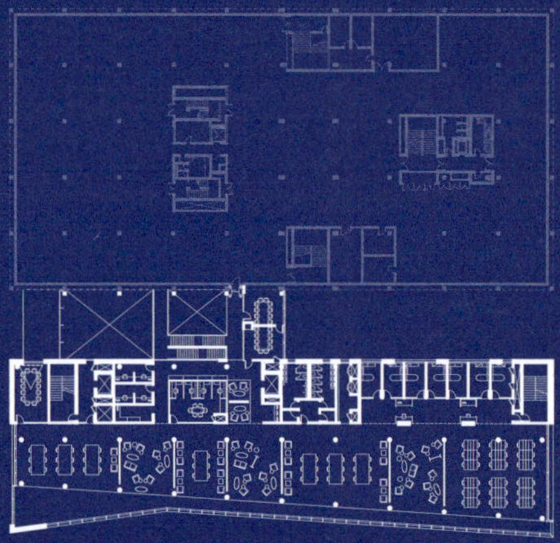

16

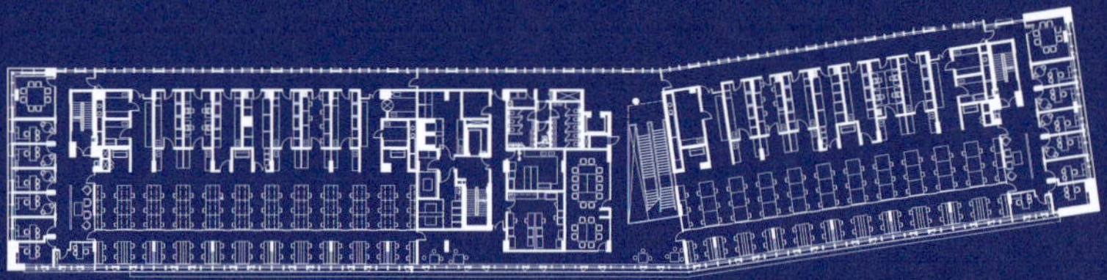

17

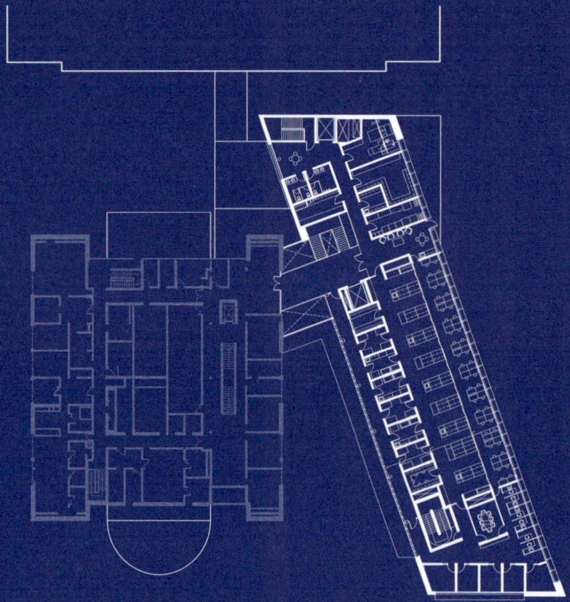

18

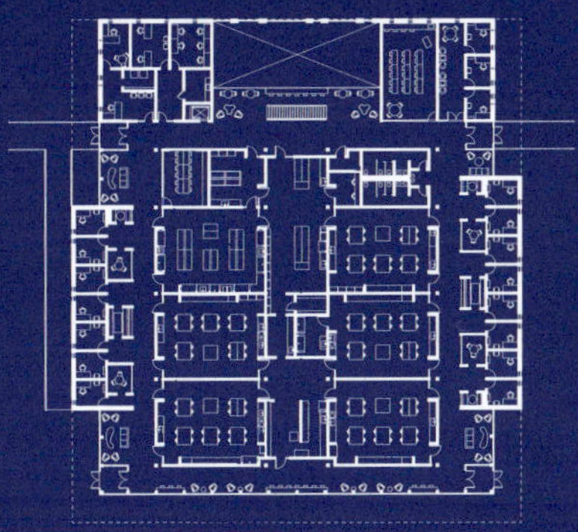

19

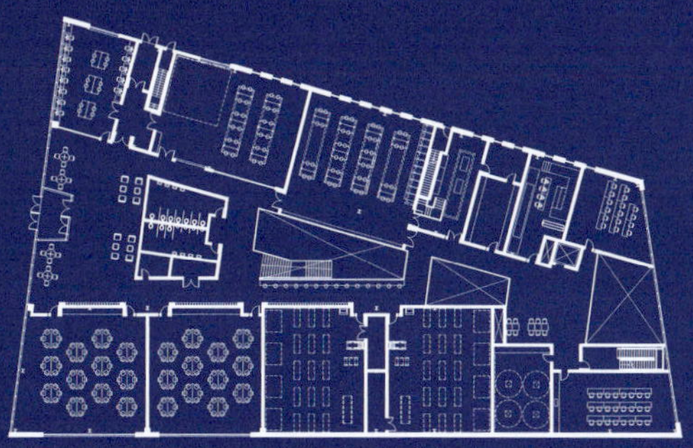

20

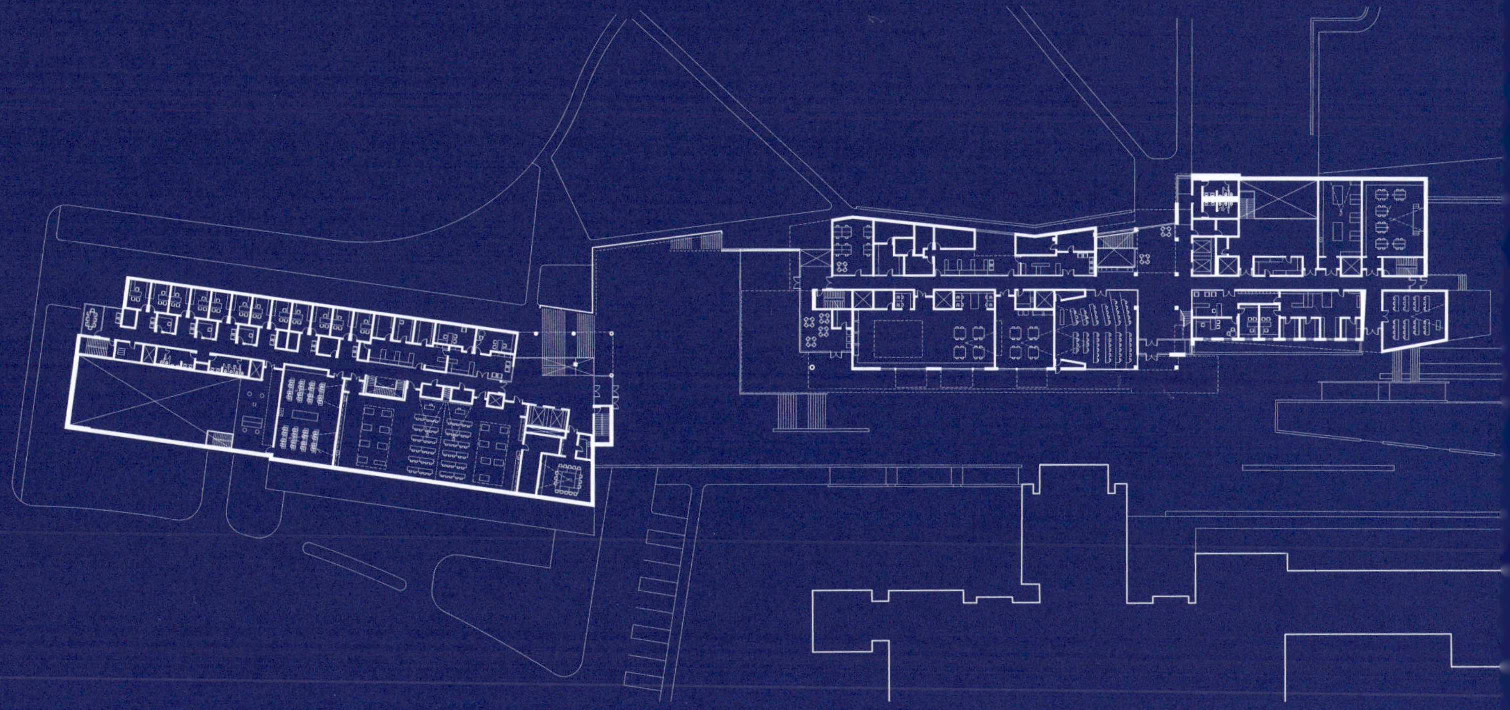

21

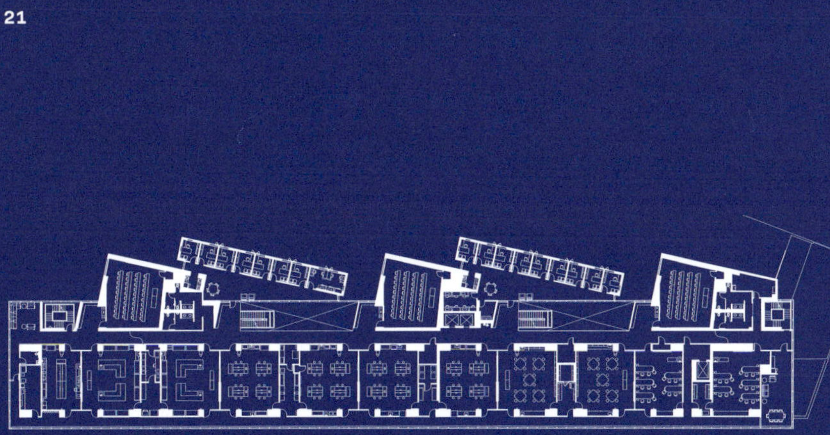

22

23 Northeastern University, Confidential Project
24 Brandeis University, Superconducting Magnet Facility
25 The Pennsylvania State University, Eva J. Pell Laboratory for Advanced Biological Studies
26 Columbia University, Gary C. Comer Geochemistry Building at the Lamont-Doherty Earth Observatory

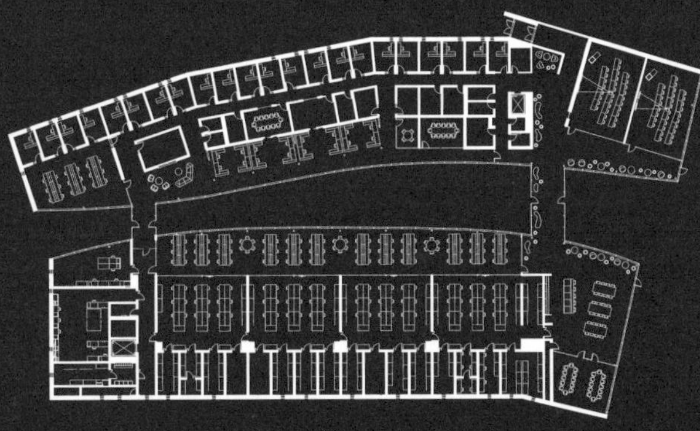

23

24

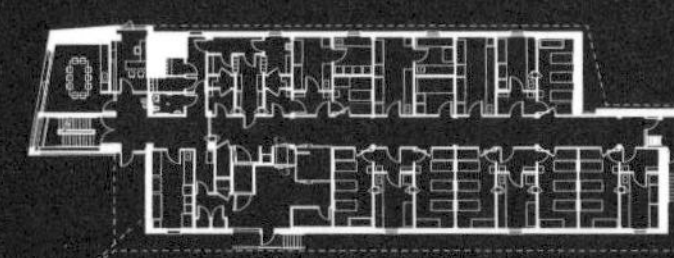

25

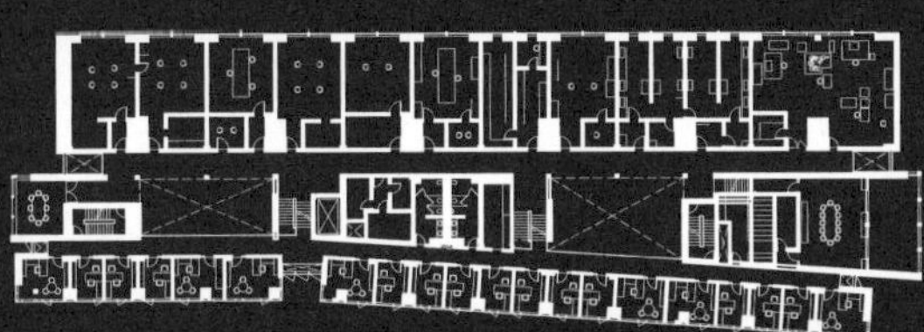

26

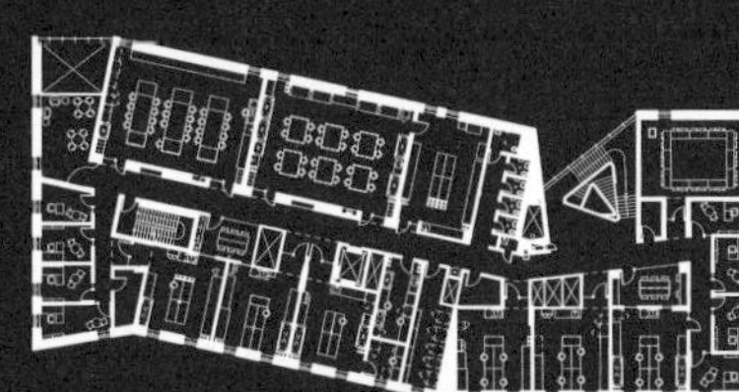

27

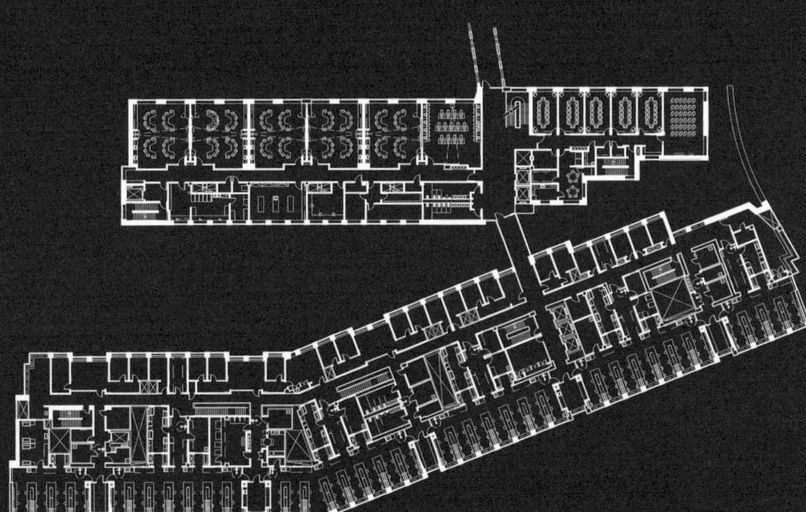

28

27 Bates College, Bonney Science Center
28 Yale University School of Medicine, Anlyon Center for Medical Research and Education
29 Jefferson Health, Thomas Jefferson University, Biomedical Research Building 3
30 Tishman Speyer, 105 West 1st Street
31 Carnegie Mellon University, Roberts Engineering Hall

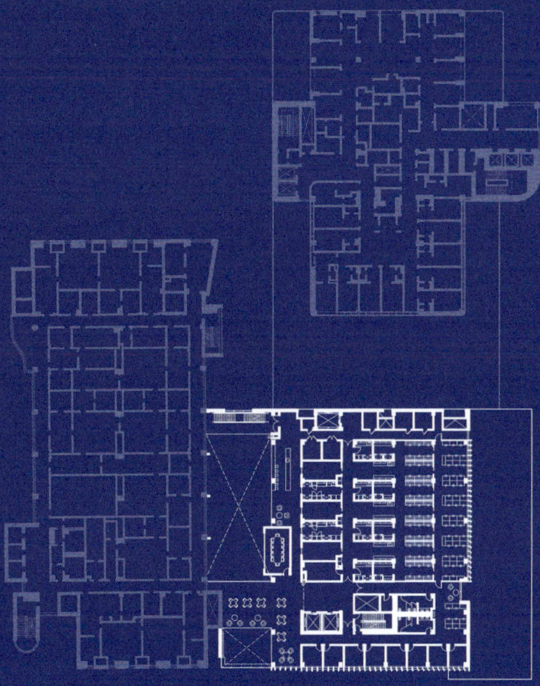

29

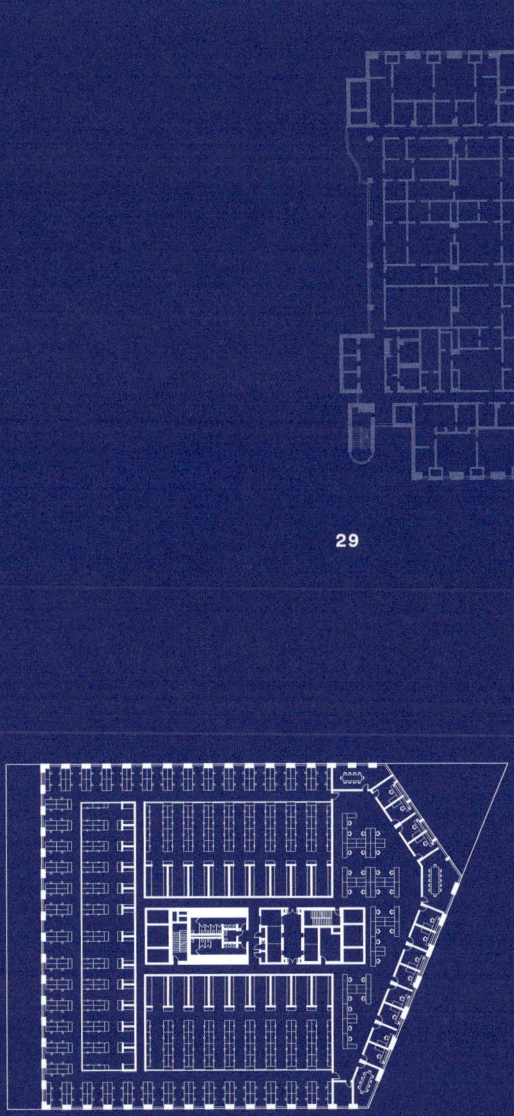

30

31

32 Bryn Mawr College, Park Science Center Renovation

33 Massachusetts Institute of Technology, PDSI Project, Physics, Department of Material Science and Engineering, Spectroscopy and Infrastructure

32

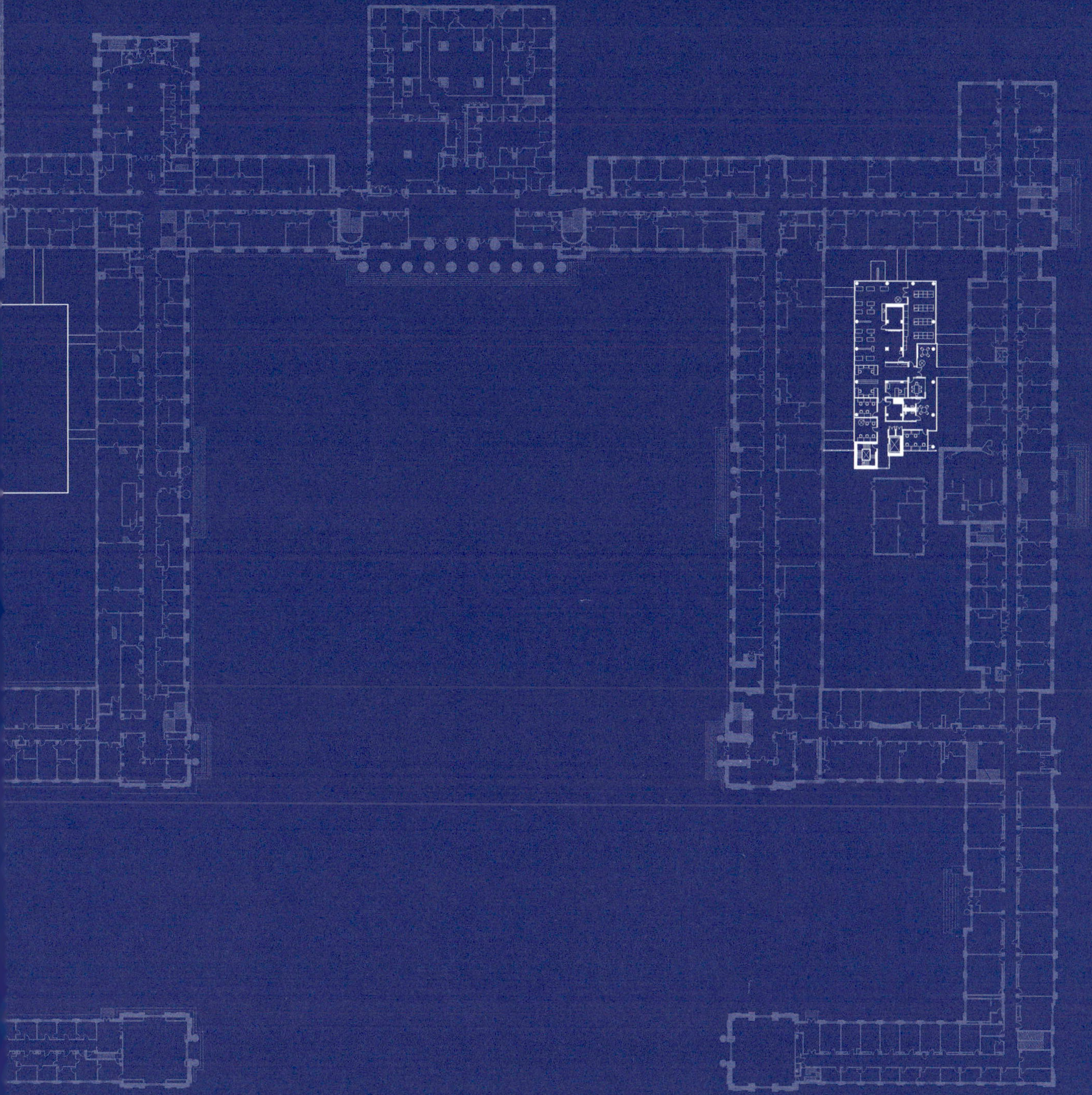

33

34 University of Alabama at Birmingham, Center for Human Genetics
35 University of California Los Angeles, The Gordon and Virginia MacDonald Research Laboratories
36 University of Alabama at Birmingham, School of Nursing Addition/Renovation
37 New York University Medical Center, Skirball Institute for Biomolecular Medicine
38 University of Alabama at Birmingham, Wallace Tumor Institute and New Cancer Center
39 University of Pennsylvania School of Medicine, Clinical Research Building

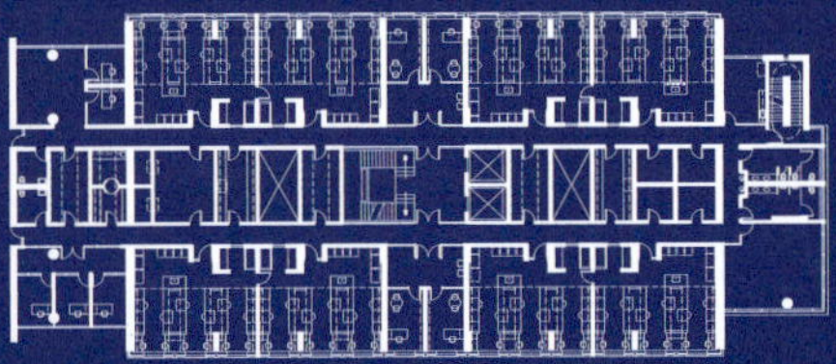

34

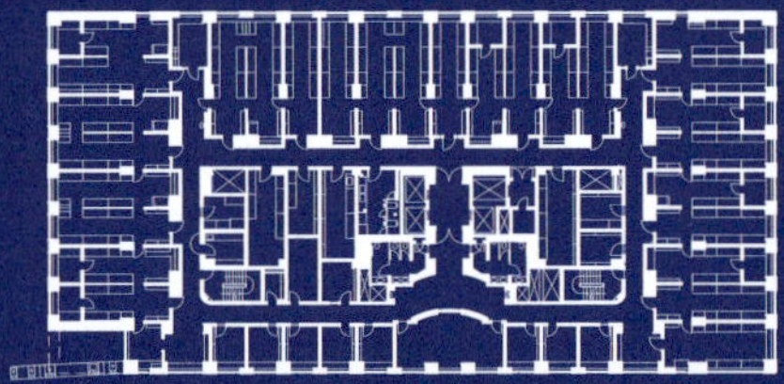

35

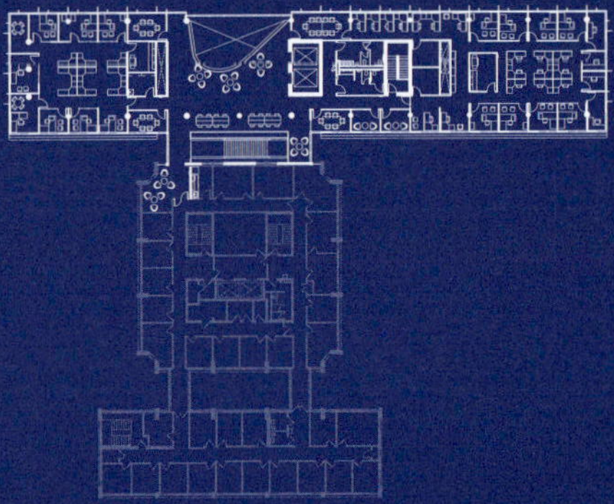

36

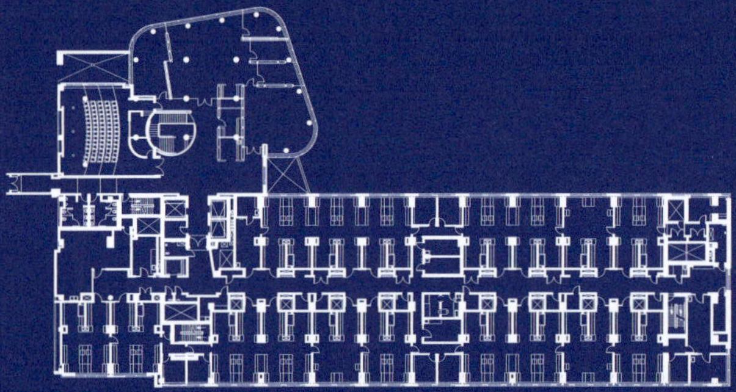

37

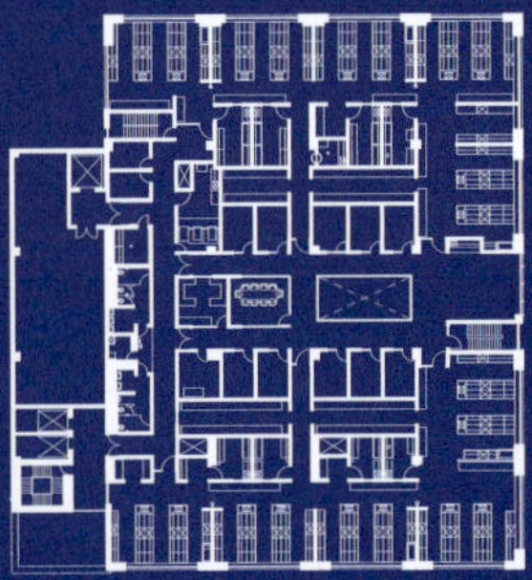

38

39

40 Massachusetts General Hospital, Center for Aging and Neurodisorders – Building 114
41 University of Pittsburgh, School of Medicine, Biomedical Sciences Tower III
42 University of Pittsburgh, School of Medicine, Scaife Hall Master Planv
43 West Virginia University, Life Sciences Building

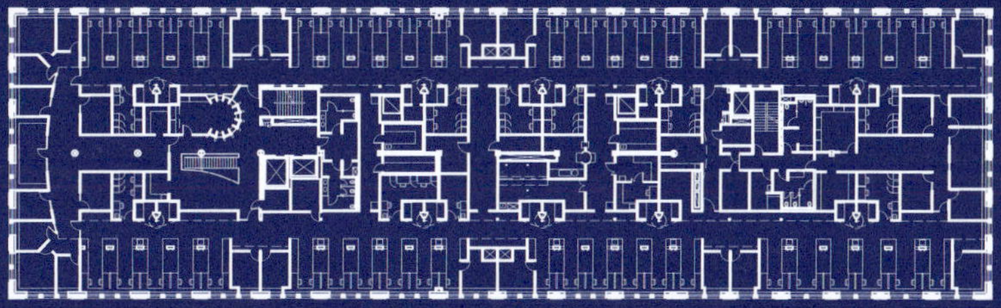

40

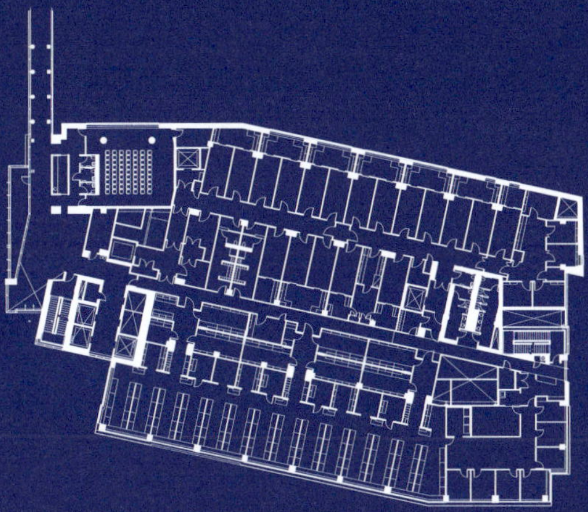

41

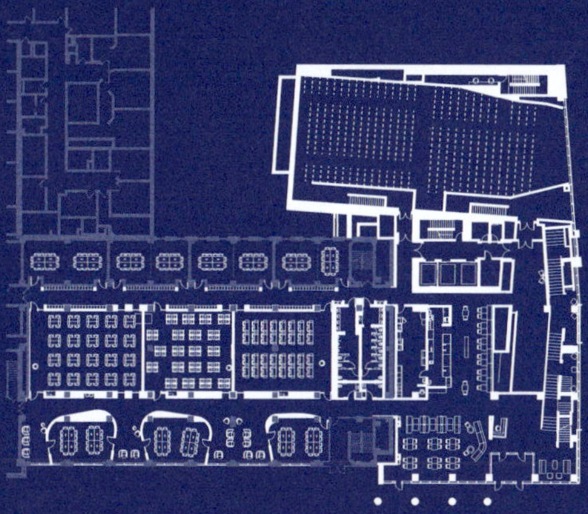

42

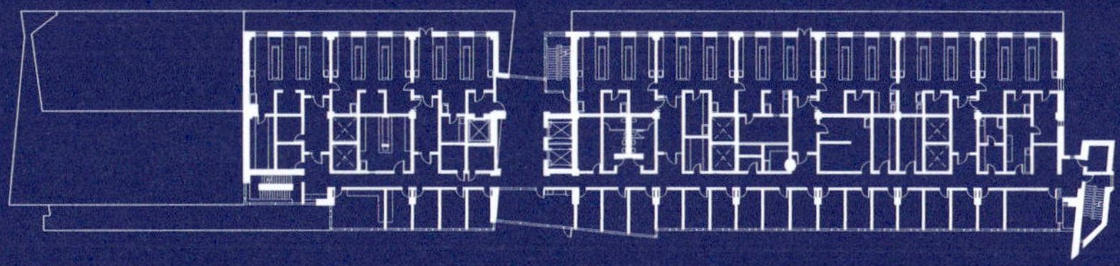

43

44 Case Western Reserve University School of Medicine, Richard F. Celeste Biomedical Research Building
45 Rutgers University and the Robert Wood Johnson Medical School, Center for Advanced Biotechnology and Medicine
46 Schepens Eye Research Institute (affiliated with Harvard School of Medicine), Laboratory Renovation
47 Wyeth BioPharma (formerly Genetics Institute), Building G
48 Massachusetts General Hospital, Wellman Research Building
49 University of Maryland at Baltimore School of Medicine, Health Science Facility Phase II

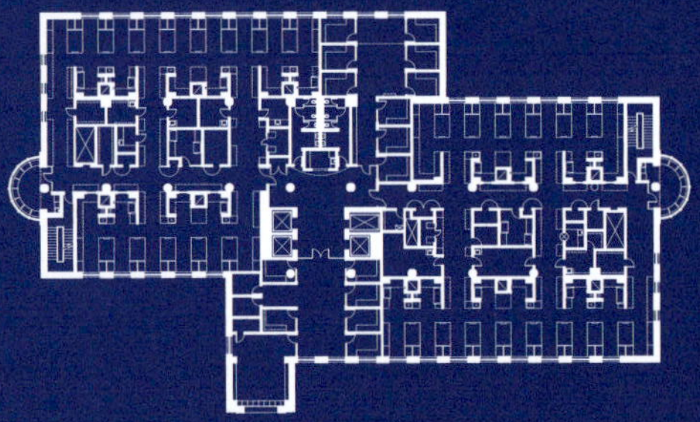

44

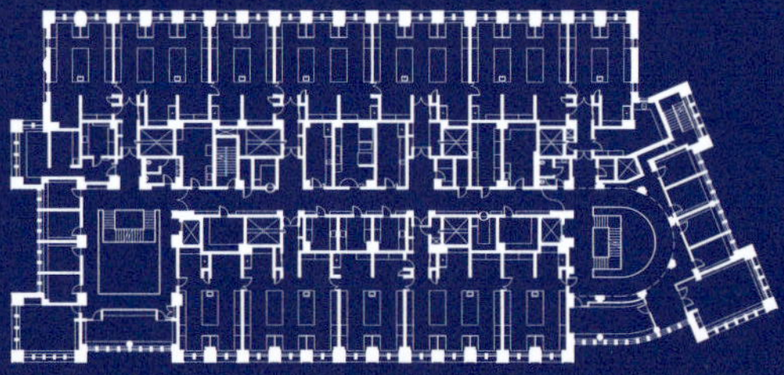

45

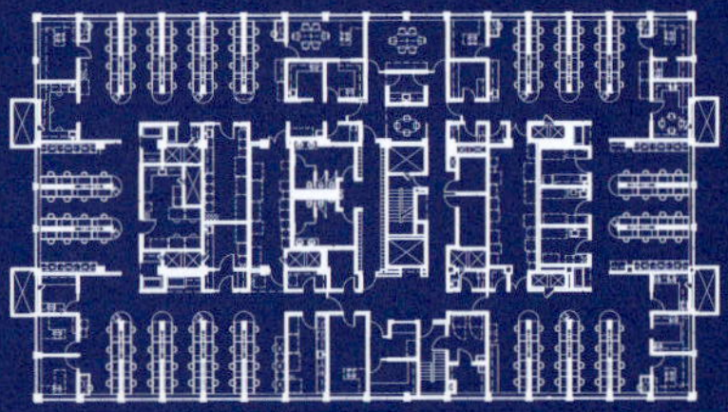

46

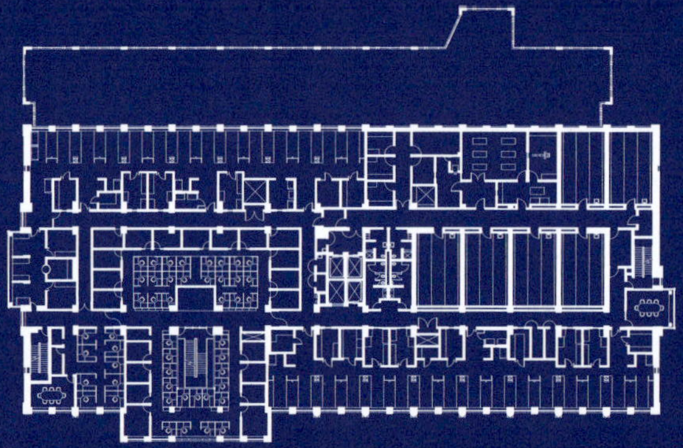

47

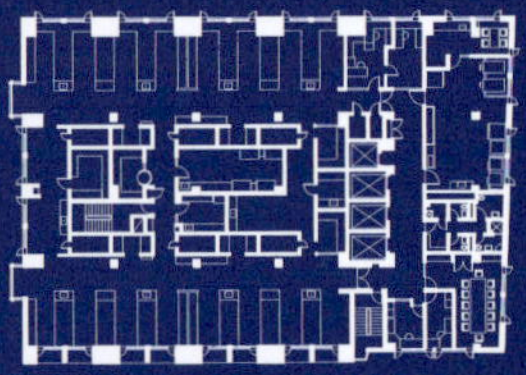

48

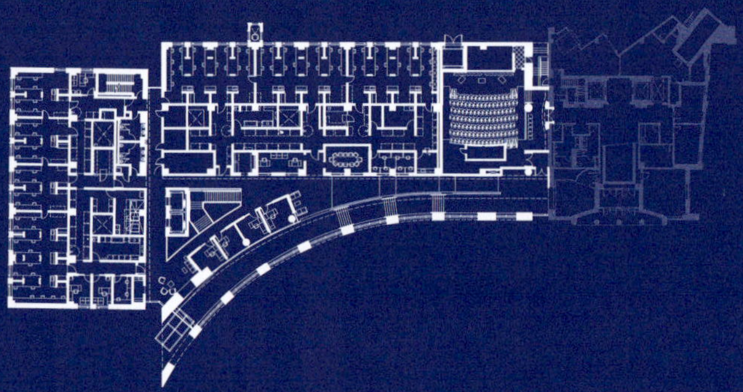

49

50 Cornell University Medical College, Lasdon Biomedical Research Center
51 Brown University, Charles Giancarlo Engineering Laboratories
52 Albert Einstein College of Medicine of Yeshiva University, Michael F. Price Center for Genetic and Translational Medicine, Harold and Muriel Block Research Pavilion
53 Vanderbilt University, Stevenson Chemistry Building
54 University of Massachusetts, Amherst, CNS Research & Education Greenhouse
55 The University of Texas at Austin, Norman Hackerman Building Greenhouse Addition

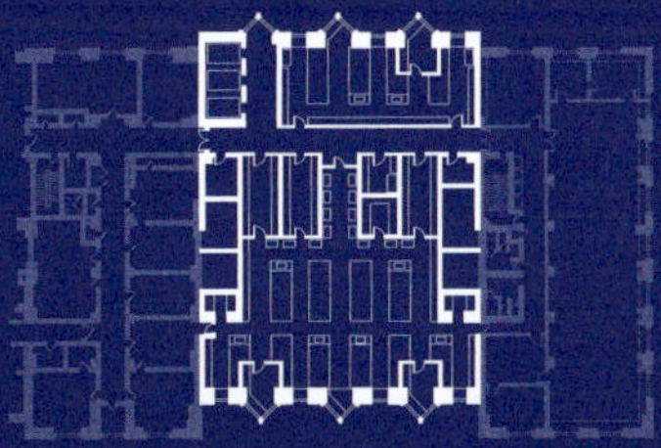

50

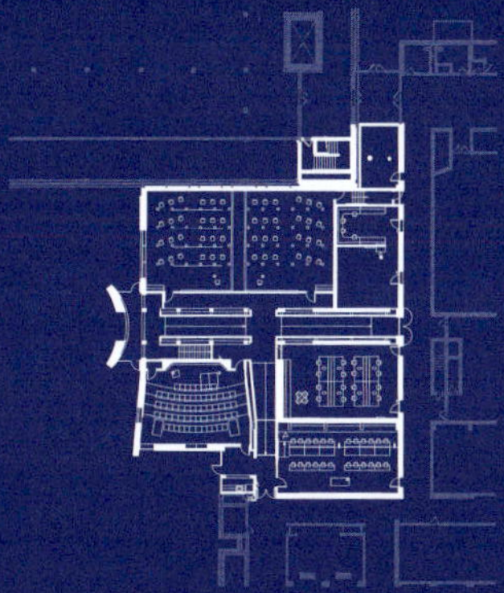

51

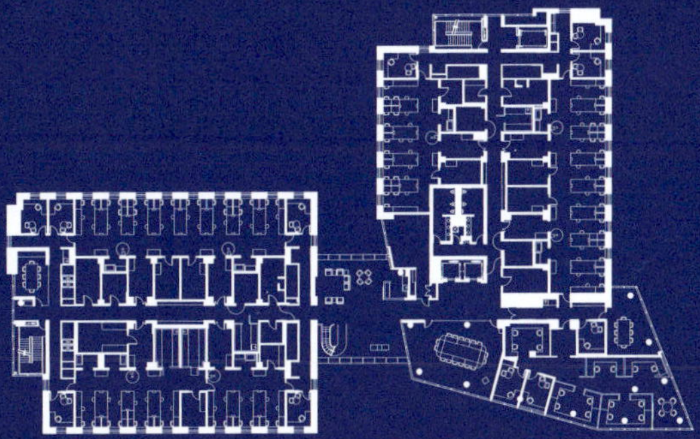

52

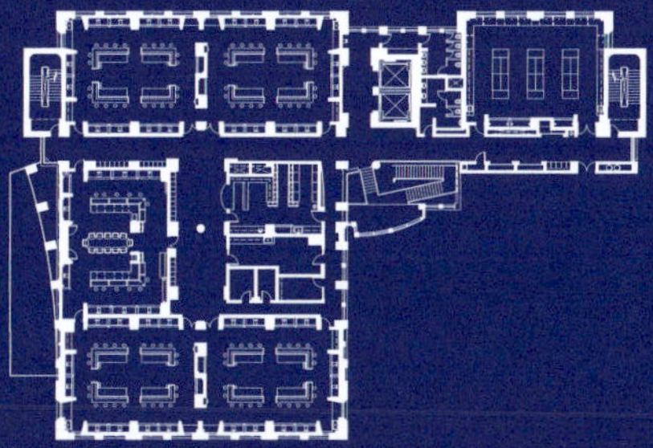

53

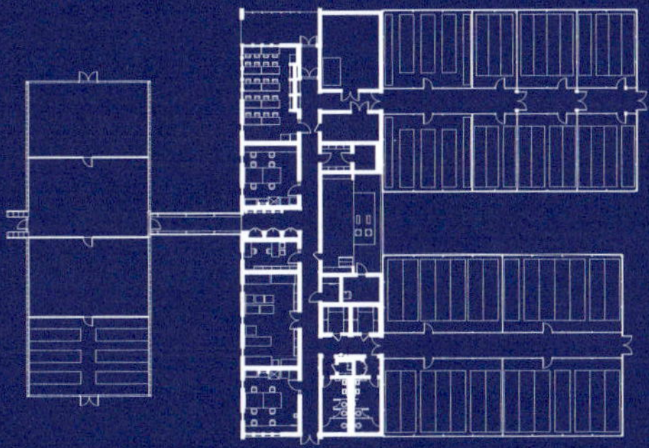

54

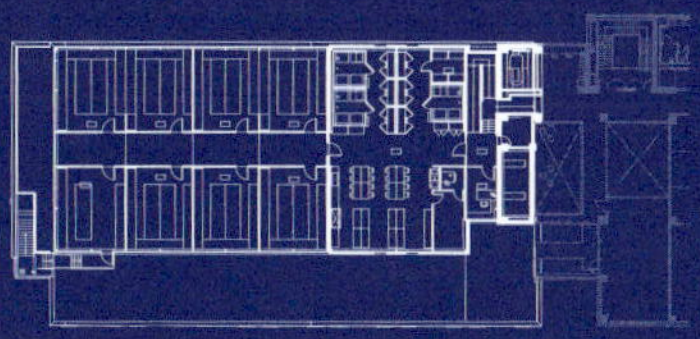

55

56 Emory & Henry College, Academic Center
57 Amherst College, Beneski Earth Sciences Building and Beneski Museum of Natural History
58 Washington and Lee University, Science Center
59 Connecticut College, New London Hall Addition and Renovation
60 College of Wooster, Severance Chemistry Building Addition

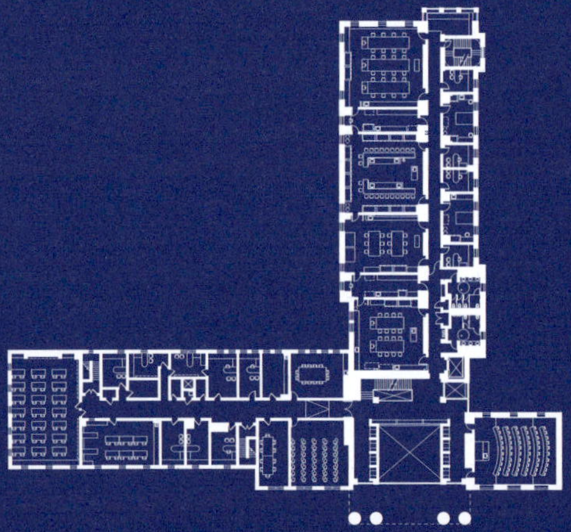

56

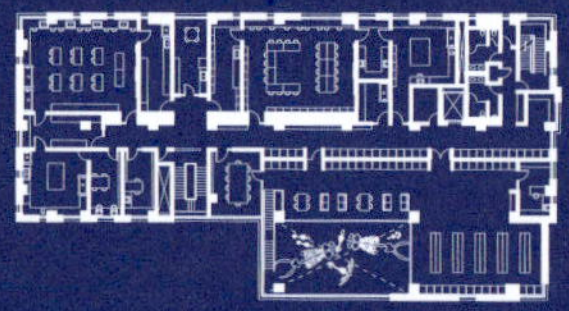

57

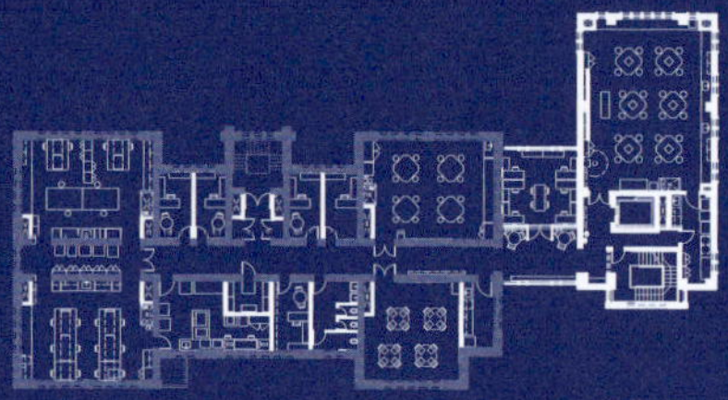

59

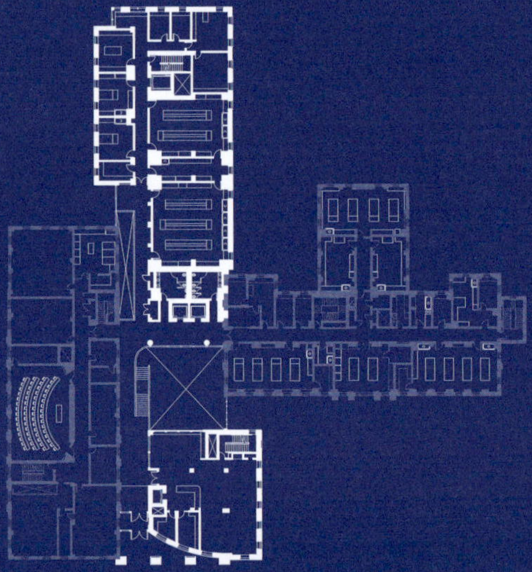

58

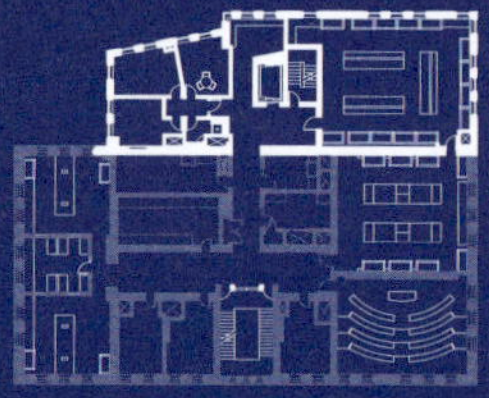

60

61 Gordon College, Ken Olsen Science Center
62 Lafayette College, Rockwell Integrated Sciences Center
63 Boston College, Schiller Institute for Integrated Science and Society
64 University of North Carolina Charlotte, Science Building

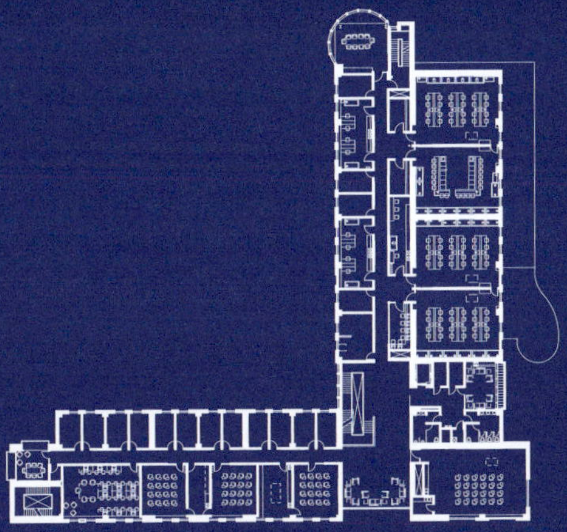

61

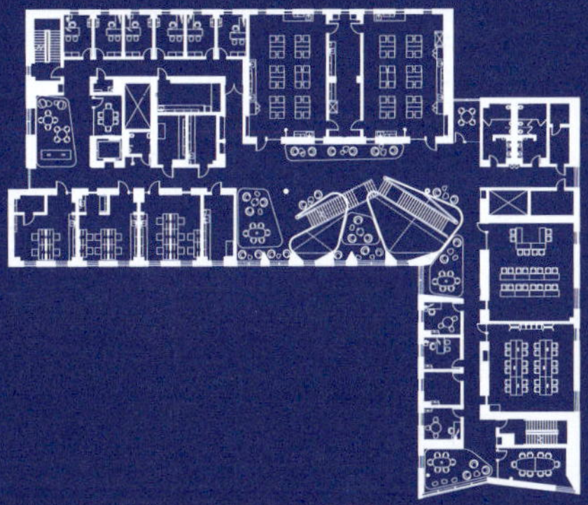

62

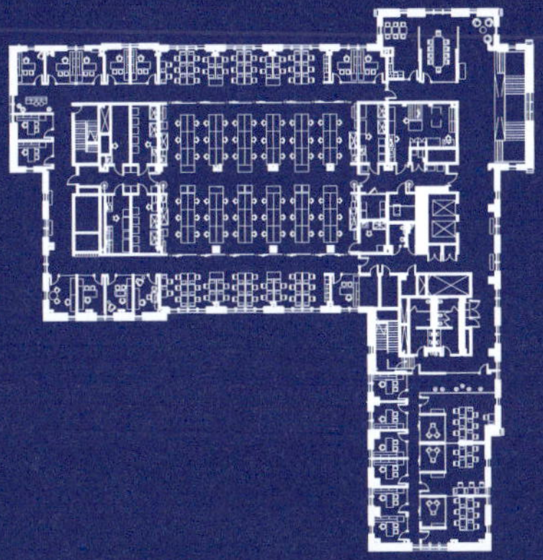

63

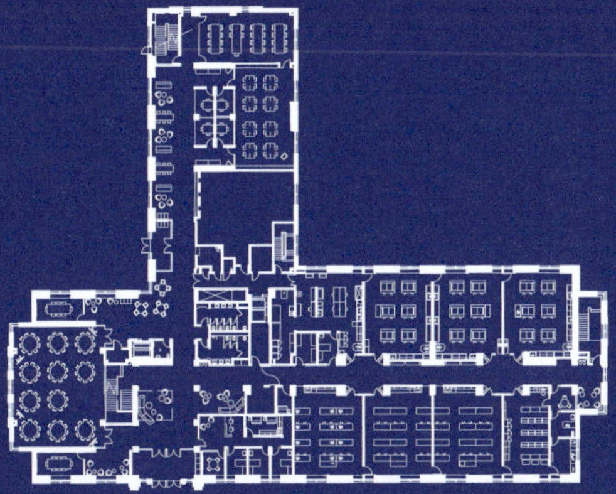

64

65 Bridgewater State University, Dana Mohler-Faria Science and Mathematics Center
66 Middlebury College, McCardell Bicentennial Hall

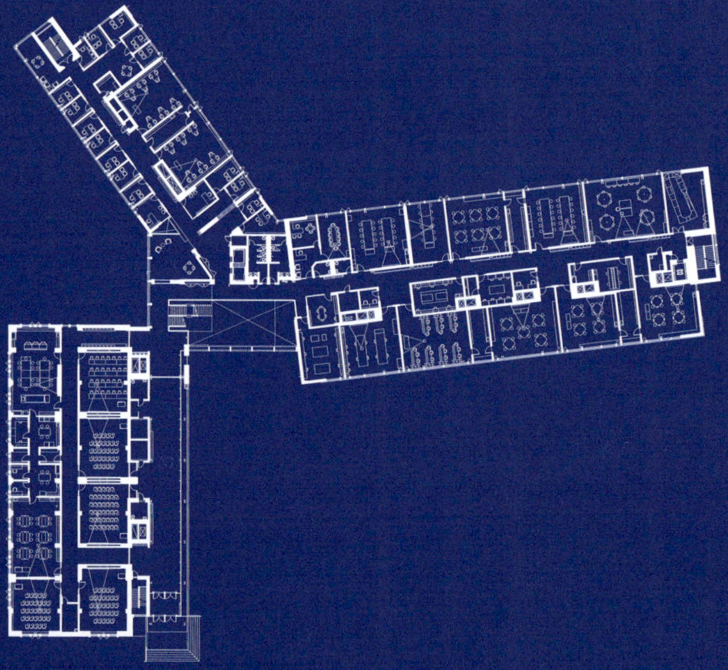

65

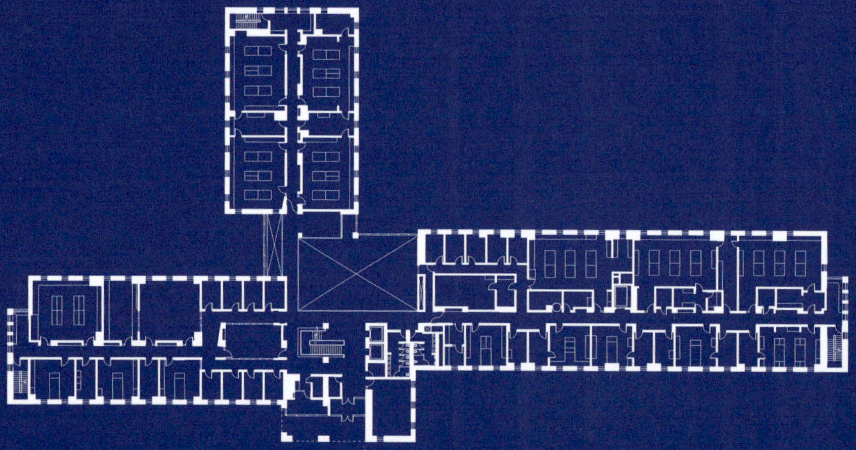

66

67 Virginia Commonwealth University, Schools of Engineering and Business
68 University of Kentucky, Don & Cathy Jacobs Science Building

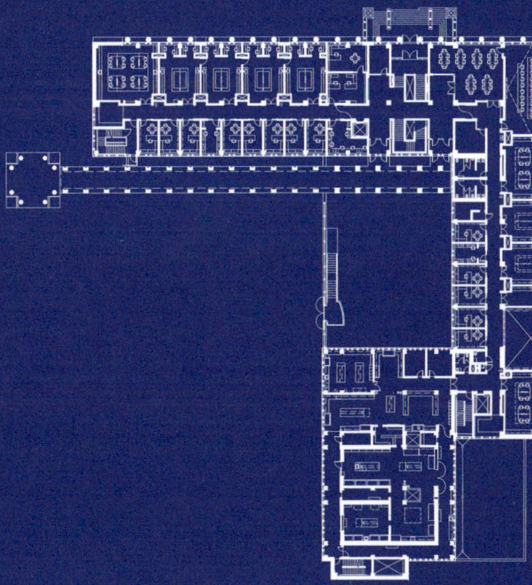

67

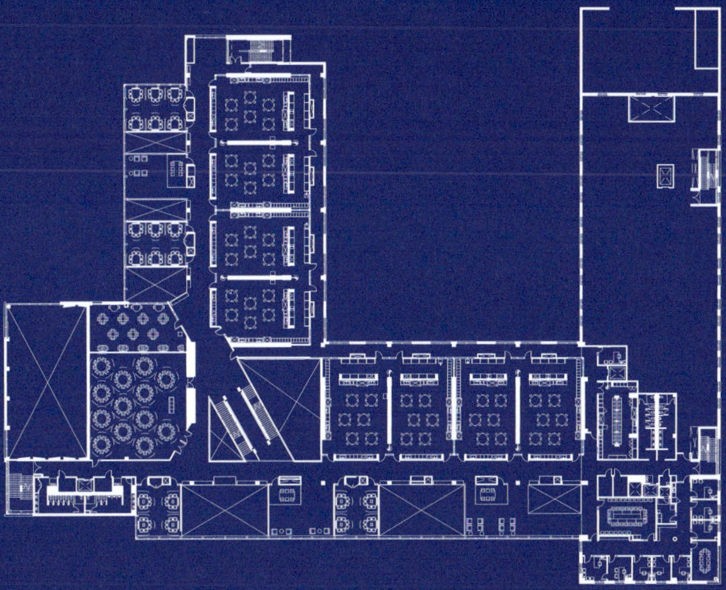

68

69 University of Massachusetts, Amherst, Integrated Sciences Building
70 Georgetown University, Regents Hall Science Center
71 Wheaton College, Science Center
72 Skidmore College, Center for Integrated Sciences
73 The University of Vermont, Health Sciences Research Facility, New Research Laboratory & Given Building Renovation

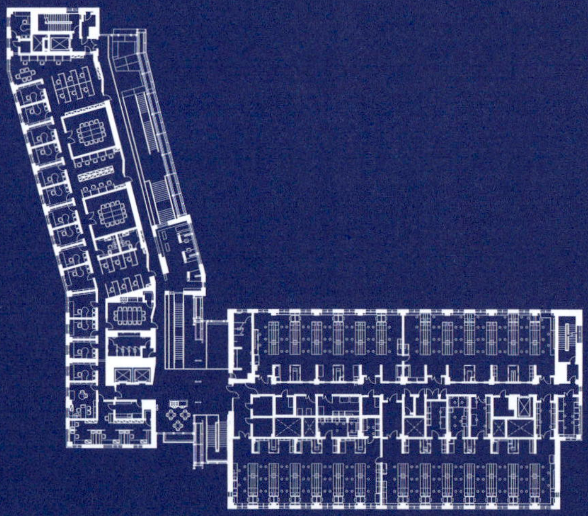

69

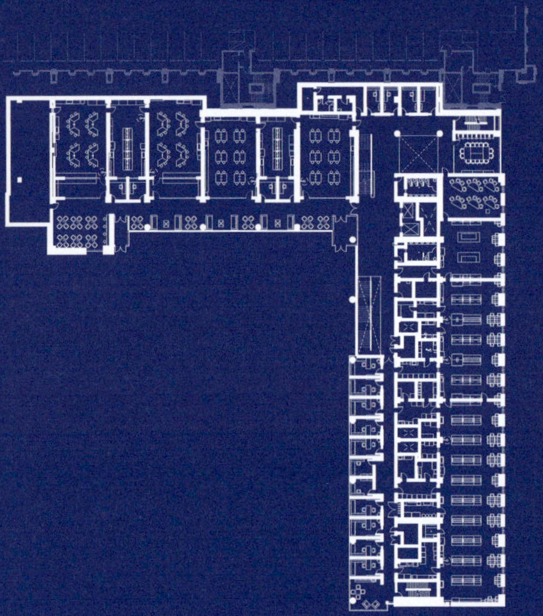

70

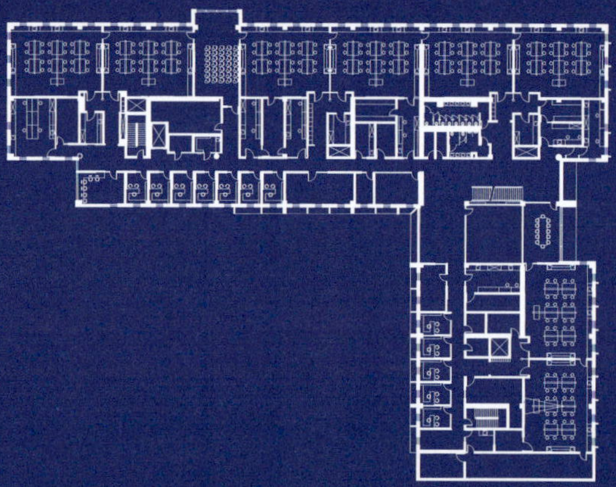

71

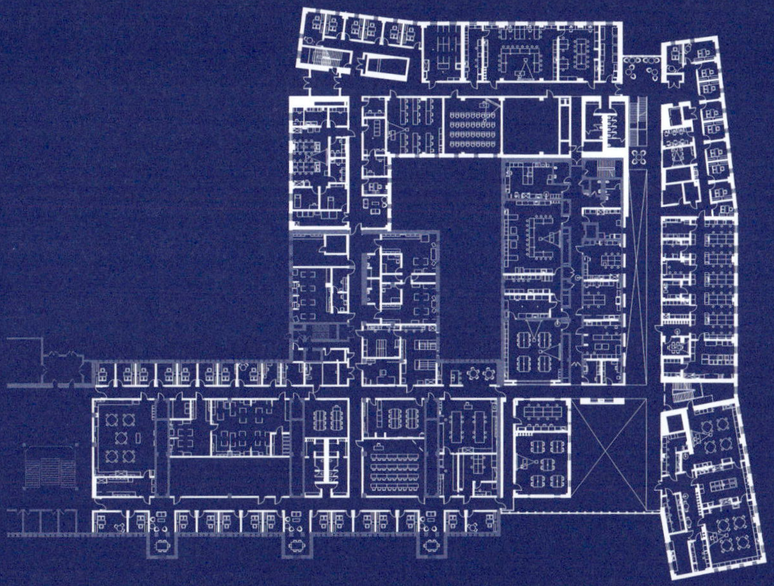

72

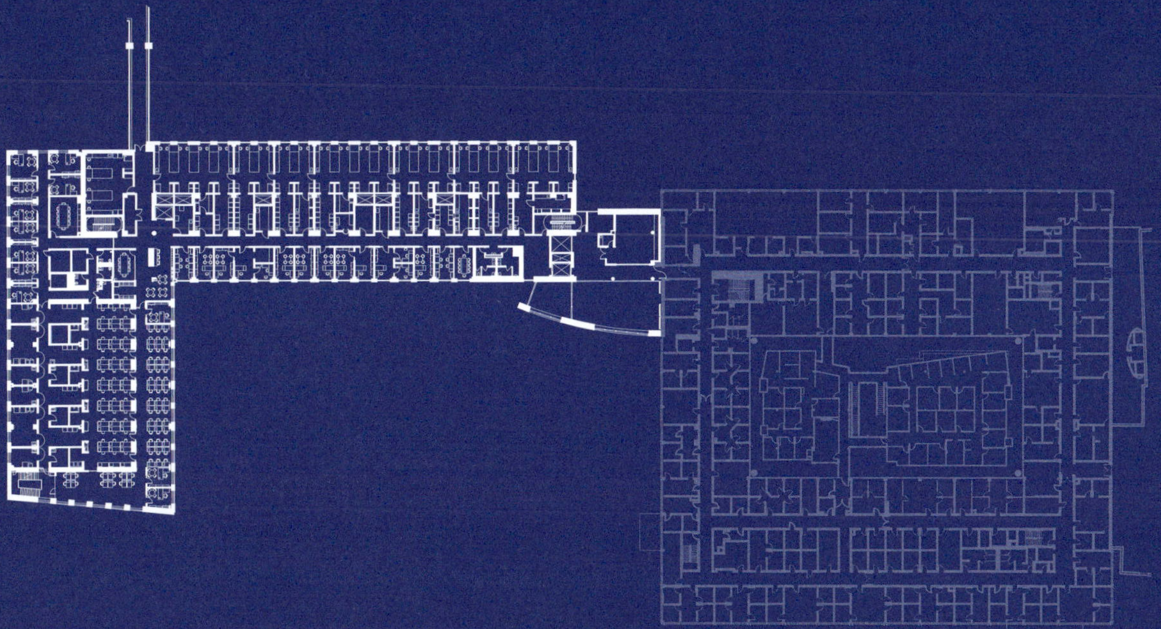

73

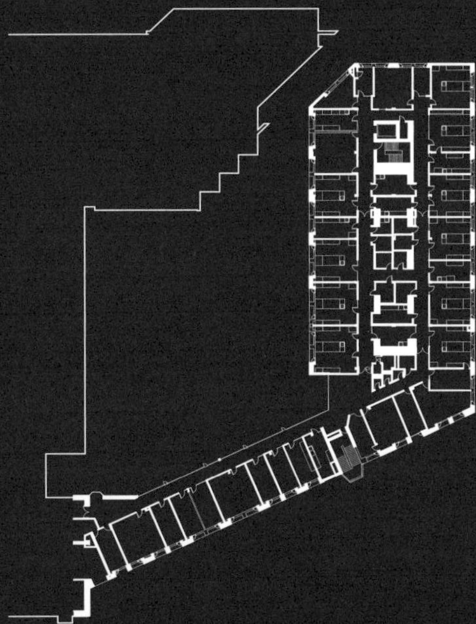

74

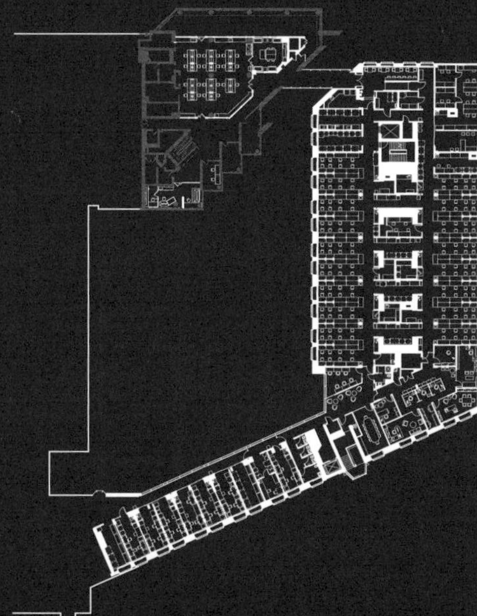

75

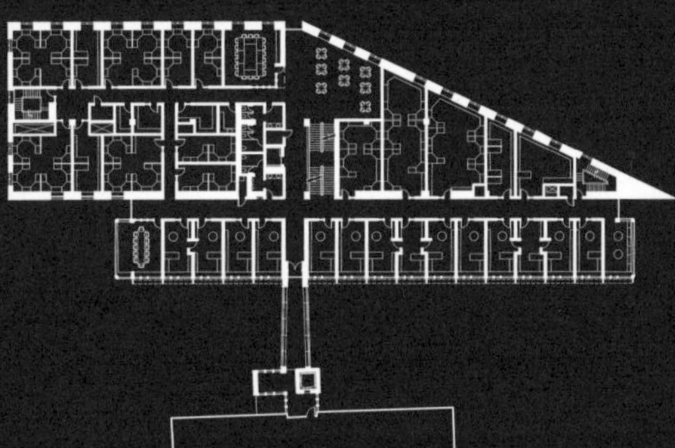

76

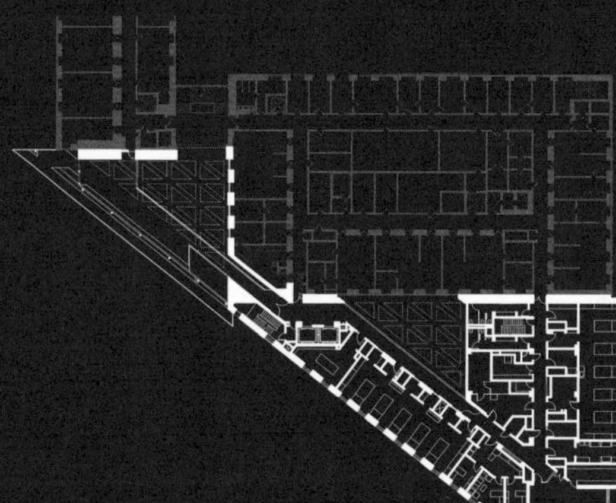

77

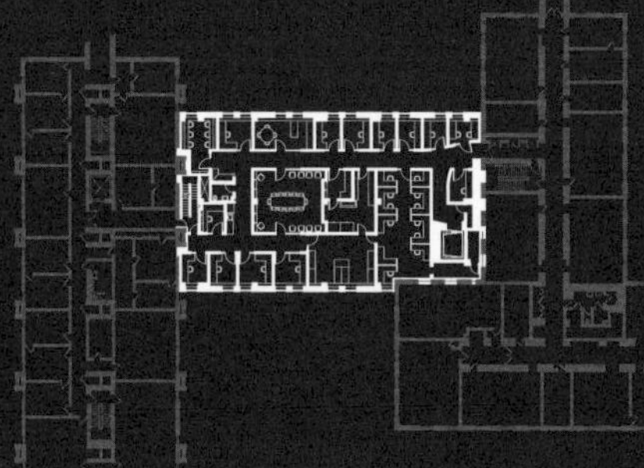

78

74 Harvard University, Sherman Fairchild Biochemistry Laboratory
75 Harvard University, Sherman Fairchild Renovation for Stem Cell and Regenerative Biology
76 Harvard University, Maxwell Dworkin Laboratory
77 Harvard School of Public Health, Francois-Xavier Bagnoud Building
78 Harvard University, Chemistry Link Building
79 Harvard University, Allston Science Complex Laboratory Planning and Programming

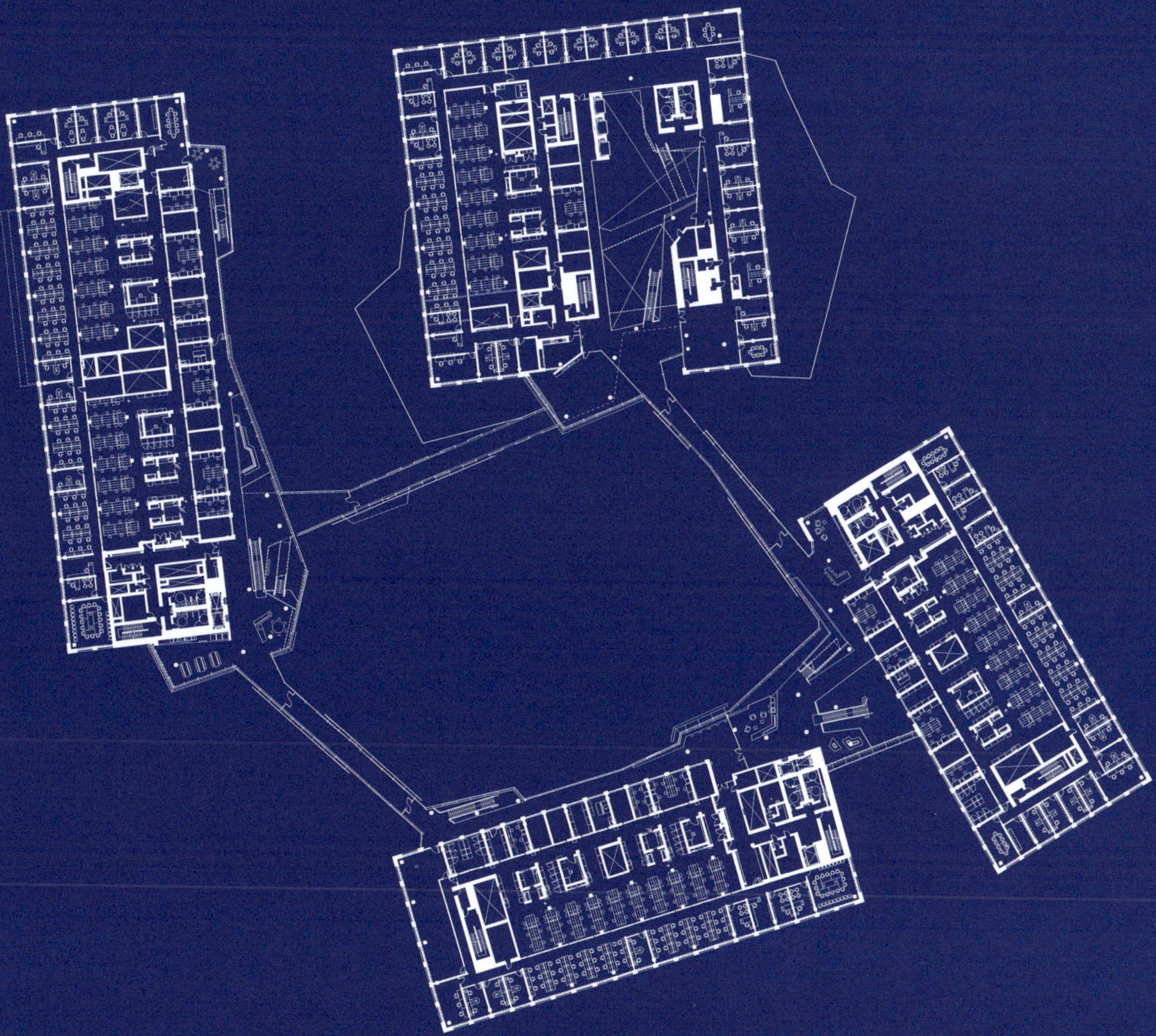

79

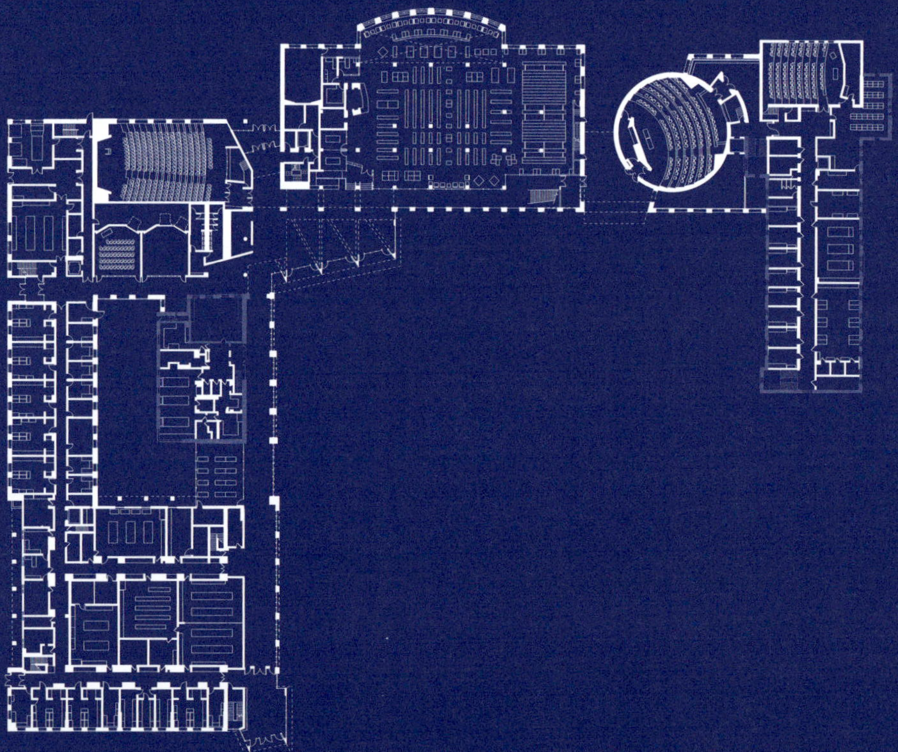

80

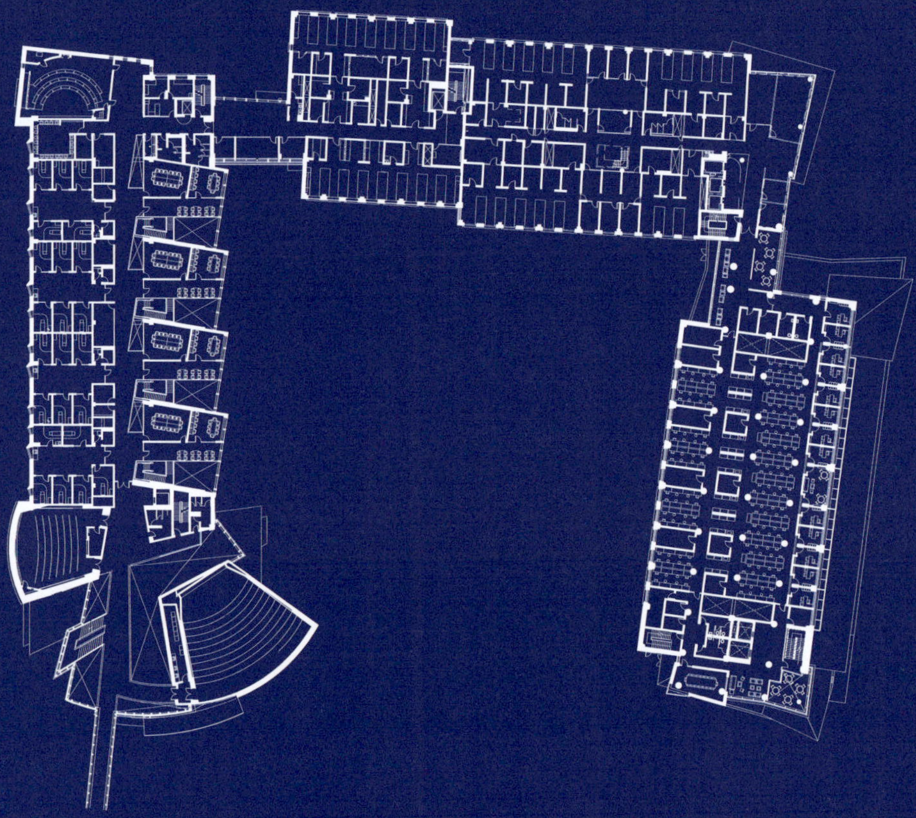

81

80 Oberlin College, New Science Center
81 University of Iowa College of Medicine, Medical Education and Biomedical Research Complex
82 Ohio Wesleyan University, Conrades Wetherell Science Center
83 International Vaccine Institute

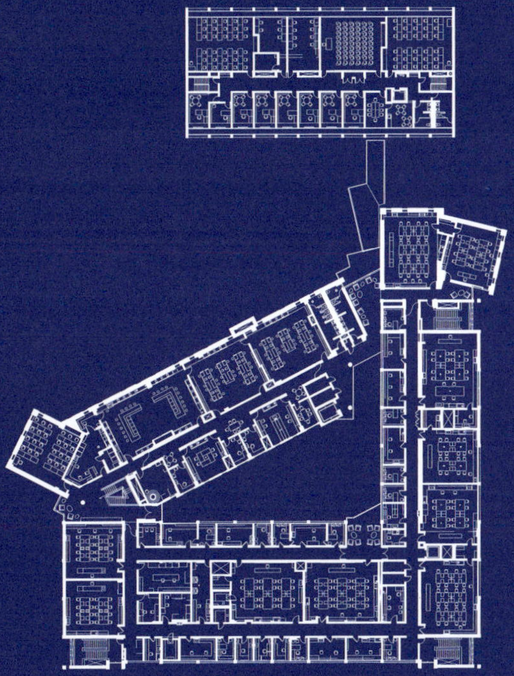

82

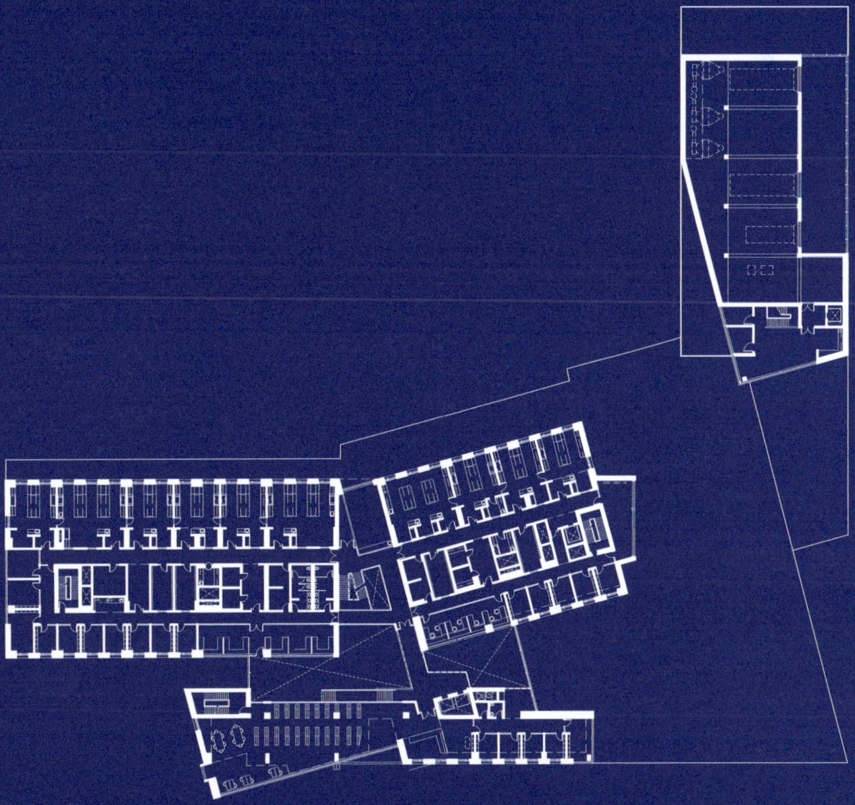

83

84 The University of Texas at Austin, Welch Hall Renovation
85 University of Illinois at Chicago College of Medicine, Research Building
86 Johns Hopkins University School of Medicine, Broadway Research Building
87 Wesleyan University, Molecular Life Science Building

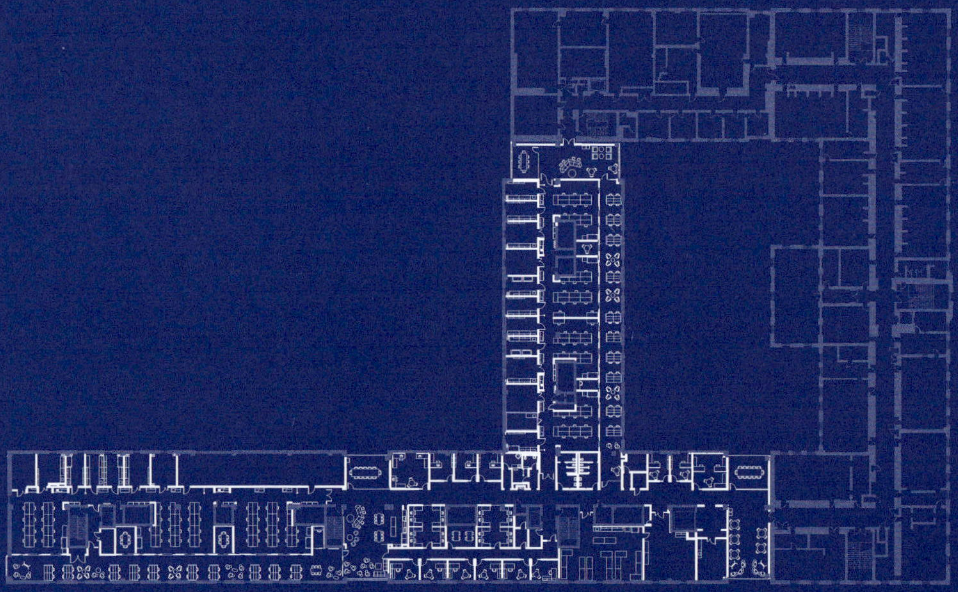

84

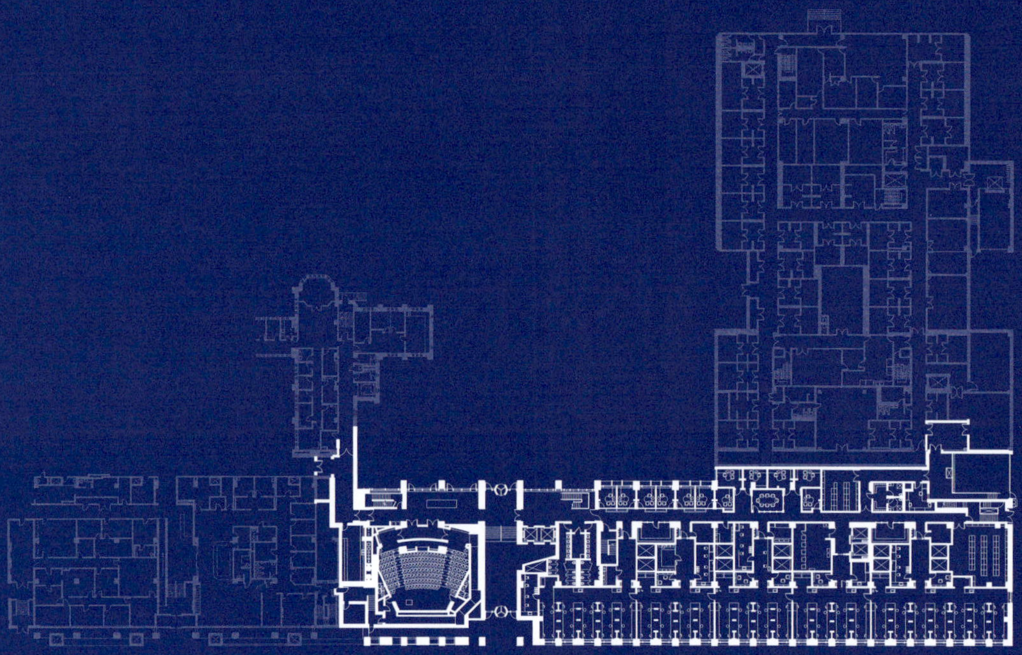

85

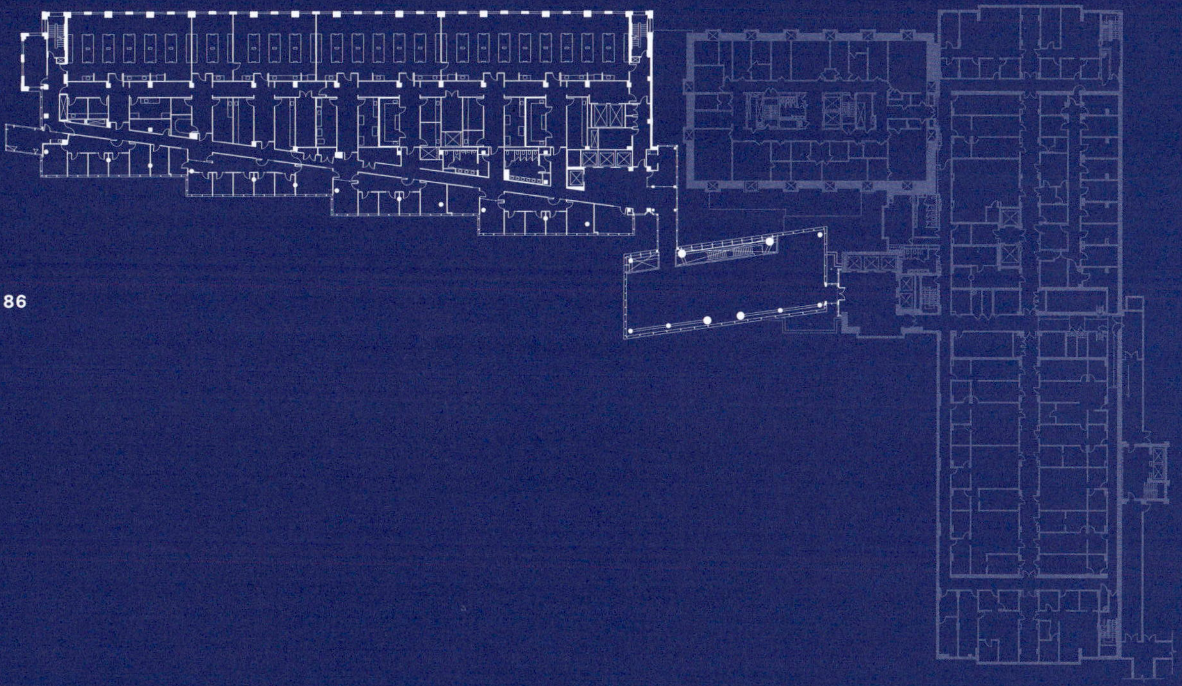

86

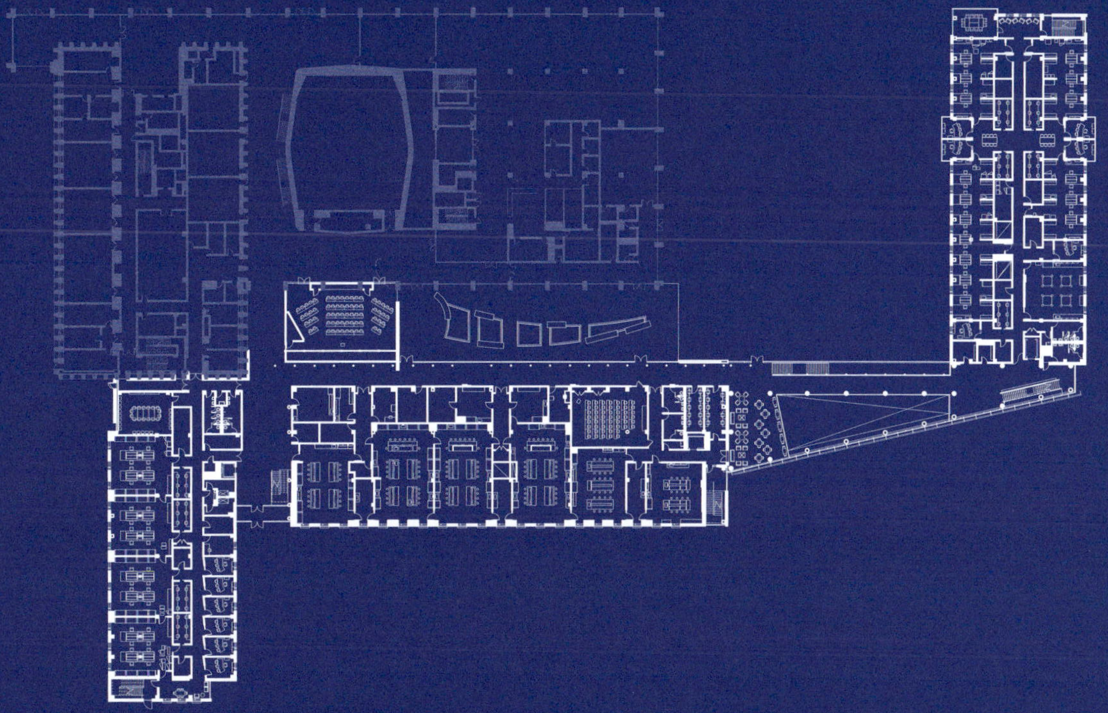

87

88 The University of Connecticut, New STEM Research Center (Science One)
89 MEDITECH, Fall River, Computer Science Building
90 MEDITECH, Foxborough, Computer Science Building
91 Alexandria Real Estate Equities, Lab/Office Building at 75/125 Binney Street
92 Biogen, Building 8: Biological Research Facility and Building 9: Research Facility
93 Biogen, Building 6: Corporate Research Facility
94 The Jackson Laboratory, Genetic Research Building

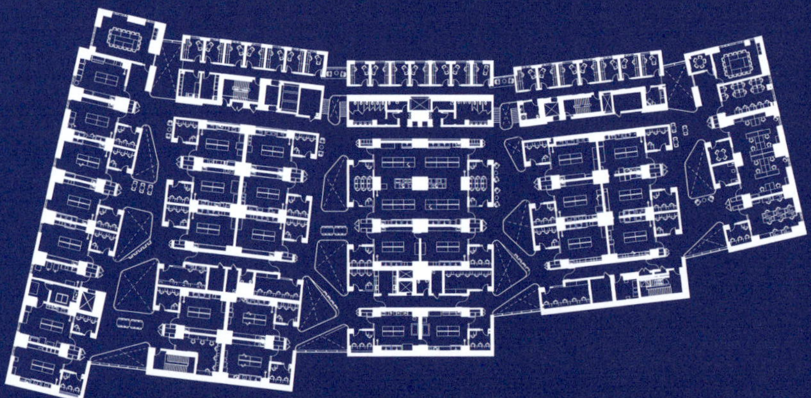

88

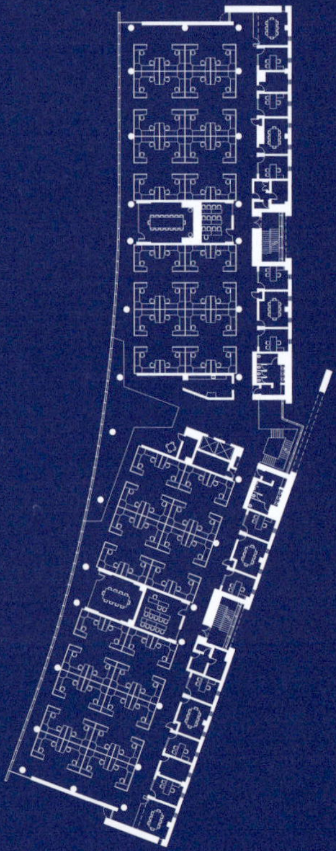

89

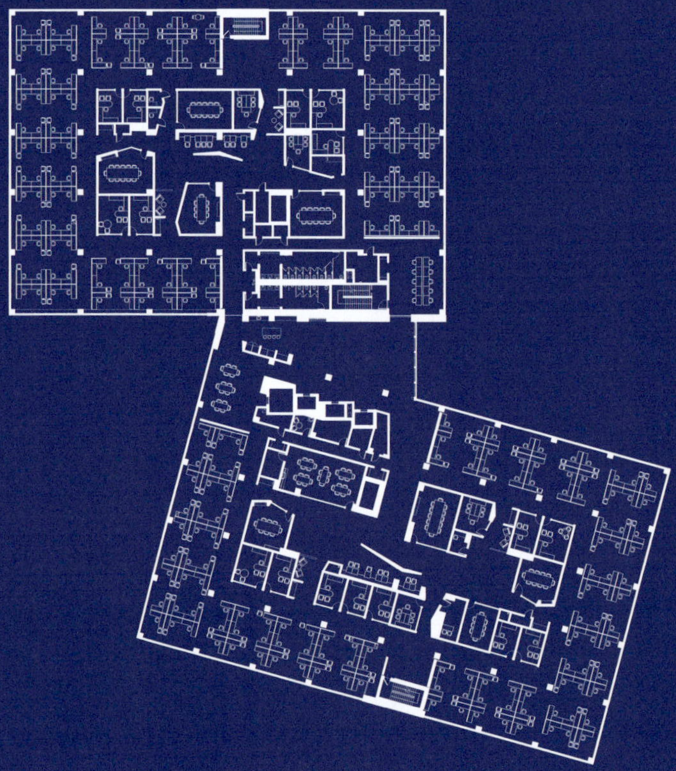

90

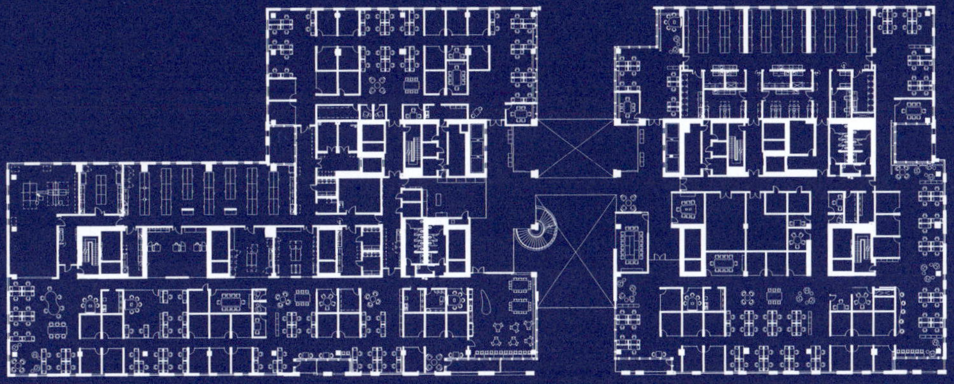

91

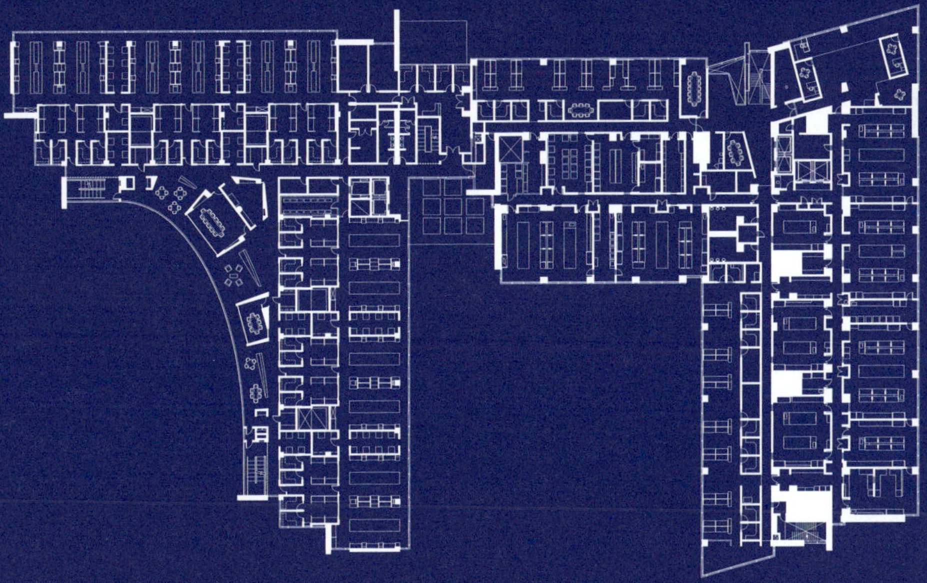

92

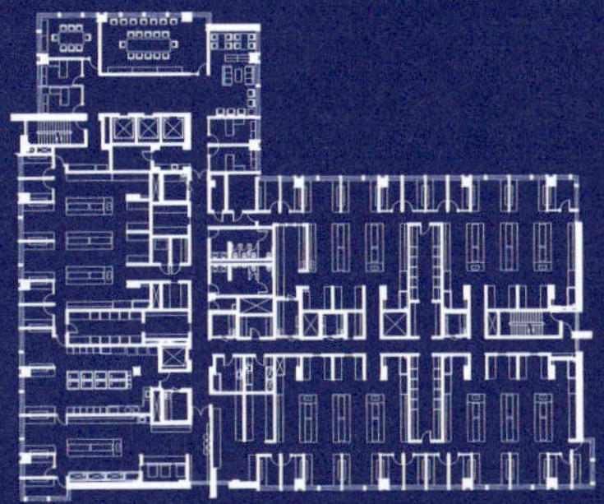

93

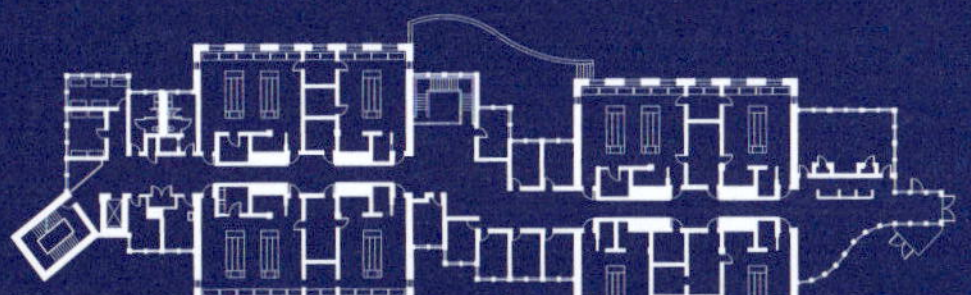

94

Healthcare

95 Penn State Health, Milton S. Hershey Medical Center, Cancer Institute and Children's Hospital

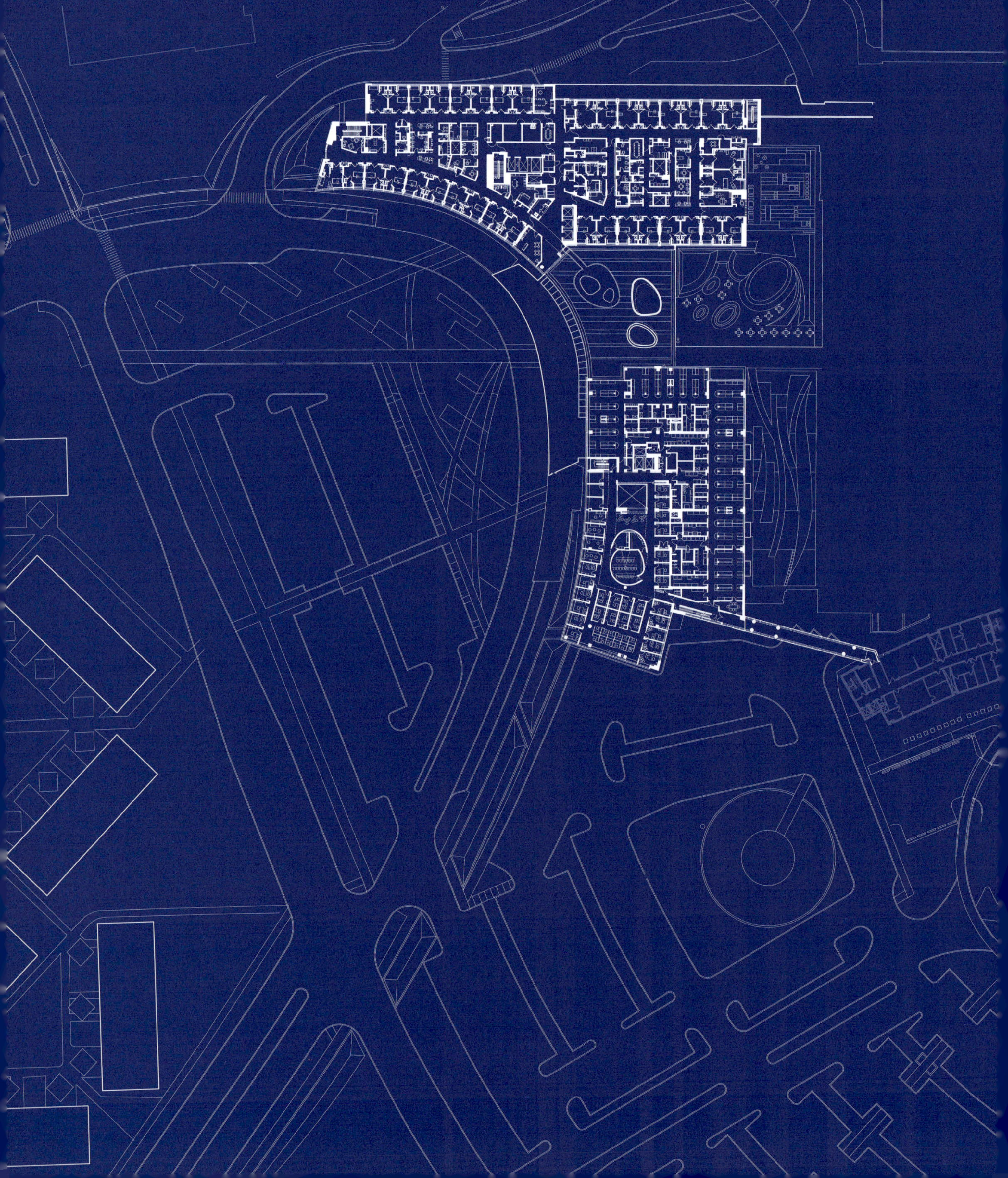

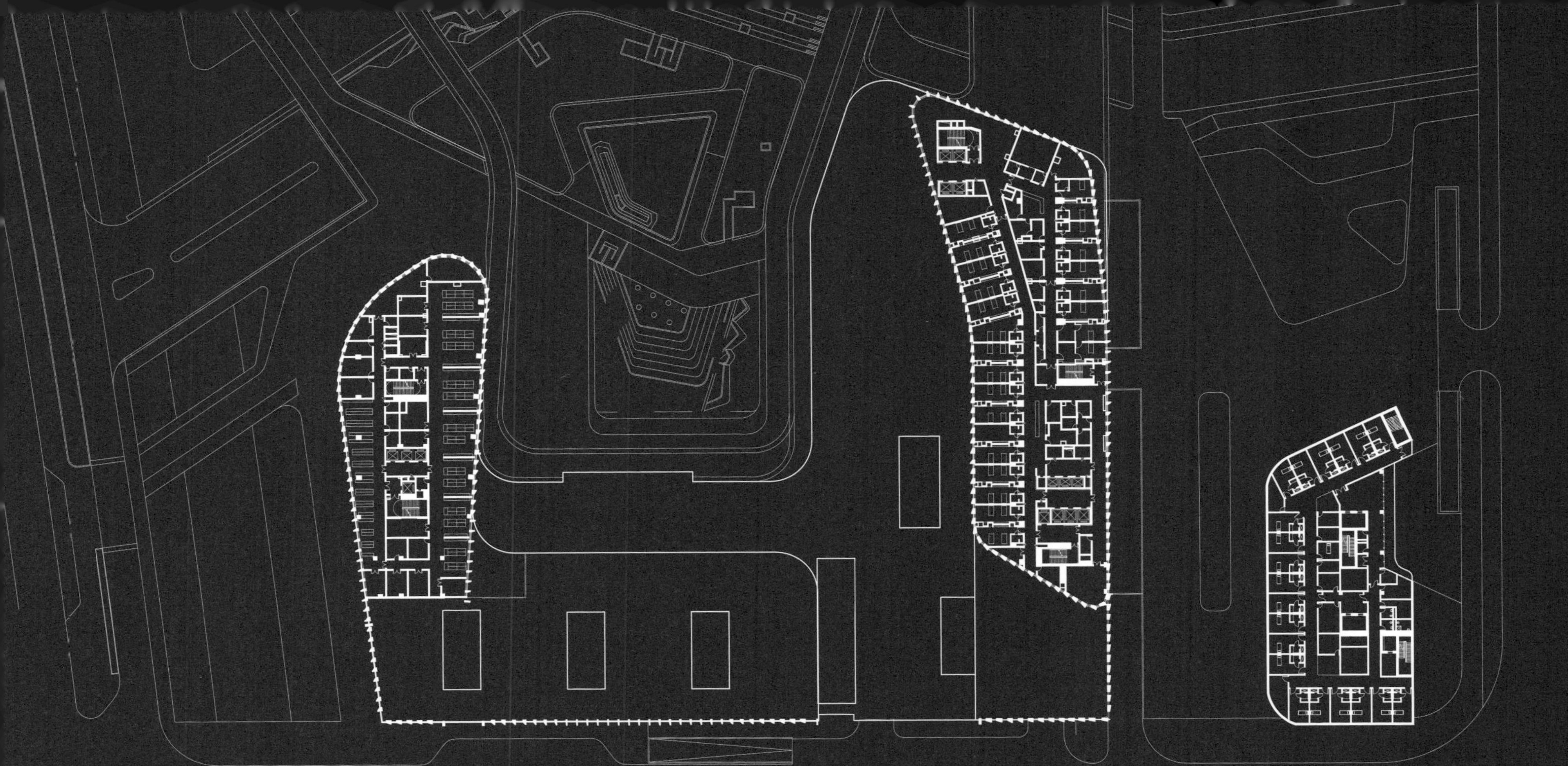

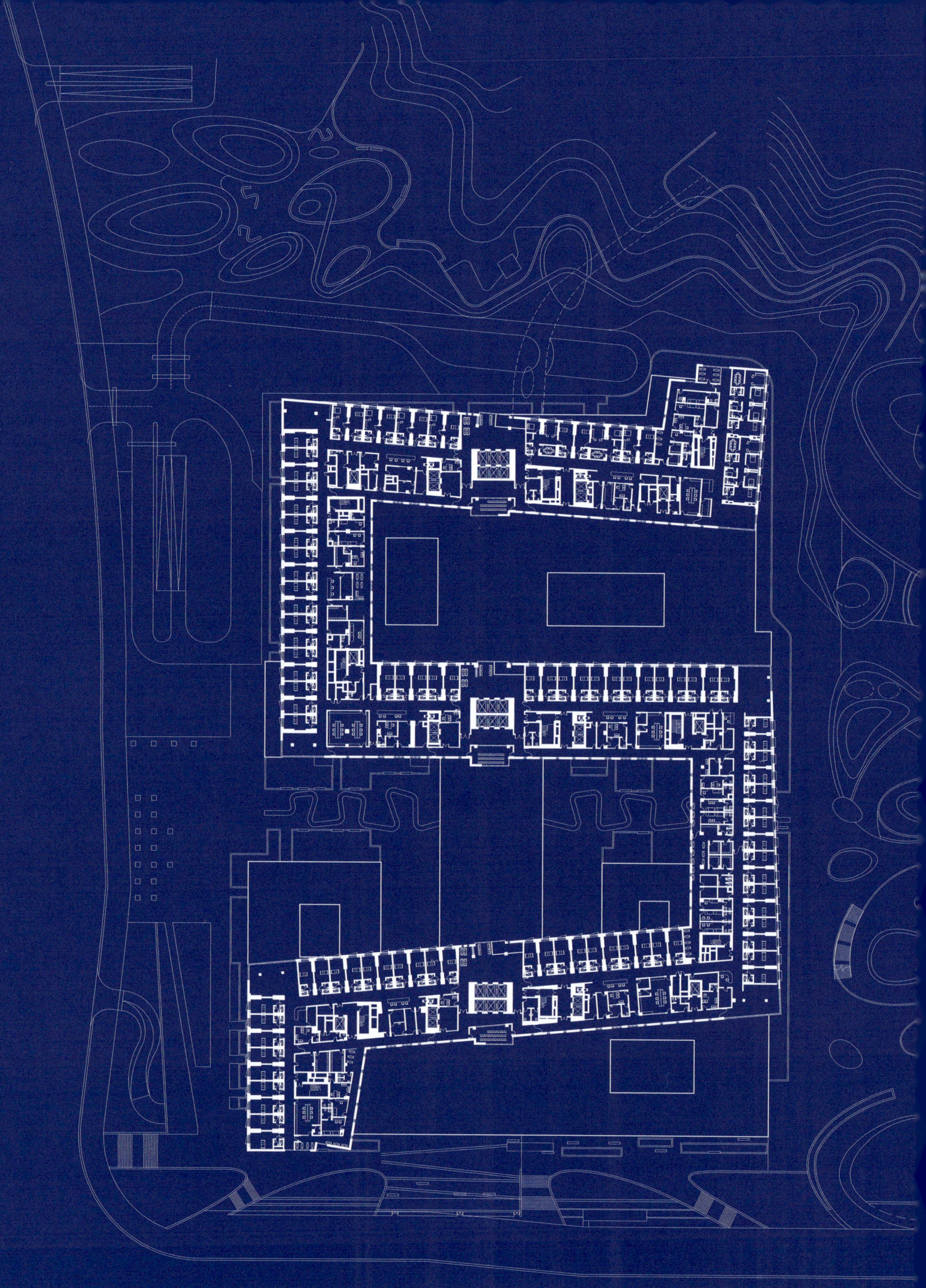

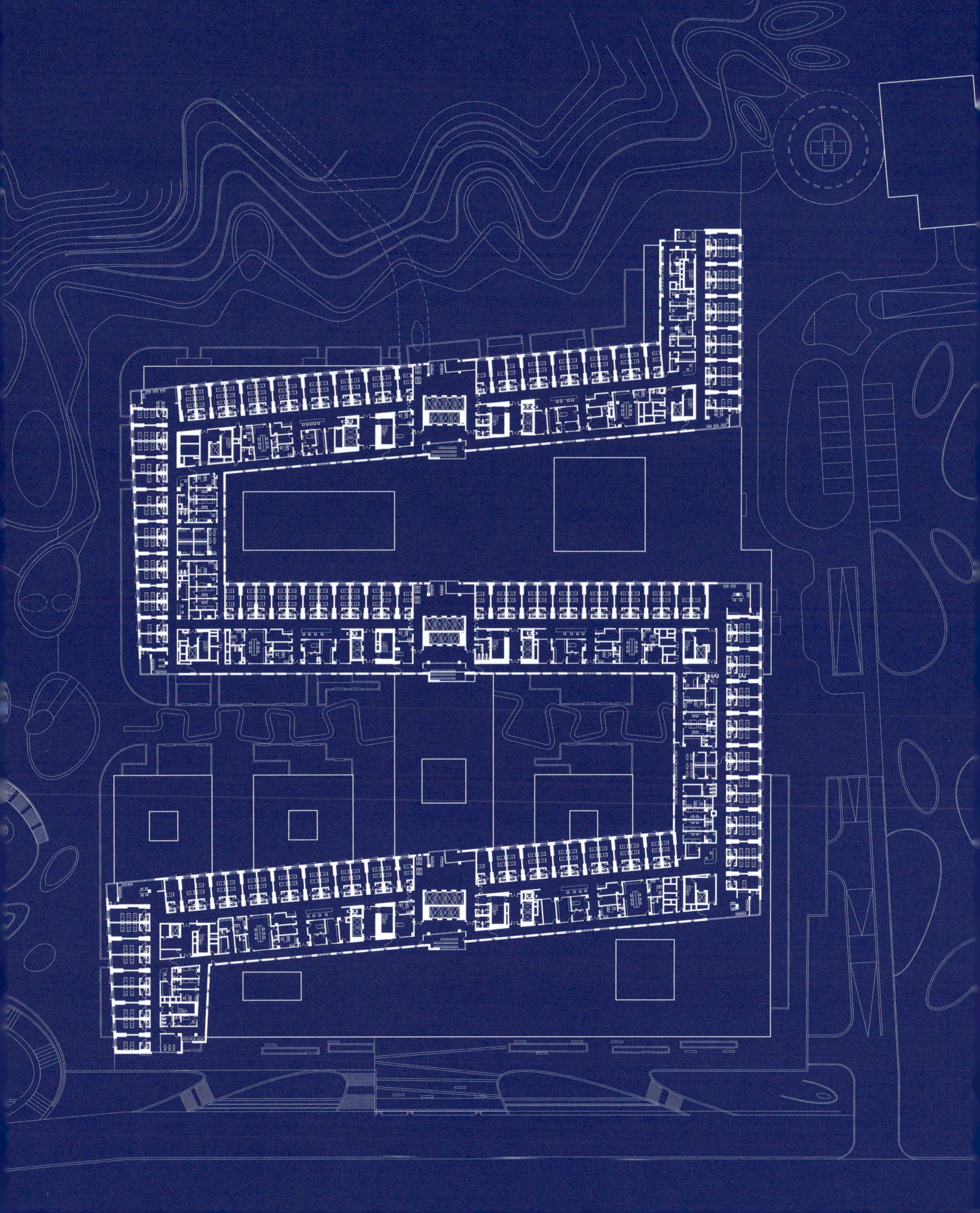

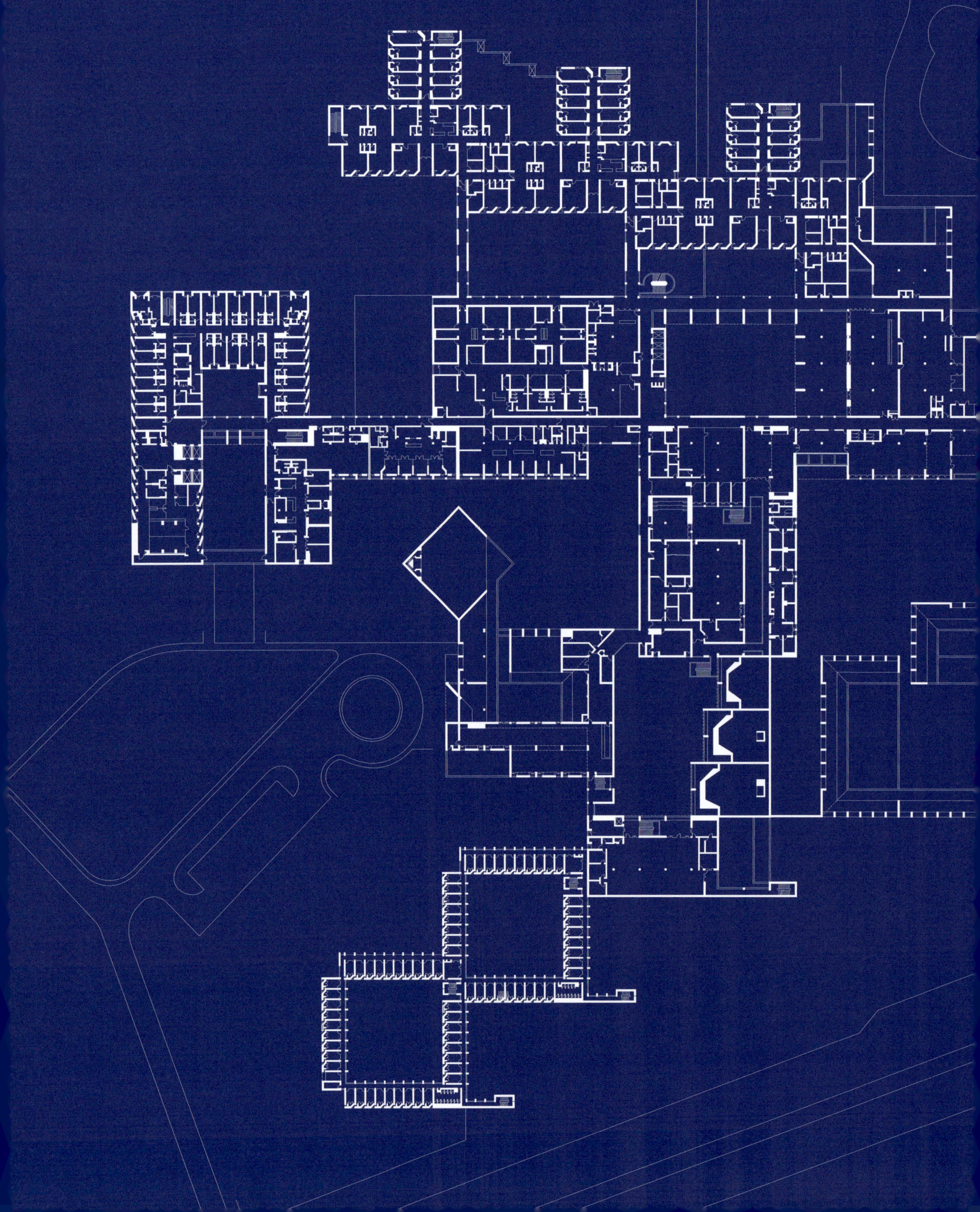

99 Mid Coast Hospital, Master Plan

100 Veterans Affairs Medical Center, Brockton, Spinal Cord Injury Long-Term Care Facility

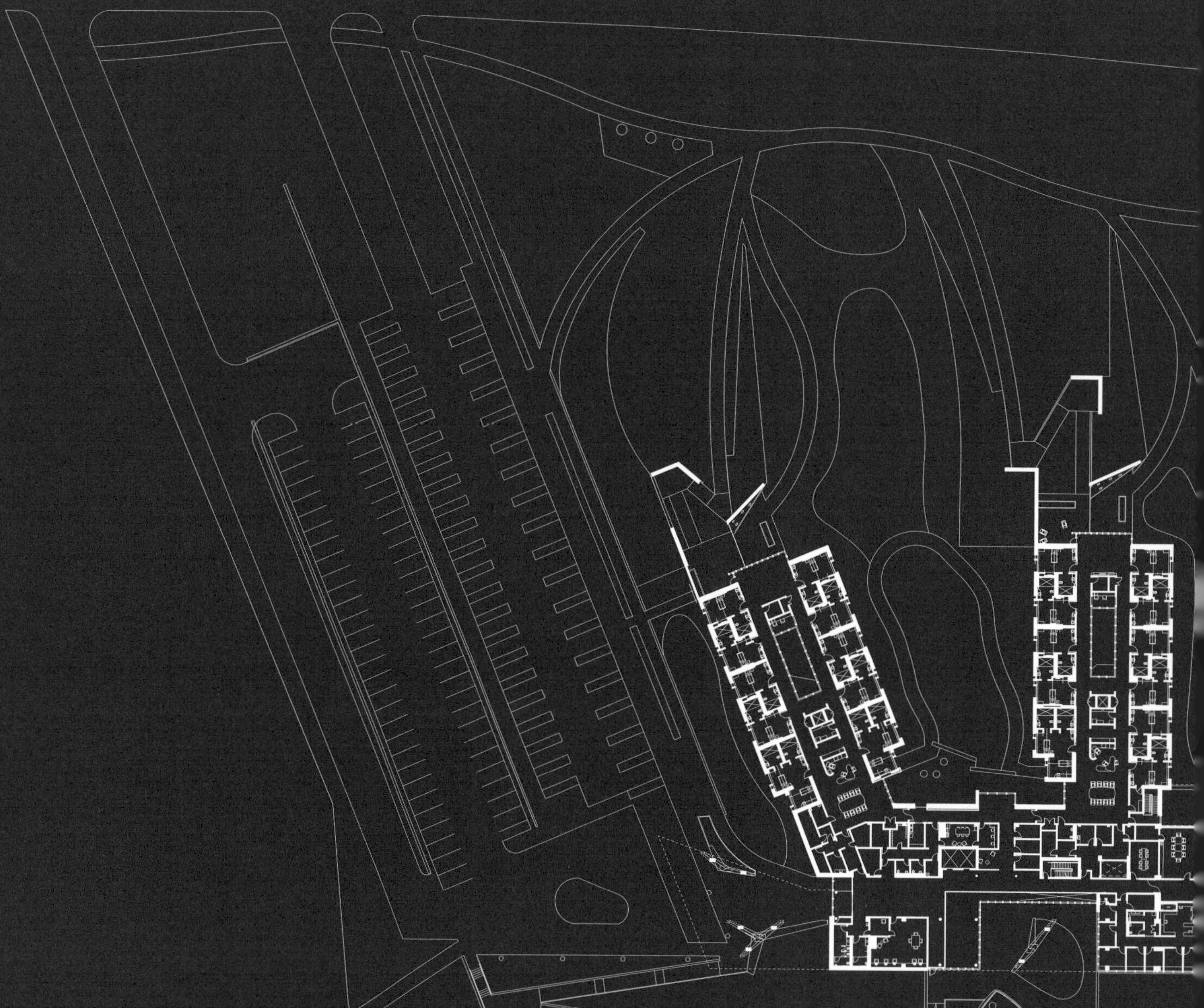

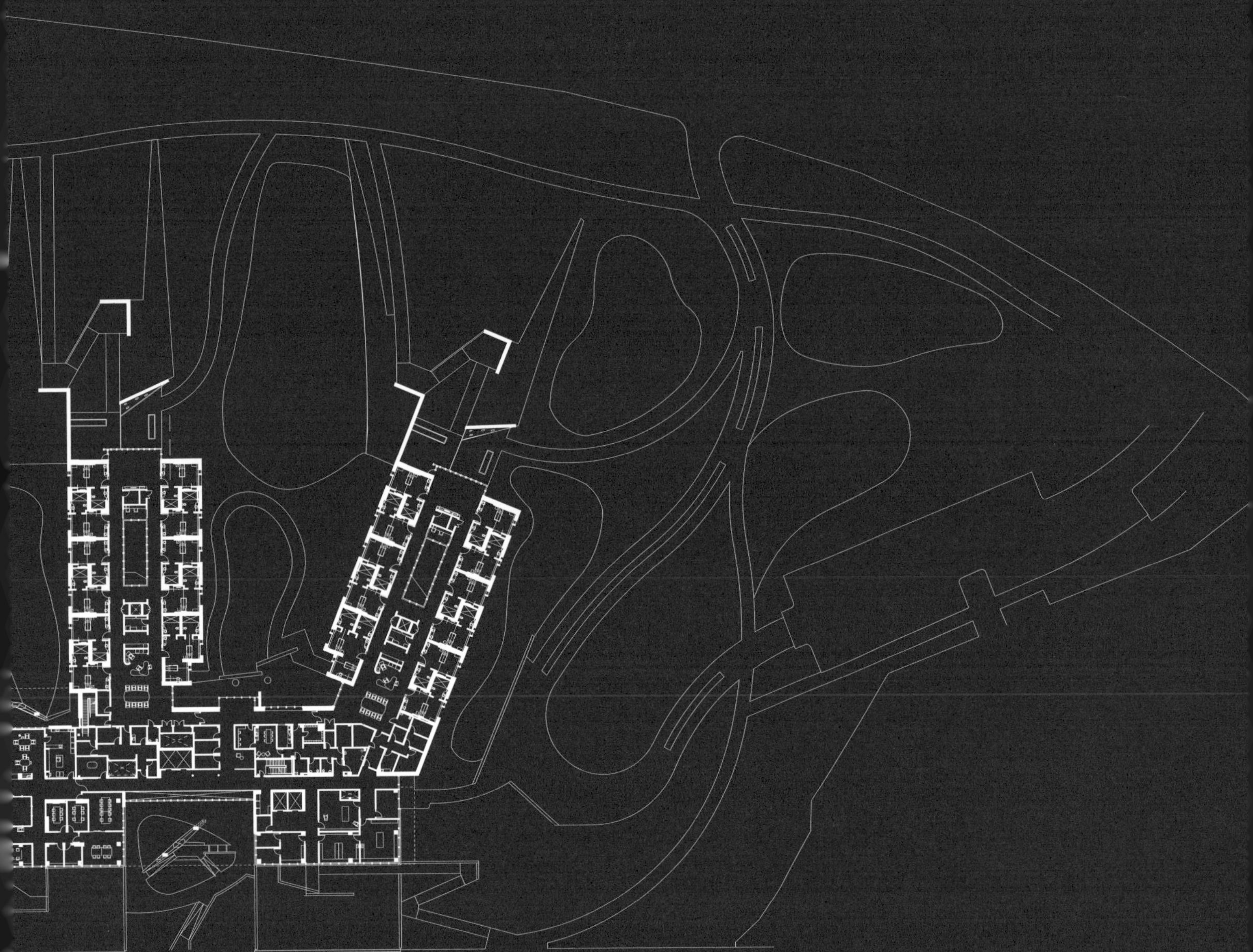

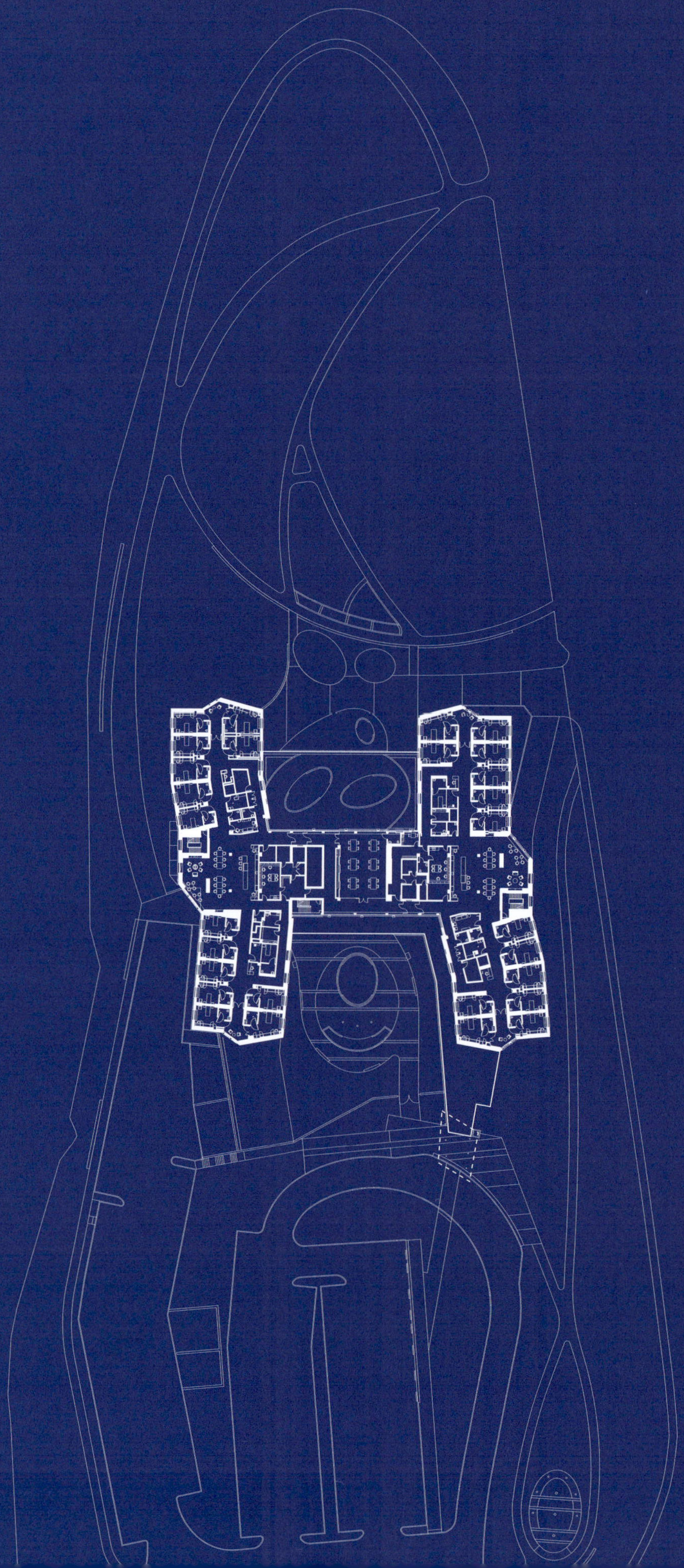

101

101 DCAMM Chelsea Soldiers' Home, Community Living Center and Campus Framework Plan
102 Confidential Healthcare Client, Psychiatric Behavioral Health Hospital

103 Veterans Affairs Medical Center, Providence, Ambulatory Care Addition and Renovation
104 Veterans Affairs Medical Center, Boston, Ambulatory Care Addition
105 The Johns Hopkins Hospital, New Outpatient Center
106 Jefferson Health, New Ambulatory Care, Cancer and Orthopaedic Hospital
107 University of Massachusetts Medical School, Ambulatory Care Center
108 St. Boniface Hospital, Maternity Ward and Neonatal Care Unit
109 Wing Memorial Hospital and Medical Centers, Surgical and Inpatient Addition

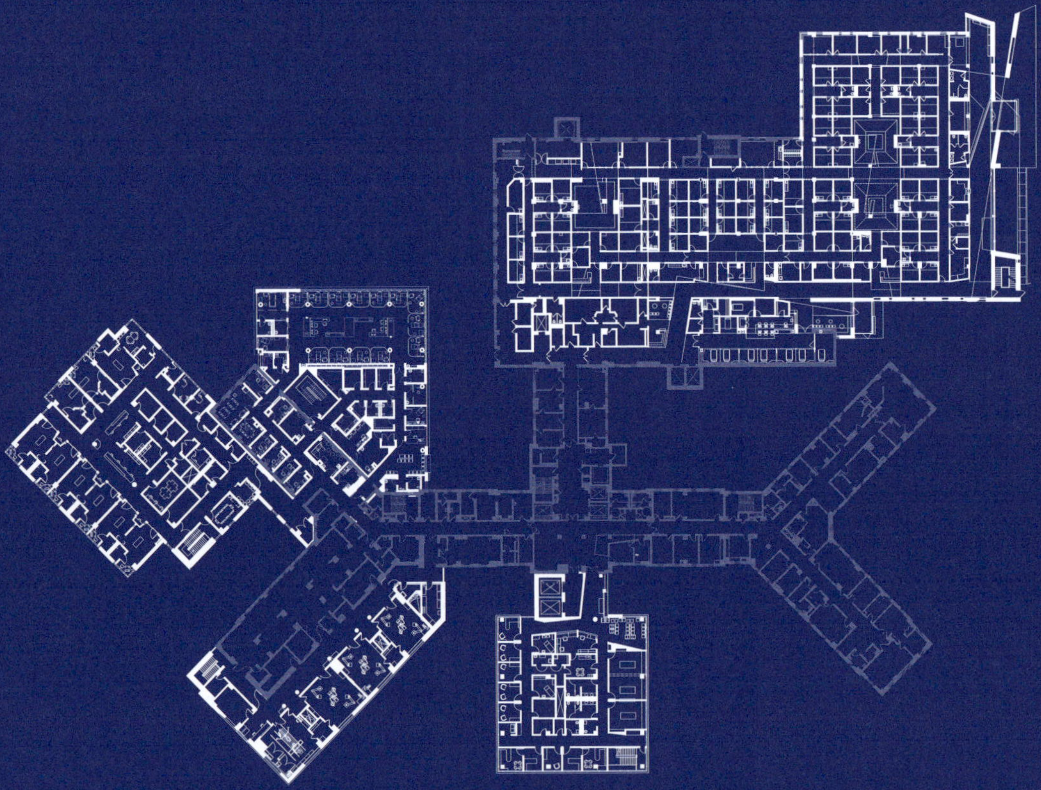

103

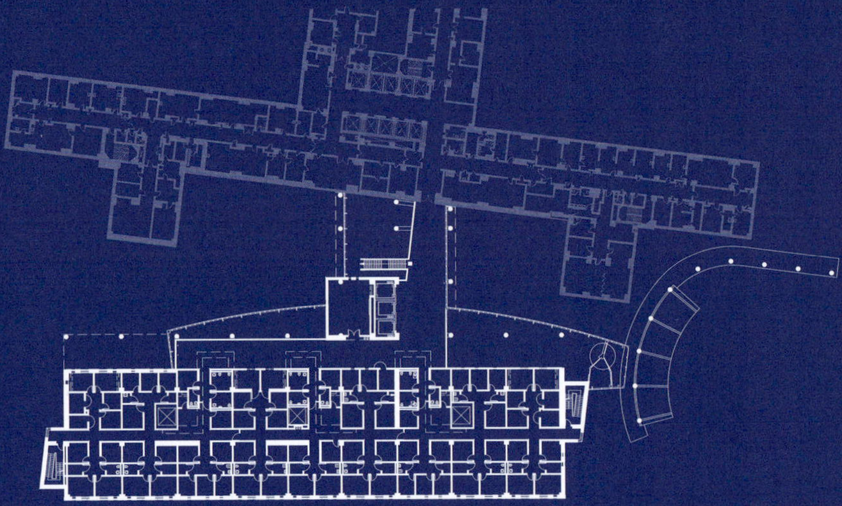

104

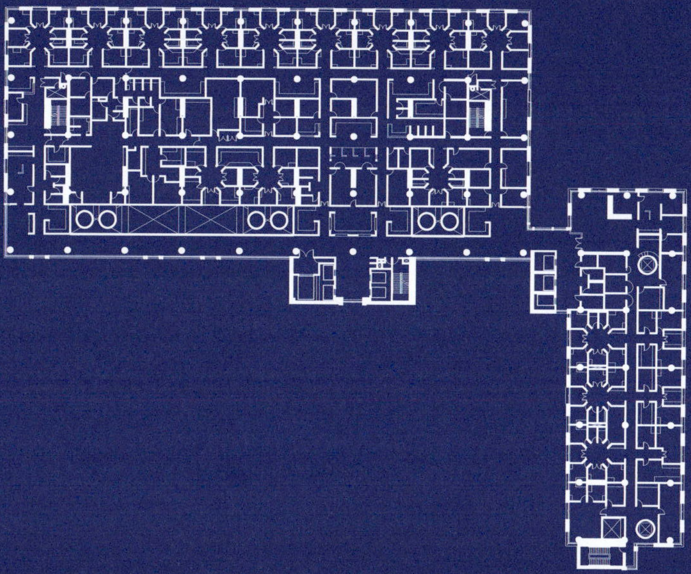

105

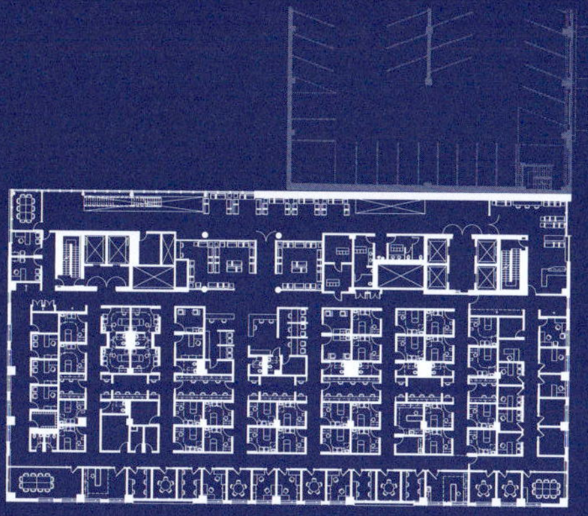

106

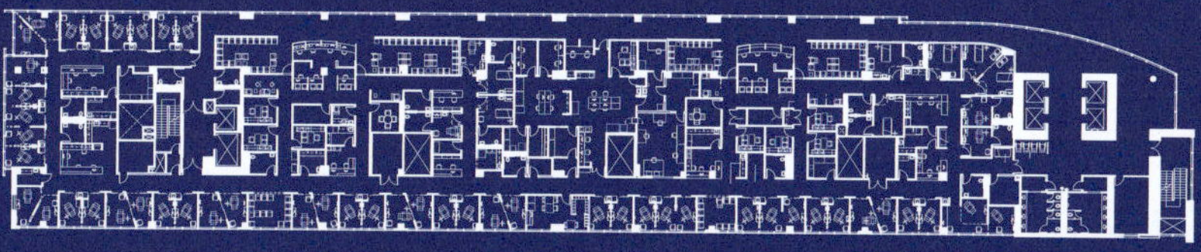

107

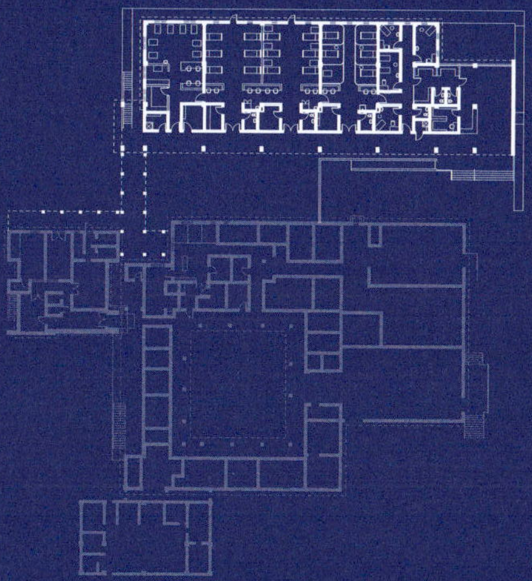

108

109

110 Boston Children's Hospital, James Mandell Building

111 Dartmouth–Hitchcock Medical Center, Center for Surgical Innovation

112 Beth Israel Deaconess Medical Center, New Inpatient Building

113 Boston Children's Hospital Waltham, Satellite Hospital

114 Jordan Hospital

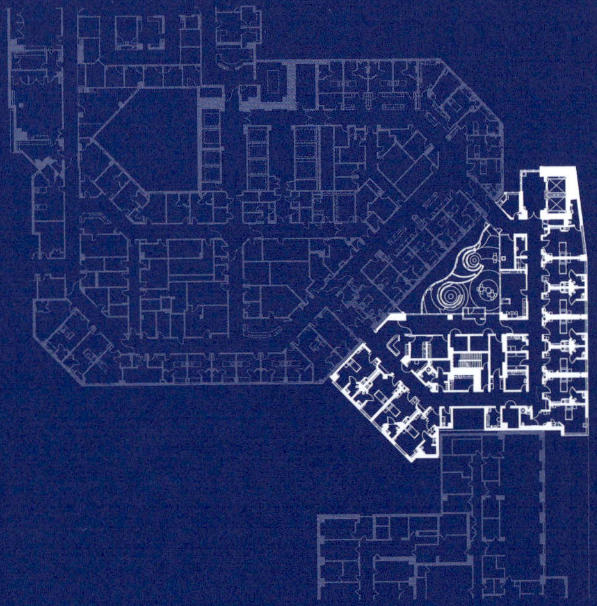

110

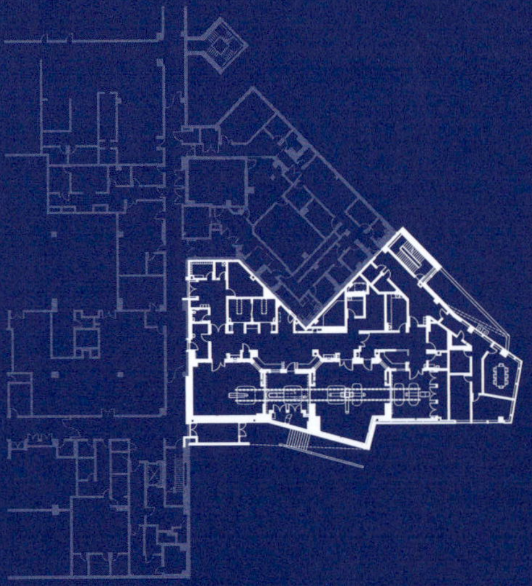

111

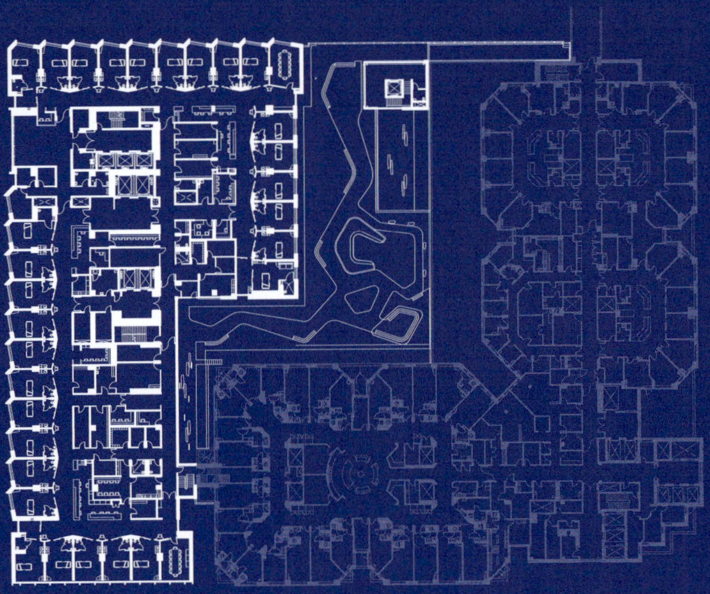

112

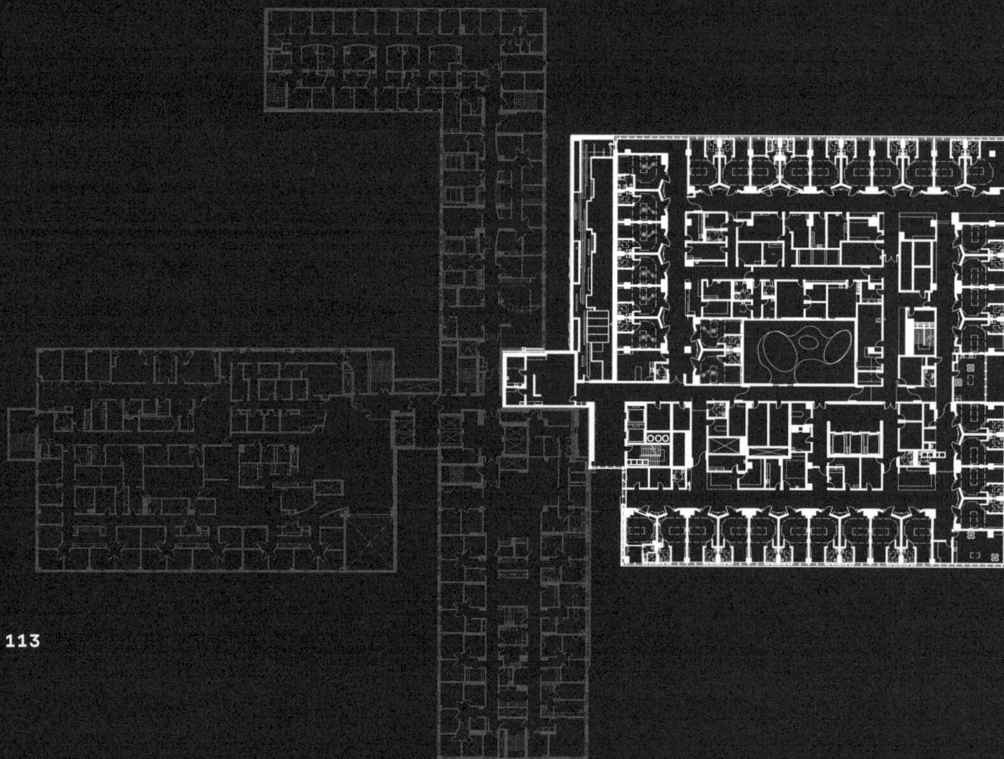

113

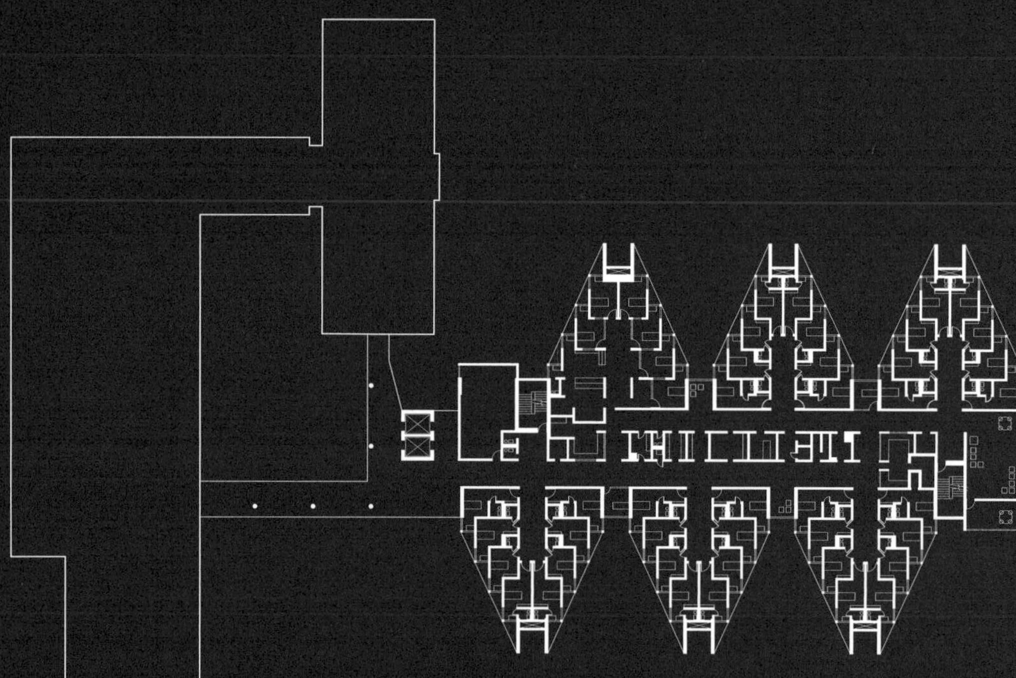

114

Culture at Payette

In the practice setting, with its demanding schedules and distracting contingencies, we can't count on our values sustaining themselves. Sustaining them is cultural work, so we are deliberate in how we structure our practice, form teams, and inhabit our space.

We reject the notion of singular authorship and promote collaborative inquiry, vigorous debate, and the synthesis of the best ideas, irrespective of origin. Our partnership structure encourages multigenerational dialogue and flattens hierarchy. Hackathons let us upend our teaming structure and share knowledge and inspiration across building typologies. With humor and humility, we submit our work for collective critique in firm-wide design forums where everyone has a voice.

We believe that diversity spurs creativity and innovation, both because it broadens the reservoir of ideas and because it enables us to better comprehend the needs of our buildings' diverse populations. Accordingly, we're working to build a more diverse firm. Three of our most recent partners are women, each successive staff level is increasingly diverse, and we are implementing processes for equitable advancement.

To strengthen our collaborative culture, we cross-pollinate project work and research. Since its founding, our Building Science Group has enlisted sixty-nine people from across the practice in research that both informs the project at hand and deepens our knowledge. Because making has always been part of our DNA, we do the same with our FabLab, involving project teams in crafting full-scale mock-ups that live alongside drawings and model studies in our design alcoves.

We believe in the single-office, single-floor, single-city model. One studio on one floor in one office is essential to optimize design potential and collaboration on every project.

Boston is an ideal home for us, a vibrant center of scientific research, healthcare advancement, and architectural education. We draw on its institutions and give back to them as teachers and collaborators.

27% of our staff were born overseas

we hail from **32 countries** and **22 states**
we work in **20 countries**

175 staff work collaboratively in a single floor studio in Boston

46% of our staff have worked on research projects

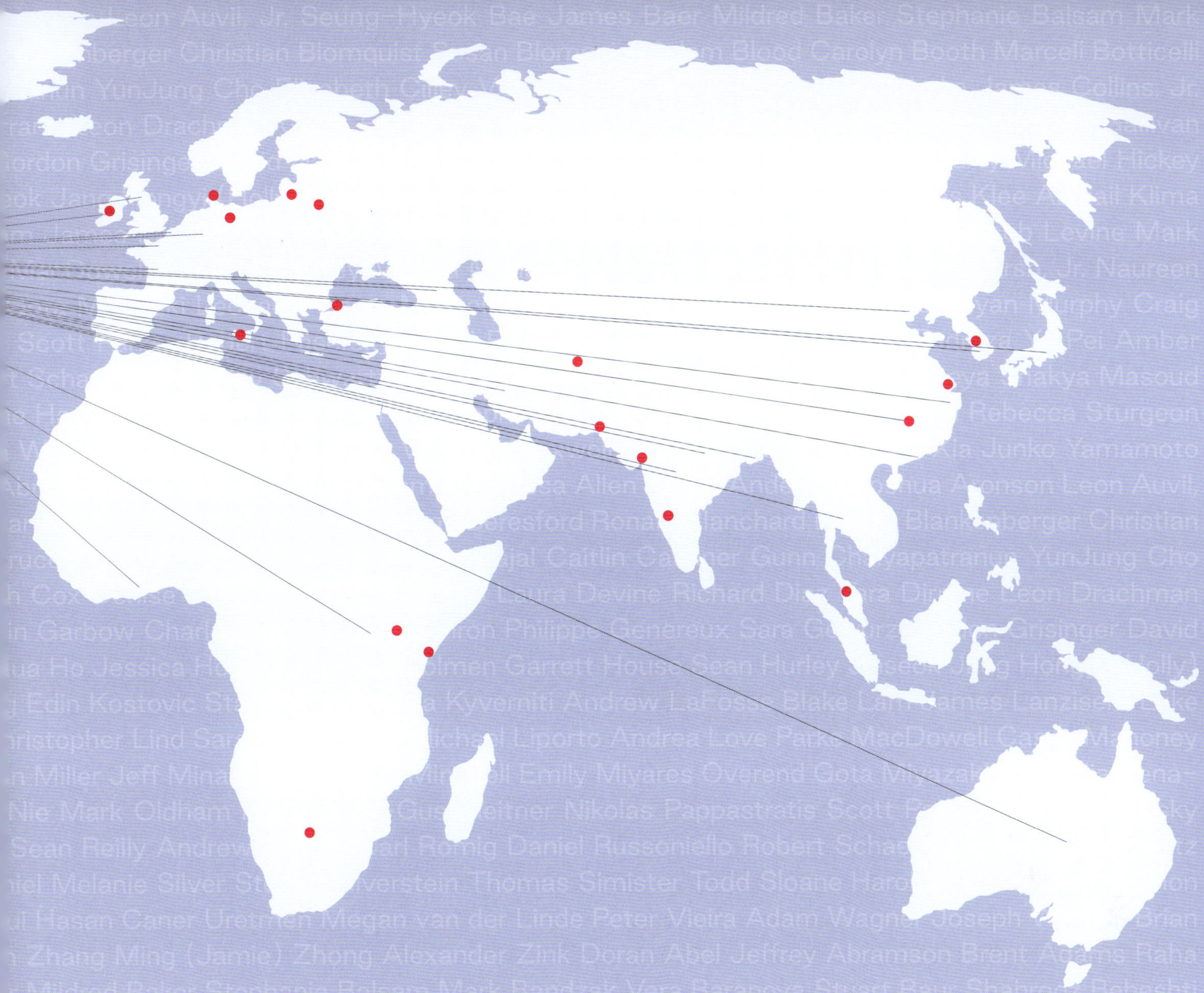

56% of our staff volunteer in their communities

28% of our staff are minorities

81% of titled staff have been at the firm for 10 years or longer

45% of our staff are women

Acknowledgments

I am grateful to all the talented people who have contributed to the Payette practice in so many ways through the years to make *Fusion* possible. Although this book captures a moment in time, highlighting our most current thinking and selected work from the past five to ten years, it was greatly influenced by our long history, shared values, and commitment to bring innovation and beauty to buildings for healthcare and science. It was a story we wanted to tell to push us forward, so in many ways, this book marks a new beginning for us.

The concept for the book was largely born as we crafted our AIA Firm Award submission when we realized that our approach, the fusion of design and performance, was worth sharing to bring greater clarity and understanding of our work and its purpose. Both efforts, the AIA Firm Award submission and the book, have, in their own way, helped us grow and articulate the goals and ambitions for our practice. Z Smith has been a tireless advocate throughout this process as we refined our message and he in turn encouraged us to dig deeper to bring to the surface the many themes of our practice that we took for granted. The fact that Z was passionate about all the same things we were—design, performance, and sustainability—made it a pure joy. Z just gets us, and I am particularly thankful that Z did not laugh at us when I mentioned "Performalism" for the first time. We are also especially grateful to Tim Culvahouse for all his editorial guidance, patience, and willingness to accept all of our foibles to help us craft our message and tell our story. We are a complex group, a collaborative with many strong, vibrant voices, so this was not an easy task, and Tim helped us to capture the storytelling that is so much a part of our design thinking.

I am grateful for the friendship provided by my colleagues at Payette, especially people like Bob Schaeffner, George Marsh, and Jim Collins who are always pushing us to do better work and who provide a constant source of encouragement. We are proud to be part of the rich history of the Boston architectural community and have been honored to practice side by side with so many talented firms. The dialogue and comradery provide an invaluable source of energy for us. Over the past several years, I have also enjoyed my discussions with Mark Lee as two old classmates have matured as architects. Mark's well-crafted observations and thoughts about our practice are not only insightful, but also provide inspiration.

I was reminded during this process how much working on a book—with its rigor, cadence, and storytelling—is like designing a building and all the similarly detailed processes that come with it. A great building cannot happen without a great team and a book is no different. Special and sustained thanks to the "book team": Chris Grimley and Shannon McLean from OverUnder, and Denise Dea, Ben Garbow, Jennifer Hegarty, Amanda Holmen, Mark Lewis, Mi Li, Leocadia Monteiro, Andrew Ringler, and Karen Robichaud from Payette. I am also very grateful to my fellow authors including Jim Collins, Leon Drachman, Andrea Love, George Marsh, Mark Oldham, Robert Pasersky, Wes Schwartz, and Peter Vieira. Our goal was not simply a monograph, but a different type of book that captured our culture and a sampling of the many voices that define Payette. We are extremely proud of the result and were very fortunate to work with editors Alan Rapp and Jenny Florence and are grateful that The Monacelli Press believed in us enough to let this idea for a book come into being.

—Kevin B. Sullivan, 2019

A Renewable Life Source: Payette Principals

We have structured our leadership paths to support the evolving goals of the practice. The fifteen partners bring complementary knowledge and skills essential for our success, but each plays a role in design, marketing, and management. Half have spent their entire careers at Payette, while the others bring fresh insight from past experience elsewhere.

Our partners form a continuum, sustaining the ethos of the firm across overlapping generations. The Sages have been with the firm for half its life; they understand our roots, and they possess extraordinary expertise. The New Core have found their voices in firm leadership and act as a bridge between past and future. The Agitators look resolutely ahead, pushing new ideas and provoking change. Promoted over the past three years, they represent consistent effort to diversify our leadership.

We are striving for equity in the next generation of leaders, which is already in the pipeline. Drawn from a deep bench, this generation will continue to bring new skills and ideas to the practice. The cycle of regenerative leadership is poised to renew itself once again.

James H. Collins, Jr., FAIA, LEED AP, has defined our science practice. Devoted to the discovery and solution of our clients' problems, he reminds us to invest our egos in the ideas and their execution rather than in ourselves. His quest to advance the collaborative dialogue between designers and users has been marked by a concomitant shift in the way science is taught in academic settings and applied in the laboratory.

Jeffrey H. DeGregorio, AIA, LEED AP, possesses a rare ability to balance design management, mentoring, and prototypical design thinking, which he has applied to both high-technology projects at a large scale and carefully crafted small projects. Jeff is particularly focused on the intersection of education and architecture and is invested in working with young staff.

Leon W. Drachman, AIA, LEED Green Associate, is driven by a passion for collaboration. His leadership is informed by a comprehensive grasp of architecture and urban design, healthcare and science, the big picture and the details. Leon believes that design is found between the specifics of each project (client, site, program) and the core realm of architecture (knowledge, expertise, research, and inspiration).

Michael Hinchcliffe, AIA, LEED AP, has both a depth and a breadth of award-winning projects for academic science, research, and healthcare. His leadership advances teams on projects that achieve balance between elegant design, technical program complexity, and high performance sustainability. Michael is committed to integrating research, education, and mentoring into daily practice.

Ching-Hua Ho brings encyclopedic knowledge of healthcare design and technology to the leadership of our healthcare group. In addition to healthcare planning and design, her passion is exploring exterior building envelopes, working with specific contexts and programs to complete a building's total expression. Ching believes there should be no boundaries in design between different project typologies.

Charles S. Klee, AIA, LEED AP, grew up wandering the corridors of the National Institutes of Health. Interning in labs through high school and college, he grew up in an environment that emphasized exploration and rigorous thought. In addition to his project work, Charlie leads the firm's Research Initiative with our Building Science Group, bringing new ideas and technology to the practice.

Sarah N. Lindenfeld, AIA, LEED AP, has over fifteen years of experience in architecture and design, both domestically and internationally. Her project experience ranges from academic science buildings to performing arts centers and libraries. Sarah has been an active participant in the Women in Design Committee at the Boston Society of Architects, including serving on the Mentoring Sub-Committee and Steering Committee. She currently sits on the BSA Honors and Awards Committee.

Andrea Love, AIA, LEED Fellow, leads our Building Science Group, working across projects to integrate performance-modeling tools into the design process. Her role is to redefine what great design can mean when it incorporates provable performance. She leads a number of the firm's internal research projects, and also teaches building envelope performance at MIT and Harvard.

George E. Marsh, Jr., FAIA, brings a deep understanding of the history of hospital architecture, from Florence Nightingale forward, to the design of progressive hospital and laboratory environments. He has commanding expertise in both healthcare and science. He is the firm historian who understands and honors the continuity of our practice, leading him to become a mentor to our mentors.

Mark Oldham, AIA, LEED AP, brings a generalist's architectural voice to Payette and possesses an interest in clarity and simplicity in the architectural expression of our ideas. He believes that delivering inspired architecture requires a complex and ever-expanding collection of voices with each one essential to the craft.

Scott D. Parker, AIA, LEED AP, manages the project teams throughout the design and construction process, making sure all aspects of the project progress toward timely conclusions. The primary focus of Scott's work is often a building's systemization and construction, including infrastructure planning, complex building phasing, and logistics in the large scale and the small scale.

Robert C. Pasersky, AIA, has made a significant impact on projects while also being generous with his time, providing pro bono design services to several organizations. Robert established Open House Works, and Payette joined the 1%, a program of Public Architecture, where design professionals pledge a percentage of their time to working pro bono for their community.

Robert J. Schaeffner, FAIA, LEED AP, has been an integral part of the firm's expansion into research facility design. After completing seminal research projects, he expanded the practice, helping to develop Payette's strong presence in academic science facility planning and design. He has led a number of science center projects at prestigious colleges and universities which have positively transformed entire campus precincts.

Kevin B. Sullivan, FAIA, is president of Payette. Expert in both science and healthcare, he has doubled down on the commitment to design excellence begun by Jim Collins. His work includes seminal healthcare, science, and campus planning projects, recognized for their attention to detail, social geometry, and integration of the landscape.

Peter F. Vieira Jr., FAIA, LEED AP, is interested in leading teams that intelligently conceive, creatively develop and meticulously execute challenging projects. While Peter's approach to design is highly analytical, it is also informed by years of teaching students how to visualize and represent complex three-dimensional spaces.

CONTRIBUTORS

Z Smith, PhD, FAIA
Director of Sustainability and Building Performance, Eskew+Dumez+Ripple (EDR)

EDR is one of the nation's most distinguished architecture firms and recipient of the 2014 AIA Firm Award. Z came to architecture from a career as a research scientist at Xerox Paolo Alto Research Center. Named as inventor on ten patents and author on over fifty peer-reviewed scientific publications, he teaches at Tulane School of Architecture and is a member of the International Institute for Sustainable Laboratories and the Society of Building Science Educators.

Mark Lee is the Chair of the Department of Architecture at the Harvard Graduate School of Design and a principal and founding partner of the Los Angeles-based architecture firm Johnston Marklee.

Since its establishment in 1998, Johnston Marklee has been recognized internationally with over 40 major honors and awards. A book on the work of the firm entitled *House Is a House Is a House Is a House Is a House* was published by Birkhauser in 2016, and monographs include *2G N. 67* (2014) and *El Croquis N. 198* (2019).

The firm's work spans thirteen countries and resides in the permanent collections of several museums. Together with partner Sharon Johnston, Mark served as Co-Artistic Director for the 2017 Chicago Architecture Biennial.

Project Credits

Alexandria Real Estate Equities
75/125 Binney Street
Cambridge, Massachusetts

Amherst College
New Science Center
Amherst, Massachusetts

Amherst College
Beneski Earth Sciences Building and Beneski Museum of Natural History
Amherst, Massachusetts

Boston Children's Hospital
James Mandell Building
Boston, Massachusetts

Beth Israel Deaconess Medical Center
New Inpatient Building
Boston, Massachusetts

Bridgewater State University
Dana Mohler-Faria Science and Mathematics Center
Bridgewater, Massachusetts

Boston University
Rajen Kilachand Center for Integrated Life Sciences & Engineering
Boston, Massachusetts

Brigham and Women's Hospital
Advanced Multimodality Image Guided Operating Suite
Boston, Massachusetts

Central South University
Fifth Xiangya Hospital
Changsha, China

Chelsea Soldiers' Home
Community Living Center
Chelsea, Massachusetts

Columbia University
Lamont-Doherty Earth Observatory Campus
Gary C. Comer Geochemistry Building
Palisades, New York

Columbia University
School of Engineering and Applied Sciences
Data Science Institute
New York, New York

Connecticut College
New London Hall Addition and Renovation
New London, Connecticut

George Washington University
Milken Institute School of Public Health
Washington, DC

Hengqin Island
Hengqin Hospital and Medical Campus
Zhuhai, Guangdong, China

Lafayette College
Rockwell Integrated Sciences Center
Easton, Pennsylvania

Massachusetts Institute of Technology
PDSI Project: Physics, Department of Material Science and Engineering, Spectroscopy and Infrastructure
Cambridge, Massachusetts

Northeastern University
Interdisciplinary Science and Engineering Complex
Boston, Massachusetts

National University of Ireland Galway
Biosciences Research Building
Galway, Ireland (Republic)

National University of Ireland Galway
Hardiman Research Building
Galway, Ireland (Republic)

Penn State Health
Milton S. Hershey Medical Center
Clinical Quadrangle Master Plan, Cancer Institute and Children's Hospital
Hershey, Pennsylvania

Pennsylvania State University
Eva J. Pell Laboratory for Advanced Biological Studies
University Park, Pennsylvania

Pennsylvania State University
Shortlidge Mall
University Park, Pennsylvania

Tufts University
Science and Engineering Complex
Medford, Massachusetts

University of Massachusetts, Amherst
College of Natural Sciences Research & Education Greenhouse
Amherst, Massachusetts

Image Credits

All reasonable efforts have been made to ascertain and obtain licenses to use third party images and materials. All images, unless otherwise noted below, are provided by Payette.

© Robert Benson Photography
Pages 120, 121 (top), 122 (top right), 150–152, 154–155, 157–165, 168–169, 232–233

© Chuck Choi
Pages 76–78, 80–84, 86–91, 110–112, 116–118, 121 (bottom), 122 (top left and bottom), 123–125, 172–174, 176–180, 182–185, 230–231

© Adam Detour
Pages 28–31, 42–43, 188–189, 216–217, 236–237

© Paul Ferrino
Page 35

© Ned Jackson, 2019
Pages 298–299, 302–303

© Warren Jagger Photography
Cover, Pages 20, 47 (bottom), 54–56, 58–59, 62–68, 70–71, 128–130, 132–138, 141–147, 194–197, 205, 209–211, 214–215, 223, 234, 235 (top right and bottom right)

© Ron Long / Pixels.com
Page 34

© Nebraska Methodist Health System
Page 45

© Rachellynn Schoen
Pages 139, 148

© Terry Sebastian
Page 50

© Ron Solomon 2019
Page 47 (top)

© Stephen Stimson/Stimson Landscape Architects
Page 60

© Peter Vanderwarker
Pages 203, 222 (top)

© Ayesha Vellani
Page 51

© Nick Wheeler
Page 46

© Edua Wilde Photography
Page 235 (top left)

© Keitaro Yoshioka Photography
Page 61

Current Payette Staff

Doran Abel
Jeffrey Abramson
Brent Adams
Raha Ahmad
Melissa Allen
Adam Anderson
Joshua Aronson
Leon Auvil, Jr.
Seung-Hyeok Bae
James Baer
Mildred Baker
Stephanie Balsam
Mark Bandzak
Vera Baranova
Stuart Baur
Shahrooz Beheshti
Thomas Beresford
Ronald Blanchard
Denise Blankenberger
Christian Blomquist
Susan Blomquist
Adam Blood
Carolyn Booth
Marceli Botticelli
Megan Brown
Benjamin Bruce-Julian
Nathan Butt
Ernesto Carvajal
Caitlin Cashner
Gunn Chaiyapatranun
YunJung Cho
Elizabeth Cilley
Valerie Cintolo
Dane Clark
Seth Clarke
James Collins, Jr.
Elizabeth Cooney
Elizabeth Cox
Denise Dea
Jeffrey DeGregorio
Laura Devine
Richard Diaz
Tara Dirrane
Leon Drachman
Greta Eckhardt
Kerri Estano
Daniel Estes
Mary Gallagher
Daniel Gallivan
Elizabeth Galloway
Benjamin Garbow
Charles Garcia
Luke Gehron
Philippe Genereux
Sara Gewurz
Gordon Grisinger
David Hamel, Jr.
Jennifer Hardy
Parry Heavlin
Jennifer Hegarty
Michael Hickey
Michael Hinchcliffe
Ching-Hua Ho
Jessica Hoctor
Amanda Holmen
Garrett House
Sean Hurley
Jinseok Jang
Hongyi (Holly) Jin
Jessica Jorge
Hyeyun Jung
Maria Keller
Charles Klee
Abigail Klima
Priscilla Klotz
Bohseung Kong
Edin Kostovic
Stacy Krieg
Nicola Kyverniti
Andrew LaFosse
Blake Lam
James Lanzisero
Luke Laverty
Nicholas LaVita
Alison Lesniewski-Laas
Jacob Levine
Mark Lewis II
Mi Li
Keunyoung Lim
Christopher Lind
Sarah Lindenfeld
Michael Liporto
Andrea Love
Parke MacDowell
Casey Mahoney
Mollica Manandhar
Michael Mandeville
George Marsh, Jr.
Naureen Mazumdar
Eamonn Meagher
Justin Miller
Jeff Minard
Montserrat Minguell
Emily Miyares Overend
Gota Miyazaki
Leocadia Sena-Monteiro
Shaun Morris
James Morrison, Jr.
Ryan Murphy
Craig Mutter
Avery Nackman
Xiaomeng Nie
Mark Oldham
Mali Ouzts-Gusenleitner
Nikolas Pappastratis
Scott Parker
Robert Pasersky
David Pawlak
Marissa Pearson
Yennifer Pedraza
Yu Pei
Amber Penman
Jonah Prada
Michael Quinn
Sean Reilly
Andrew Ringler
Carl Romig
Daniel Russoniello
Robert Schaeffner
Wesley Schwartz
Mark Scott
Steven Seaver
Tyla Sewell
Shreeya Shakya
Masoud Sharikzadeh
Xichen Sheng
Barry Shiel
Melanie Silver
Steven Silverstein
Thomas Simister
Todd Sloane
Harold Solie
Sarah Solomon
Christopher Stansfield
Ngaire Stuart Gongora
Rebecca Sturgeon
Kevin Sullivan
Diana Tsang
Timo Tsui
Hasan Caner Uretmen
Megan van der Linde
Peter Vieira, Jr.
Adam Wagner
Joseph Watson
Brian Webber
Maxwell Werner
Mike Wilson
Yin Xia
Junko Yamamoto
Jensen Ying
Jing Yu
Lu Zhang
Yuan Zhang
Ming (Jamie) Zhong
Alexander Zink

The image credits on page 310 constitute a continuation of the copyright page.

Library of Congress Control Number: 2019955244

ISBN 978-1-58093-534-0

10 9 8 7 6 5 4 3 2 1

Printed in China

Design: Chris Grimley and Shannon McLean, OverUnder

The Monacelli Press
6 West 18th Street
New York, New York 10011
www.monacellipress.com